THUNDER in the MORNING CALM

THUNDER
in the
MORNING
CALM:

*The Royal
Canadian Navy
in Korea
1950-1955*

Edward C. Meyers

Vanwell Publishing Limited
St. Catharines, Ontario

This book is dedicated to the memory
of my father who taught his family
the ideals of honour and loyalty.

Canadian Cataloguing in Publication Data

Meyers, Edward C.
Thunder in the Morning Calm

ISBN 0-920277-71-3

1. Korean War, 1950-1953 - Naval operations,
Canadian. 2. Canada. Royal Canadian Navy -
History. 3. United Nations - Armed Forces -
Canada. 4. Canada. Royal Canadian Navy - Military
life. I. Title.

DS919.2.M48 1991   951.904'2   C91-095080-6

Design Susan Nicholson

Vanwell Publishing Limited
1 Northrup Crescent
P.O. Box 2131
St. Catharines, Ontario L2M 6P5

Printed in Canada

CONTENTS

FOREWORD

When HMCS *Haida, Huron* and *Iroquois* made their triumphant return to Halifax on June 10, 1945, it must have seemed to onlookers and ships' companies alike that their fighting days were over. The European war had ended a month earlier, and their services would not be required in those waning days of the war against Japan.

With four Canadian-built sisters, commissioned 1945-48, and four British-built consorts of smaller size, these made up the bulk of the Royal Canadian Navy in the years immediately following World War II.

The tranquility of those years was rudely broken in the summer of 1950, when North Korean forces invaded South Korea, and the Canadian government offered three destroyers as its initial contribution to a United Nations "police action" in that region. Neither army nor air force could have responded nearly so quickly as the three west coast destroyers that sailed on July 5 for Pearl Harbour.

Between 1950 and 1955 a total of eight Canadian destroyers took part at various times in that anomalous campaign, their targets more often than not sampans, junks and locomotives. They acquitted themselves admirably, though their efforts went largely unnoticed by the public, and all have long since gone to the scrapyard except for *Haida*, drowsing at her jetty in Toronto.

In these pages, Ted Meyers tells their story. His vantage point is not that of the wardroom, but of the messdeck; not that of a military historian, but of one who was there. He recounts the excitement (infrequent), the boredom and discomfort (routine) and the frustrations of service far from home, in a war the passing years make more difficult than ever to comprehend.

His shipmates would approve.

KEN MACPHERSON

PREFACE

In 1979, during the Labour Day weekend, a couple of hundred former members of HMCS *Cayuga* got together for a reunion at HMCS Naden in Esquimalt, B.C. I was unable to attend for a number of reasons, but a few weeks later two packages arrived in the mail. One was a framed ship's crest and the other a package of snapshots taken during the celebrations. The pictures, the replica of the ship's crest, and the letters describing the festivities, were gifts from a couple of old friends who wanted to share the memories. It was at that point I decided to write a book about the ships and sailors who had served in Korea with the United Nations peacekeeping force. I decided to write it from the point of view of the ordinary sailors, the ones who had worked the ships, fired the guns and made the heroic efforts from which victories are derived. I also wanted to depict the darker side of life in those ships: the black moods, the morale swings and the resentment spawned from time to time by officers who yearned for the Canadian Navy to assume a close resemblance to the Royal Navy.

I then began a journey along what proved to be a longer road than I had anticipated. I decided to start right at the very source, and with that in mind, sent letters to various magazines published by veterans' groups, asking for information from those who had served in Korea. My requests brought many replies. A great number of those who wrote asked to remain anonymous, so to them I will say a collective thank you all very much. Your input is appreciated. I will let it go at that in the old RCN spirit of "no names, no pack drill."

There were others, however, who made no special requests, so I wish to thank them in a more public fashion. First, I must give special thanks to the staff at the National Archives in Ottawa. Those with whom I dealt were so helpful, in particular Miss B. Wilson of the State and Military Records Division, who so patiently explained the meanings of certain documents.

I extend thanks to Gordon E. Berry of Calgary, Alberta, for the use of his files on HMCS *Athabaskan*; and to CPO R. Griffins, RCN (ret'd) for information on the same ship. Thanks to CPO Jerry Stokke, RCN (ret'd) for his input on HMCS *Iroquois*; to Malcolm English of Hemmingford, Quebec, for his recollections of HMCS *Nootka*. Also, thanks to William Mushing of Dundas, Ontario, for his files of HMCS *Huron*.

I wish to thank Wally Mills and W. K. Wilson of the Korean Veterans' Association for the information they gave on the PPCLI. Special thanks to Captain Ralph Goddard, Canadian Forces (ret'd) for the crest of the *Cayuga* which set the entire idea into motion; and to Ron Stewart who brought me into contact with many former shipmates.

My appreciation goes to Ken Macpherson and John Harbron whose critiques of the first draft were so helpful; and to Professor Barry Gough of Wilfrid Laurier University who made many suggestions of a technical nature. My thanks also to Vanwell Publishing.

I also wish to thank my wife, Maureen, for being with me along the way. She spent some long hours in the archives digging through dusty files of the RCN Collection; and it was she who uncovered a number of important items I might have easily overlooked. Then she spent many lonely evenings while I sorted the data and typed and retyped the various drafts.

While this book in no way tells the complete story of the RCN in Korea, I hope it sheds a little more light on the efforts of the dedicated Canadians who served in those now almost forgotten ships.

E. C. MEYERS

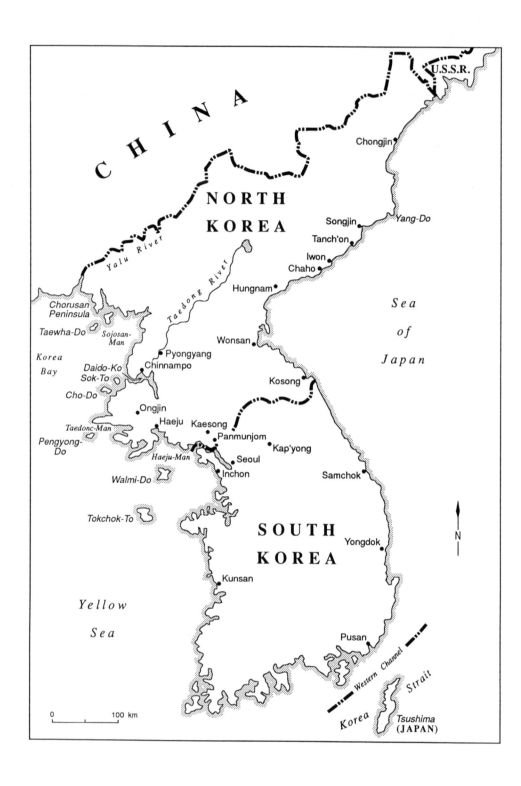

CHINA

NORTH
KOREA

Yalu River

Taedong River

U.S.S.R.

Chongjin

Songjin · *Yang-Do*
Tanch'on ·
Iwon ·
Chaho ·

Hungnam ·

*Chorusan
Peninsula*

Taewha-Do *Sojosan-
Man*

*Korea
Bay*

Daido-Ko
Sok-To

Cho-Do

Wonsan ·

Sea

of

Japan

· Pyongyang
Chinnampo ·

Kosong ·

· Ongjin

Taedonc-Man

*Pengyong-
Do*

Haeju · Kaesong ·
Panmunjom ·
Haeju-Man · Seoul
· Inchon

Walmi-Do

Kap'yong ·

Tokchok-To

SOUTH
KOREA

Samchok ·

N

Yongdok ·

· Kunsan

*Yellow

Sea*

Pusan ·

Western Channel

Korea *Strait*

Tsushima
(JAPAN)

0   100 km

Chapter One _____

ASSAULT

Throughout South Korea in the week preceding 25 June 1950, the thoughts of peasant and city dweller alike turned to the anticipated arrival of the annual monsoon, just as the thoughts of countless previous generations had turned. The monsoon, never guaranteed by the gods but reasonably dependable, meant there would be a successful rice harvest, while its failure to appear meant devastating famine. Koreans had known both, so there was never speculation about bumper crops or poor crops. The harvest would be either a success or a failure; there were never in-betweens.

When, on 23 June, the rain did indeed begin to fall, great joy was felt by all. Buddhist monks chanted prayers of thanksgiving. The assurance of a heavy rainfall plus the unusual heat ensured a crop of great abundance. The harvest was certain to be a success.

While South Koreans were watching the storm clouds building in the skies, a storm of a different nature had been brewing in North Korea. For weeks the warnings had been visible but no one heeded the signs.

On 8 June, the North Korean state press had published a short article entitled 'The Manifesto of the Central Committee of the United Patriotic Front." Almost overshadowed by its title, it announced that a general election would be held throughout the entire peninsula on 15 August 1950. It went on to state that the duly elected representatives would guide the nation in unity under the Red Banner. It made no mention of those already in office in the south. Neither did it mention the recognition of South Korea by the United Nations, or that body's refusal to recognize North Korea.

The manifesto was later published by both Tass and Pravda, the official news agencies of the Kremlin, thereby putting Russia's stamp of approval on the document. However, it was printed without editorial comment, possibly to give western readers the impression that Russia had no real interest in the article.

No attention or comment was forthcoming from any of the western capitals. Neither was any notice given to two other warnings.

On 10 March, a coded message had been sent to Washington from the Tokyo Headquarters of General MacArthur. It detailed major troop movements just north of the 38th parallel and along its entire length. It gave the strength and composition of the involved units. The Pentagon made no reply. Two days later a report from a contact in Pyongyang, the North Korean capital, informed MacArthur that Kim Il Sung, the North Korean premier, had approved the invasion of South Korea. Kim had apparently told his chief of staff, General Chai Ung Jun, to prepare his troops and to formulate a plan of battle. The report mentioned June as the month of invasion but gave no date. This warning was also ignored.

So, throughout May and June life went on normally in South Korea. The large American colony in Seoul went about its business, as did the smaller British enclave. The Koreans watched the sky and talked of rice and rain. No one was aware that in the cloistered, forbidden land to the north General Chai was shuffling his troops, briefing his commanders and preparing for the day of unification.[1]

On 23 June, Chai called upon Kim. With utmost confidence he told the premier that all was ready. As if to emphasize his great confidence, he told Kim an order would be given that Seoul must be taken within seventy-two hours of the initial assault.

* * *

In Seoul, General Chae Byong Duk enjoyed his position as Deputy Commander of the Armed Forces of the Republic of Korea. He liked the long title, and revelled in the social life his rank afforded. His only superior was President Syngman Rhee, who did not interfere in military affairs so long as things went smoothly. As a result, the general had a virtual lock on the office.

Chae, referred to privately as "Fats" by the Americans because his 5'5" frame was not adequate for his 250 pounds, had little interest in the topic of rice and rain. He was interested only in reports he was receiving about troop movements north of the border. He was concerned about the silence which had settled over areas normally swarming with guerilla groups.

12

The rotund little general, while hardly a good strategist, was not a fool. His love of tailored uniforms adorned with ribbons and medals, of the idle gossip of cocktail parties and the attentions of the ladies never interfered with his sense of duty. It was this sense of duty that caused him to seek out his two American military advisers at the American Embassy.

He spoke to them of the stillness along the border. According to most sources the advisers were not concerned. Being more used to the procedures of European military campaigns than with Asian history, they obviously felt the monsoon was responsible for the lull. Chae reminded them that Asians were quite used to rain, that several important battles in centuries past had been fought in the rain, and that the troop increase along the border could well signify that a major offensive was in the works. The advisers either did not know of the two pieces of information which had been recorded in Tokyo or had chosen to ignore them. Whatever their reasons, they downplayed Chae's worries.

Chae may not have been totally convinced, but he left feeling less worried. He had great faith in the Americans, mainly because they had defeated the hated Japanese but also because they had introduced him to *TIME* magazine.

TIME, in its issue of 3 June 1950 had lavished high praise on the South Korean army. The article had gone so far as to inform readers that South Korea was well protected by "the second best army outside the United States." In his ignorance of the world in general, Chae assumed TIME meant that his troops were second only to those of the United States. This naive belief afforded him comfort, and he cannot be faulted too much. In the more innocent world of the 1950s, many people looked upon TIME as the world's oracle. TIME had proclaimed his army as being Asia's best and, therefore, it must be so. He would still worry, but not as much.

On the evening of 24 June 1950, General Chae, resplendent in a new uniform tailored especially for the occasion, attended the gala opening party of the newly built Officers' Club, secure in the belief that *TIME* was omniscient, that the second best army was guarding the border and that North Koreans had no taste for fighting in the rain.

* * *

At 2100, 24 June 1950, the commanders of the North Korea's No. 1 and No. 2 corps received battle orders directly from headquarters, Pyongyang. It was the first glimpse either had ever seen of the plan and they were amazed at its simplicity.

13

The two officers, separated by many miles and with no knowledge whatever of the plans as they affected the other, called together their regimental and divisional commanders for final briefing.

At 0100, 25 June, all battalion, company and platoon leaders learned the roles their respective troops were to play. By 0300 all was in readiness. At 0350, the commander of the 105th Armoured Brigade gave the order that started the engines of forty T34 tanks. Five minutes later the powerful machines began their relentless roll southward. The Korean War had begun.[2]

The entire operation had begun in complete secrecy. Up to 2100 no one—possibly not even Premier Kim—had known the exact time set for the attack or even where the initial attack would be. Chae had kept the plans entirely in his head, refraining from writing anything which might have been seen by prying eyes. Thus, although the uncertified spy had learned that an attack had been authorized, he had been unable to provide any details. From 2100 until 0300 only three men had known the plans—and two of them had been kept totally ignorant of anything not concerned with their own sectors. There had never been any chance of a leak.

The battle plan prepared by Chai was basic simplicity. He knew the weaknesses of his enemy, knew the element of surprise would almost assure a quick victory, and that surprise would be best attained by a series of attacks having the appearance of small, unrelated raids. So, he began his invasion a little at a time, then hit the entire front once the length of the border was under attack.

At precisely 0400, 25 June, the 14th Regiment and the 23rd Brigade moved swiftly against the ROK 17th Regiment in the Onjin Peninsula. At 0415 another attack began. At intervals thereafter similar attacks were begun.

It was some time, therefore, before it was realized that the attacks were part of an overall invasion. Each ROK commander had been of the opinion that his sector was the only one engaged, and the attack nothing more than a nuisance raid. Hence there was a time lapse before signals were dispatched to Seoul.

At 0600 a frantic signal from the 17th Regiment in Onjin was received. The attack against it, the signal read, was so intense that defence was no longer possible. A full-scale retreat was in progress.

LSVP craft were quickly sent out from Inchon. Within hours the shattered remnants of the 17th began an evacuation by sea to temporary safety in Inchon.[3]

The North Koreans, working methodically and effectively, struck each point along the border to full advantage. As a result, the ROK defenders were caught largely unprepared. Most of the ROK commanders had granted weekend passes to many of the men in their units. Consequently most of the units were at half or even one-third strength when the attacks began. Those still on duty were hard-pressed to put up a decent fight. Within hours most of the units were in total disarray, and some were in panic flight.

* * *

At 0930, 25 June, Kim Il Sung went on the air from Radio Pyongyang to tell the world that a state of war existed between the two Koreas. He accused South Korea of initiating unprovoked attacks on North Korean units. While he was describing the heroic and desperate struggles of his beleaguered army against the barbaric aggressors from the south, his army was already many miles into South Korea.

Those in Seoul were well aware the invasion was full-fledged and that the Reds were pushing rapidly toward the city. The Red advance had been so relentless that already the city of Uijongbu was in danger of falling. A mere ten miles to the north of Seoul, it was the closest line of defence. The total panic which would soon grip Seoul was not yet in evidence but the confusion was great.

Chae Byung Duk, despite having laid out plans for just such a crisis, quickly realized that plans which look good on paper are often useless in practice. Worse, he was not in control of himself. He had come to rely too heavily on his advisers but, being representatives of a foreign government, they had no authority to assume even minor command positions.

Chae, now alone at the top, gave orders which were at best tentative and at worst stupid. In what would be the first of many errors, he gave orders to all reserve and militia units to report to Seoul instead of going directly to the front where they were needed. By the morning of 26 June, Seoul was crowded with troops. Few knew where to go or to which units to report. The situation was made worse by the congestion caused along the roads by hordes of fleeing refugees.

To make matters worse, the ROK army had no mobile equipment. It had no personnel carriers, no tanks and the few trucks on inventory were mostly unserviceable because of a severe shortage of spare parts. Still, many ROK soldiers found their way to the front using personal vehicles which ranged from ox-carts to bicycles. Many walked.

15

The city of Uijongbu fell at 1900 on 26 June. A few hours later two North Korean divisions linked up with the 105th Armoured Brigade and the combined force began a relentless drive toward Seoul. There was less than eight miles to travel.

* * *

When news of Uijongbu's surrender became known in Seoul the city became a scene of pandemonium. Much has been written of the terror and confusion which gripped Seoul for the next twenty-four hours. Frank Gibney of *TIME* and Marguerite Higgins of the *New York Herald Tribune* managed to get out of the city just as the first group of North Korean troops entered. They both filed reports of South Korean troops in panic flight, of the blowing up of bridges without warning those already on them, and of thousands killed by misdirected shells and wild gunfire.

The South Korean government fled without giving notice to anyone, including the British and American ambassadors. Foreign nationals were left to their own devices. Fired by President Rhee because he failed to stop the enemy advance, General Chae had been one of the first to leave the city.

The American ambassador, John Muccio, with a large contingent to worry about, managed to secure passage for them all aboard a small Norwegian freighter. The *Reinbolt*, a tramp steamer berthed at Inchon taking on a load of fertilizer, had accommodations for only fifteen passengers. Her captain was not inclined to remain in Inchon any longer than was absolutely necessary, but agreed to take the Americans aboard provided they could get there before the day ended.

Ambassador Muccio somehow managed to herd his entire group to the port city before the final hour and the *Reinbolt* slipped its lines and headed into safe waters, loaded to overflowing with fertilizer and 682 miserable passengers.

The Americans were lucky. The British ambassador, believing the North Koreans would grant foreign nationals safe conduct, made no efforts to evacuate his people. Most of them never saw Britain again. The fact that London had recognized Red China only a short time before made no impression on the North Koreans. The British ambassador had pinned his hopes on that recognition.

The Reds took Seoul on 28 June, one day after President Rhee and his officials fled to Suwon, south of the Han River. The North Koreans now held all the territory north of the Han, and their plan of battle was only twenty-four hours behind the original schedule.

16

The invaders paused to regroup and resupply in preparation for the final great thrust and the anticipated victory.

On the other side of the world, Canadian politicians were slowly emerging from their initial state of shock over the unexpected attack. The gears of External Affairs slowly began to turn and then mesh with those of the Department of National Defence. Many hours would pass before the two began to move in concerted effort.

Chapter Two _____

INVOLVEMENT

Korea has a time difference from Ottawa of fourteen hours. Thus, when the North Koreans crashed across the border at 0400 on Sunday, 25 June, Ottawa was basking in the hot sunshine of a Saturday afternoon. The clock in the Peace Tower had just tolled 1400, and residents and visitors alike who heard the chimes went about their business unaware that the bell had, at least indirectly, tolled for them.

Four hours later, when most of them were enjoying their supper, the first news from Korea was beginning to occupy the thoughts of newscasters. Most simply used the news as a headline story without much detail. The seriousness of the situation would not become evident until the following morning.

Up to then the only Canadians who had any idea of the events in Korea were those who staffed the Canadian Embassy in Tokyo. They had been aware of the fighting from its earliest hours and had sent a series of signals to Ottawa. Although fully cognizant of the intense excitement in the American Embassy, the Canadians simply notified Ottawa and sat back to await a reply.

Those signals arrived late Saturday evening, but it was not until Sunday morning that anyone in External Affairs took notice. Fifteen hours would elapse from the arrival of the first signal to the beginnings of some excitement.

Ottawa, in 1950, was not in contact with the world as it is today. The nation's excellent wartime intelligence service had been cut back to almost nothing when World War II ended, and as a result, Canada lost its best finger on the world's pulse. Furthermore,

External Affairs at that time was not fully operational during the weekends. From Friday evening to Monday morning minimal staff attended the teletypes and took the few incoming phone calls.

Because the signal from Tokyo had been sent routine priority, the duty clerk had no reason to inform anyone in authority. Only urgent or immediate priority signals were considered important. The high priority signals did not begin to arrive until Sunday.

The delay in notification would probably have gone into Monday had not Mary MacDonald, Lester Pearson's secretary, been listening to CBC Radio when detailed reports from Korea were broadcast on the Sunday morning news. She deemed the news serious enough to warrant a disruption of Ascot Reid's weekend. In order to notify Reid, an official in External Affairs, she had to drive to Lake Gaureau, then row a small boat to the middle of the lake where Reid was quietly fishing. He was totally unaware of the proceedings in the outside world and immediately headed for Ottawa. Mary MacDonald then drove north to Brunet where the Pearsons were spending the weekend. The two then drove back to Ottawa.

While Mrs. MacDonald was on her travels, the duty clerk in External Affairs had received a top priority signal from the State Department in Washington spelling out in some detail the plans the United States was formulating for action on the Korean matter. They obviously wanted Canada's support. The duty clerk immediately notified Douglas LePan of the United Nations Division. LePan phoned Prime Minister St. Laurent, who had also fled Ottawa for the weekend. Parliament was to resume sitting the following Monday, so St. Laurent had hoped to spend one final weekend in peace and quiet before the new session.

LePan also contacted Under-Secretary of State A. D. Heany in New York. Heany, well aware of the situation, was already preparing to go to Lake Success for the expected Emergency Sessions of the General Assembly and the Security Council of the United Nations.

By the time St. Laurent, Pearson and Reid arrived in Ottawa, LePan was able to present a complete briefing on the situation in Korea. Almost twenty hours had elapsed since the first salvos had been fired across the 38th parallel.

Events now unfolded quickly. At 1400 the U.N. General Assembly met for the debate on Korea, and a three-point resolution sponsored by the United States was quickly passed.

The Security Council also met in an emergency session to await the resolution from the Assembly. Of the ten members comprising the council, all were present except the Russian representative. Yugoslavia, a temporary member, announced it would remain strictly neutral on the Korean question and would not vote either way on the expected resolution. The four other temporary members—Cuba, Ecuador, Egypt and Norway—were all pro-west and would vote in favour. The five permanent members—Britain, France, Nationalist China, Russia and the United States—all held veto power, but Russia was absent and the resolution was assured passage. Once the resolution had passed both the General Assembly and the Security Council it became official.

Trygve Lie, then the secretary general of the United Nations, deserves full credit for the passage of the resolution because he moved before Russia could abandon a boycott upon which it had embarked the previous January. Had the Russian delegate been in attendance that day he would have used his veto, nullified the bold resolution and changed the situation completely.

The Russians had stormed out of the 10 January session in protest against the council's refusal to unseat Nationalist China in favour of Red China. Jakob Malik, the chief Russian delegate, then stated that all future sessions would be boycotted by Russia until Red China was seated.

The Russian display of petulance that day made it possible for the United Nations to show some mettle. By a vote of nine to zero the Security Council passed the resolution denouncing North Korea for breaking the peace. The resolution was amended the following day to increase the U.N.'s mandate in Korea. It called for an immediate cease-fire, immediate withdrawal of North Korean troops to positions north of the 38th parallel, and for all member nations to give aid to South Korea.

With the way now clear for actions of intervention, the various nations were free to make whatever plans they deemed appropriate. The Americans, secure in the knowledge that any action on their part had United Nations sanction, rushed troops to Pusan from bases in Japan. Within hours they were at the front lines.

These troops were for the most part young, untried and poorly trained. They were totally unprepared for the rigors and dangers they were to face. Having grown fat and undisciplined by the easy life in Japan, they fared badly against the hardened peasants who comprised the army of North Korea. The Americans were not prepared for Korea in any way, and only their sheer numbers slowed the Red advance.

The young, frightened Americans were thrust into a situation they could not handle. Day after dreadful day they were mauled. Each day saw them retreat further south, suffering grievous losses. Hindered more than helped by the remnants of the ROK army, they retreated toward Pusan for the last stand.

While other nations were pledging—and sending—ground troops to Korea, Ottawa was characteristically avoiding the issue.[1] Canada had promised three destroyers, and that commitment was being seen to with efficiency. The matter of ground troops was quite another issue, and despite heated debate in the House of Commons (members of the House were overwhelmingly in favour of such a commitment), the Cabinet remained adamant that no such action was needed. The three destroyers, Ottawa declared, would be sufficient.[2]

Canada was in no position to send troops to Korea. As usual the nation was unprepared for a military venture. The Canadian army was small, designed to handle problems at home and fulfil certain obligations in Europe. The Royal Canadian Air Force was a transport service and home defence force, unable to contribute the type of aircraft needed in Korea. Only the Royal Canadian Navy was prepared to undertake a full operational commitment half a world distant. So Ottawa pledged the ships, hedged on any other kind of commitment, and hoped the whole thing would resolve itself somehow. No one in Ottawa felt the tiny war could possibly culminate in anything other than quick capitulation by the South Koreans. In the early days of the fighting, all signs pointed to a North Korean victory. Had it not been for the gallant stand of the small force— mostly Americans—fighting under the banner of the United Nations, all indeed would have been lost. That small group, having fallen back to a confined area which became known as the Pusan Perimeter, held their ground long enough for reinforcements to arrive. By 30 July, South Korea's immediate future began to look a little more optimistic.

Chapter Three_____

IN ALL RESPECTS, READY

Once more unto the breach, dear friends, once more.
Shakespeare, *King Henry V*

When the first news of the fighting in Korea was heard by Canadians they exchanged glances with whomever they were with, made a comment or two (as often as not the comment was only an enquiry as to Korea's location on the globe—somewhere near China, isn't it?) then resumed whatever pressing conversational item the news had interrupted.

Canadians, on 24 June 1950, were little interested in the troubles of the world. Life was good. The nation's employment rate was at a record peacetime high. Wages averaged $50 a week, adequate for the reasonable cost of living. A pound of prime steak sold for 45¢, a pound of butter was 35¢, a quart of milk was 25¢. A glass of draft beer was still 10¢. Fuel for the brand new $1800 Ford, Chev or Dodge in the driveway was plentiful at three gallons for $1.00. Canadians who wished to travel by train from Toronto to Vancouver could do so for less than $50. The same trip by bus would get the traveller back home for the same price.

Canadians were smugly content. Louis St. Laurent, whom they had nicknamed "Uncle Looie," was prime minister, having finally taken over from the enigmatic MacKenzie King. How could a little war in Asia compete with items of such importance as the chances of Ralph Kiner winning the American League's batting championship, which he did, or of the Montreal Alouettes going to the Grey Cup final for a second straight year, which they did not? Would the Weavers' "Good Night, Irene" be displaced on the Lucky Strike Hit Parade by Frankie Laine's "Mule Train" after ten weeks of popularity? These were the burning issues, not Korea. Korea was simply not part of Canada's world.

The lack of national interest extended to the Royal Canadian Navy. The sailors had no reason to be interested in Korea. Like the nation's civilians, few had ever heard of the tiny country. Like other Canadians they lived within the boundaries of their own interests. Most had joined the navy in search of travel and adventure. Few, if any, held illusions of glory. That possibility had ended with World War II. None, certainly, had joined for the money. An ordinary seaman (new entry) was paid $54 per month. With the usual increases over time, plus trades pay, he could look forward to about $86 a month once he made able seaman. This would take eighteen months. His fringe benefits were good. He received an initial free kit while in his twenty-four-week basic training period at HMCS Cornwallis, the huge base near Digby, N.S. The initial kit was supplemented by a small monthly sum which he could use to keep the kit up to date. He was relatively well fed. Free dental and medical care were his. He could, under normal circumstances, look forward to thirty days' paid leave (plus travel time to his home) each year. He worked a five and one-half-day week as did most civilians.

Of course, he had to put up with naval discipline which was often harsh, often foolishly applied, and usually varied from ship to ship and shore base to shore base. There were always problems with discipline, both in its application and its acceptance. These problems had plagued the RCN since 1945. In 1948 a series of incidents aboard HMCShips *Ontario, Athabaskan, Crescent* and others had occurred. Called incidents by the RCN in official documents, they were in fact minor mutinies. These mutinies had been brought about by the conduct of some senior and many junior officers in their application of "good naval order and discipline." These officers had, in effect, developed a great love affair with the Royal Navy.

In their zeal to adapt, nurture and apply the traditions of the Royal Navy to the Canadian Navy, and at the same time foster the idea of an elite officers' corps within the RCN, they alienated the men of the lower decks. The sailors of the RCN had no use for the class system prevalent in the RN. As a result of this difference of opinion, there were underlying currents of mistrust and resentment toward the officers which would continue for years.

This resentment reached its peak in 1948, but during the period of the Korean War lay dormant. There was one incident in 1950 aboard *Cayuga*, but it was resolved quickly.

Considering, then, the problems Canadian sailors were having within their own service, plus their lack of interest in anything not connected with their way of life, it is small wonder the news of the Korean invasion caused barely a ripple. In Halifax and Esquimalt, the sites of the two principal naval bases, there were few sailors who considered the news to be of "well, here we go again" significance. Even among the higher ranks there was little show of concern. An alert signal was sent out to all units from naval headquarters in Ottawa. Such signals were sent whenever troubles broke out anywhere in the world and just as routinely filed away.

The Halifax-based ships had for the most part spent June in the continuous comings and goings of routine training. On 24 June, all the ships except two frigates were at home. Most of the ships' companies were on leave.

At Esquimalt the bulk of the Pacific Fleet lay in harbour, with only minimal activity planned for the next few weeks. May and June had seen the ships confined mainly to local waters on a day-to-day basis. This routine pleased nearly everyone. June had been a month of clear, sunny skies and calm seas. Sailing had been most pleasant. The nights at home were equally appreciated.

The Pacific Destroyer Command—CANDESPAC—comprised five destroyers, of which only three were in commission at any given time. When Korea broke into the news HMCShips *Cayuga*, *Athabaskan* and *Sioux* were operational, while *Crescent* and *Crusader* were the out-of-commission units. Moreover, the three ships in commission were in varying stages of refit at the time. Thus they too were for all intents and purposes not operational. It was unusual for a naval squadron to be incapacitated in its entirety, but the world was at peace and there were no indications of trouble anywhere.

The refits had been deemed timely, for the three ships were slated for a lengthy journey to Europe in the company of three east coast ships—*Magnificent*, *Micmac* and *Huron*. It promised to be a great tour, and the ships' companies were looking forward to it, particulary the young, eager newcomers whose first ships these were.

The Pacific Command ships were to proceed down the coast to San Diego, through the Panama Canal, across the Caribbean Sea to Jamaica, then northward to Halifax and their rendezvous with the carrier and the two destroyers. The six ships would then travel across the Atlantic to Europe. The ports of call were to include Copenhagen, London, Oslo and also principal ports in Sweden, France and Belgium. For the western ships the stay away from home was to be lengthy.

The sailors on the west coast first heard of the fighting in Korea from the noon newscast over station CJVI, Victoria. Although they may have routinely discussed it, none felt any concern.

The following day their mood changed, and by Monday, although no official word had come down, the general feeling aboard the ships was that Europe was about to be overridden by Asian affairs. However, the routine continued as normal throughout the day. The refitting went on as the "dockyard mateys," with their miles of electrical cable lying stretched out along the decks, went unhurriedly about their work. The normal noises of shipboard activities were punctuated by the hissing and sparking of the welding and cutting torches.

Tuesday 27 June saw a decided change of pace which told all concerned that Europe was indeed "out" and Asia was "in." The Communication Centre at HMCS Givenchy, the naval station in HMC Dockyard, received the first of a series of signals, all top priority. One stated that Captain Jeffry V. Brock, RCN, would arrive 29 June to assume overall command of preparations for the sailing of three destroyers with a tentative departure date of 5 July. There was no mention of a destination.

* * *

Jeffry Vanstone Brock, DSC, RCN, slated to take command of *Cayuga* effective 5 July, was on leave when the news from Korea broke. He was recalled to Ottawa for a briefing, from which he left immediately for the west coast. He was to prepare the three destroyers for a voyage westward. The ultimate destination would be announced shortly.

While Brock's appointment to *Cayuga*, and with it the title of Commander Destroyers Pacific—COMDESPAC[1]—had been made weeks before, the coincidence was to prove fortunate. The navy could not have made a better choice than the talented Brock. At age 36, he was the youngest man ever to hold the rank of captain in the RCN. He had been connected with the navy from his earliest years, having started out as an officer in the Reserve at HMCS Discovery, Vancouver. Because of his availability for immediate service when World War II commenced, he moved quickly up the promotional ladder. Canada, as usual, had been unprepared when Hitler started his war, so large numbers of Canada's fighting men were seconded to Britain's forces. Brock was among them.

He spent most of the war in RN ships in a variety of capacities, did his work well and was noticed by those in high places. At war's end he returned to the RCN and continued his rise. An excellent tactician, Brock knew naval strategy well. In a course he attended at Whale Island, the elite RN gunnery school, he raised eyebrows and much envy by placing first among all in attendance, including many who had been considered by the RN as being the best in the military world.

Described by *TIME* in a 1950 article as a "Sundowner," Brock came to know troubled times in the peacetime navy.[2] He had been generally considered the main cause of the 1948 mutinies aboard *Ontario* while that ship was in Mexican waters—a series of incidents resulting from a routine too harsh for a ship in tropical waters.

Brock was only part of the trouble. However, he was high profile with his share of jealous rivals, and as he had been in command of the troubled *Ontario*, was singled out as the likeliest cause of the problems. His case was not at all helped by his admiration for the Royal Navy's "pusser routine" which he had come to know and love during his years with the RN. The strict routine, which worked well enough in British ships, did not go down at all well with Canadians, who have always tended to be freer spirits than their British counterparts. It had been only a matter of time before the breaking point was reached.

Ottawa, alarmed at the severity of the complaints from the sailors involved, moved hurriedly to alleviate the situation. Adm. Rollo Mainguy was instructed to make an in-depth investigation. His final report, the *Mainguy Report*, was the result.[3]

The report did much to solve the navy's ongoing problems, but misguided admiration for the Royal Navy's disciplinary methods on the part of many RCN officers continued to give troubles into the 1960s. Because of Brock's involvement in the incidents, his reputation, so far as the lower decks were concerned, was badly tarnished. His appointment to Ottawa, and a desk job, was not bemoaned.

In due time Brock would be exonerated by a Royal Commission appointed to look into naval affairs*, but reputations die hard. In 1950 there were many serving in *Cayuga* who were less than happy at the prospect of serving under his command. To Brock's credit he quickly dispelled their fears and, as events unfolded, it became

---

* The report by the Royal Commission is still on the classified list. It will not be available to the public for many more years for a number of reasons, not the least of which was a promise by the Commission members to keep the identities of the sailors who testified before it a closely guarded secret.

obvious that no better commander could have been chosen to lead the three ships into an uncertain venture.

* * *

Though the sailors were not informed of what was happening, the good citizens of Victoria were very well informed of the secrets of the RCN. The talk in the city by Monday was of the war in Korea and the probability of Canadian involvement. How the supposedly classified or top secret information reached the public ear is easily guessed, and it was soon obvious that civilians could be informed while those involved remained in the dark.[4]

Bartenders, barbers and gas pump attendants seemed well informed of the plans to send ships, but the RCN did not get around to informing its sailors of their impending voyage to Korea until 30 June. By that time an official proclamation was unnecessary; the news had already been proclaimed by any number of civilians.

By 29 June, activity aboard the three ships had become hectic. Brock had arrived to take control of the preparations with the cool professionalism that had become his trademark. He took a quick look around and decided to cancel most of the remaining refit work for *Athabaskan*. She was, he decided, ready for immediate duty. *Cayuga*, though out of dry dock, still had much upper-deck work to do. Brock ordered that only the most needed work be completed. The lesser work could be left for the shipwright as an at-sea project. *Sioux* was refloated a day ahead of schedule. He then ordered the ships moved to No. 10 jetty. The enormous task of resupplying would be accomplished more quickly with the ships in a concentrated area.

That same day all leaves were cancelled. A total of 198 officers and ratings were hastily drafted from other ships and bases across the nation to bring the destroyers from peacetime to wartime status. *Cayuga*'s crew was increased by 76 to a total of 15 officers and 271 men. *Sioux* took aboard another 37 for a final total of 16 officers and 271 ratings. *Athabaskan* swelled her roster to 16 officers and 239 seamen of all ranks, an increase of a record 85.

While most of the newcomers were new entry trainees who had known naval service for less than eighteen months and just recently graduated from Gunnery, Supply, Communications or Engineering schools, some were members of the RCN Reserve. These men had taken leaves of absence from their civilian jobs to answer a call to action. Of the draftees, several had been pulled from their classes before they could graduate. These men were entitled to wear their trade badges and use the designations of their trades. They would, however, be required to add the letters NQ after the designation. A gunner, for example, would be designated 12345-E Smith, John, J. OSQRS(NQ). This meant that he was considered to be an ordinary seaman gunner who had not yet passed all his final tests. The *E* after his official number indicated he was of the Pacific fleet. Atlantic Command sailors were designated by an *H*.

The final days of June and the first three days of July were days of feverish activity and long hours. With the sudden influx of those newly arrived, living conditions in the ships, never comfortable at the best of times, became critical. As there were not sufficient hammock bars for all concerned, some of the sailors in each mess had to sleep on the locker cushions. As a makeshift bunk a locker was not uncomfortable, but would prove to be less than dependable in rough seas when any lurch of the ship could tumble the sleeper to the deck. The fall was nearly fifteen inches and nearly always threw the sleeper against a metal leg of one of the tables, which proved hard on the ribs.

Turmoil prevailed. The mateys still milled about with torches, cables and hoses. Adding to the confusion was a seemingly endless parade of supply trucks which disgorged boxes and crates containing everything from canned goods to spare engine parts. As if this abnormal congestion was not enough, a constant, annoying procession of high-ranking officers came and went in parties of threes and fours to oversee the proceedings.

The congestion of busy workers plus the clutter of crates and boxes made movement along the upper decks difficult. The racket of the drills and pneumatic hammers prevented normal conversation. The atmosphere reeked with the odour of truck exhaust, the fumes from cutting torches, the smell of fresh paint, the essence of cooking from the galleys and the omnipresent odour of diesel fuel, the singular essence of all ships.

To the casual onlooker the scene would appear to be one of total confusion. It was, in fact, a finely organized operation which came to its conclusion well within schedule. Sometime during the morning of 3 July, the final box was tucked away into its proper storage place, the mateys gathered up their cables and hoses to depart for work elsewhere and the final party of brass made a last tour. Just before noon the three ships moved across the harbour to the naval magazine where the stocks of ammunition were replenished. Dusk saw them all back at No. 10 jetty.

The following morning, 4 July, in short ceremonies, Capt. M. A. Medland, RCN, turned over command of *Cayuga* to Captain Brock. A few yards away, aboard *Sioux*, Cdr. Paul D. Taylor, RCN, took command from Cdr. David Groos, RCN. These command changes had been promulgated weeks earlier. They were in no way influenced by the intended dispatch of the ships to a war zone.

The ships were now in all respects ready for sea.

* * *

When Brock arrived in Esquimalt on 29 June, he was caught in a bit of an awkward position. Medland, in command of *Cayuga*, was COMDESPAC and would be until 4 July. Brock, however, had been placed by Ottawa in charge of all preparations for the as yet unannounced departure date and the ships' destination. There was some confusion until it was decided that Brock would assume overall command, but would leave Medland in charge of his ship to deal with the daily shipboard routine and the minor details. The arrangement seems to have pleased both men. Certainly it played a major role in saving the necks of two young seamen a few days later.

Whether *Cayuga*'s Entertainment Committee had planned the smoker for some time or only at the last moment, is not known, but it seemed a good idea, if only to take the crew's minds off the crowded conditions. Besides, it was viewed as an excellent chance to say goodbye to the departing Medland and hello to Brock. The sudden plans which had changed the European cruise to a trip to Asia were also part of the decision, certainly.

The Entertainment Committee announced on 29 June that a smoker would be held on Saturday 1 July from 1930 to 2300, in the wet canteen at HMCS Naden. Blue Boats would be available to transport the revellers to Naden from 1830 to 2000; and would begin return runs to the dockyard at 2200. The last boat would depart Naden at 2330.

A smoker, in the heyday of the RCN, meant a rowdy evening. The ale flowed unabated at no cost and, as there were never women present, the songs, jokes and stories were ribald and without fear of the censor's knife. The smoker of 1 July in the austere canteen of Naden was no exception. A strong ale, one brewed specially for the navy by the Silver Springs Brewery of Victoria, was plentiful.[5] The old songs were sung and L/S Jim Tyre, by popular demand, recited his legendary versions of "Young Albert at the Zoo," "In the Corvette," "On Parade" and several other of the lad's many misadventures. By several accounts a great time was had by all.

Two ratings had *too* good a time. They were among the last to leave when the doors closed, and as a result, arrived at the Naden floating jetty just in time to see the last Blue Boat disappear into the darkness. Chagrined at the thought of having to walk two miles to the dockyard, they decided to solve the problem by borrowing a

THUNDER IN THE MORNING CALM

large boat tied to the jetty. It would, they thought, be a simple matter of starting the engines and running the boat across the bay. No harm would befall the boat, and it would be found the next morning.

With that in mind the two clambered aboard, flashed up the twin Chrysler Marine engines and pushed off into the stream. How they managed all that without alerting the sentries aboard *Ontario*, one hundred yards distant, was never explained. The engines had no sooner roared into life when the reason for the boat's presence at Naden became clear. It was there for repairs. The boat could not be steered properly and the throttle for the port engine was stuck on "full ahead." This combination caused the boat to swing to starboard at high speed. To make matters worse, it was on a collision course with *Ontario*.

With the engines roaring at full throttle, and *Ontario* looming larger as the distance closed, one of the sailors leapt to the tiller and swung it over in a desperate effort to veer the boat away from the cruiser. At the same time, the other cut both engines. Deprived now of power, the cutter slid under the bows of the ship. The miss was by scant inches. It shot then, with a gut-wrenching crunch, between two barnacle-encrusted pilings before coming to an abrupt stop atop a jagged rock, which splintered the boat's bow planks. The sea rushed in through the wounds.

The boat began a slow settling beneath the surface as it slid sideways from its perch atop the rock. A sentry aboard *Ontario*, alerted belatedly by the noise, raised an alarm. Within minutes the cruiser's upper deck became a hive of confused activity. Several watchkeepers rushed down the gangway to the jetty in the direction of the shattered cutter.

The moment the boat hit the rock and began its slide into the cold depths the two miscreants, their minds now firmly set on escape, leapt over the side into the chilling water. Half swimming, half scrambling through the waist-deep water, they struggled up and over rocks made slippery by slime and clinging seaweed. Panting with cold-induced exhaustion, the two gained the shore to flee into the darkness offered by Naden's many buildings. Unable to leave by the main gate, they fled to the west fence, scaled the wire near "B" Galley and ran pell-mell in the general direction of the dockyard. They thought they were free and clear. They were wrong.

The following morning brought a shock. The senior of the pair —an able seaman—realized his wallet was missing. He immediately went to the regulating petty officer's office to report it missing—an action which ultimately saved his skin. Twenty minutes later he was recalled to the RPO's cabin. There Chief Petty Officer Robert Weber informed him the wallet had been found in the bilge of the doomed cutter, that he was under open arrest charged with wilful damage to naval property, and that he would be well advised to urge his partner-in-crime to give himself up in order to save a lot of trouble for the investigating officers.

The seaman was almost immediately brought before the ship's executive officer, Lt. Cdr. C. R. Parker, RCN. The charges alleged the seaman to be guilty of theft and destruction of naval property in that "to the prejudice of good naval order and discipline, [the accused] and an as yet unidentified accomplice [had stolen the cutter], property of HMCS *Ontario*, from its moored place at the jetty of HMCS Naden." "The defaulter," the charge continued, "did willfully and with malice run [the cutter] at high speed [onto the rocks] causing it to sustain serious and severe damage to its bows and keel. Although pursued [by watchkeepers from Ontario] the accused did escape in the darkness. A search [of the cutter] revealed a wallet, the property of [the accused]."

Parker wanted nothing to do with the case. He hurriedly ordered it over to Captain's Report. He ordered a complete investigation be mounted "forthwith" to apprehend, if possible, the accused "unknown accomplice."

At Captain's Report, convened a few hours later before Medland, the charges were once again read. Medland in the meantime had received an urgent request from *Ontario*'s commanding officer, Capt. Hugh F. Pullen, RCN, asking that the culprit be transferred to the cruiser. Medland, who would be *Cayuga*'s skipper for less than twenty-four more hours, had no wish to deal with either the case or with Pullen's request. To his way of thinking there were too many loose ends, not to mention the coincidence of the accused having reported his wallet missing before it was found in the cutter. Medland felt there was a possibility the wallet had been found by the real culprit and planted to throw the investigators off his track. Medland ordered the case set aside for the incoming Brock.

Because of the hectic pace under which the ship had been operating, no Captain's Report was scheduled before it would be at sea. Thus the sailor was spared transfer to *Ontario* and the tender mercies of Pullen. Pullen, however, was not so easily put off. He moved his venue of request to the office of the Flag Office Pacific, the redoubtable Rear Adm. Wallace Creery, RCN. The rear admiral applied mild pressure on both Medland and Brock. Medland refused to budge from his initial position, while Brock replied that he was far too busy to spare any time for the case. Brock replied he would deal with the matter at his scheduled Captain's Report on 7 July. Creery, who also had more pressing problems on his desk, informed Pullen his request was denied and the matter was dropped.

During the morning of 7 July, as *Cayuga* plied her course toward Hawaii, Brock heard the case, considered the evidence and dismissed all charges as "not proven." He left no doubt, however, in anyone's mind that he felt the sailor probably was the culprit, but he was not about to make a decision based on probabilities. At the same time he managed to convey to the crew that his patience with impulsive and exuberant young men was not without limits.

Brock and his crew came to an understanding that morning. As time passed a mutual respect and trust grew. It prevailed throughout the duration of their months together. For many it prevailed for years.

* * *

The morning of 5 July dawned upon an almost serene dockyard. Gone now was the frantic scurrying and bustling that had marked the previous week. The three destroyers, prim and gleaming in coats of fresh paint, rode motionless alongside the jetty. The sky was cloudless, the water below was clear, unrippled. Cormorants skimmed inches above the surface in search of the small fish upon which they fed. Overhead the ubiquitous gulls dipped and cavorted, their shrill screams piercing the quiet of the early morn.

By 0800 the dockyard was once again a bustling hive. Sailors and civilian workers hurried to their ships or places of work. Those who served aboard the destroyers had been granted extended leave—to 1000—but few took advantage of the extra hours. By 0900 the crews were nearly at full strength. By 1005 both *Sioux* and *Athabaskan* were able to report "all hands present and accounted for," but *Cayuga* was to report one man missing. He was pencilled into the ship's log as AWOL.[6]

Departure was scheduled for 1500. At 1300 wives, family members, girlfriends and reporters began to arrive. By 1330 the jetty was crowded with well-wishers. At 1415 a short ceremony began. The fleet chaplains read the naval prayer and the band from HMCS Naden struck up the naval marches and anthems that have thrilled crowds for generations. At 1450, the bosun's calls shrilled out the familiar whistles to announce the time of departure had come.

"Out pipes. Special sea-dutymen to your stations. Hands fall in for leaving harbour. Secure the brow."

On the bridges the three captains began to replay a scene each of them had performed many times.

"Let go all springs. Stand by engines."

"Let go the forward lines. Let go aft."

"Engines slow astern. Wheel ten degrees starboard."

32

"Engines slow ahead. Wheel five degrees starboard."

So it would go until each ship had cleared the jetty to move slowly toward the harbour gate.

The three ships moved out in single file to fall into line behind *Ontario*, who had slipped quietly away from the jetty a few minutes earlier. The cruiser would accompany the destroyers to a point halfway to Hawaii, where it would refuel the smaller ships prior to heading home.

The ships steamed toward the harbour exit to the cheers of a crowd estimated by many to be in excess of fifteen thousand. The notes of the naval anthem "Hearts of Oak" echoed across the water. In reply each ship sounded the penetrating "Whoop! Whoop! Whoop!" from their sirens, the world-renowned trademark of destroyers.

The four ships steamed from Esquimalt in partial order of seniority, *Ontario* leading. Then came *Cayuga*, *Athabaskan* and *Sioux*.[7] As they made for open water the ships passed the Duntze Head Beacon. There the salute was taken by Rear Adm. Harold G. DeWolfe, RCN. In the review party were Maj. Gen. George Pearkes, V.C., Member of Parliament for Victoria. Also in the party was Capt. M. Medland.

The ships, the beacon now behind them, moved into the Straits of Juan de Fuca and into the Pacific Ocean, their destination Pearl Harbour, Hawaii. Canadian warships were to make the 2100-nautical-mile trip many times.

* * *

Coded Task Group 214.1, the four ships spent the next four days in hard training and exercises. The perfect weather allowed much to be accomplished. On 7 July, *Ontario* bade farewell and turned back. The others, now TG 214.4 continued on their way, still undergoing exercises and drills. In the early morning of 12 July, they entered Pearl Harbour. The waiting time began.

To this point the United Nations had not officially accepted Canada's offer of ships, although acceptance was expected. Besides, a totally unexpected problem had come forward when someone in Ottawa raised the question of the legality of placing Canadian ships and sailors under the command of a foreign national. The foreign national in question was, of course, Gen. Douglas MacArthur, commander in chief of United Nations forces in Korea. Also, there was one more problem: the need for ships in Korea was not pressing as warships were available in abundance. The need was for ground troops, and Canada was not about to make such a commitment. For a while it appeared Canada might not send anything to Korea.

Late that afternoon, however, a lengthy signal arrived from Ottawa. TG 214.4, it stated, was herewith assigned to the United Nations and was to proceed to Korea. Shortly after, a signal which has often been described as polite, was received from MacArthur. Obviously he had been hoping for soldiers, not sailors. The signal bade the ships welcome with a request they proceed to Guam via Kwajalein Atoll. At Guam, the signal said further orders would be issued.[8] Brock decided to remain in Hawaii until 15 July. There were some more preparations required and MacArthur's signal had not disguised the fact that another three ships were neither wanted nor needed.

* * *

The three days in Pearl Harbour were routinely spent. Time was found for anti-submarine exercises with a couple of U.S. subs, but for the most part the ships remained alongside. Leave was normal and little trouble was reported by the shore patrol. One sailor was arrested by the USN patrol and returned to his ship where he was put under "close arrest."[9]

It was during this time that the incident previously mentioned occurred aboard *Cayuga*. It came very close to paralleling the 1948 mutinies. The ship's first lieutenant, Lt. Cdr. C. R. Parker, had ordered those who worked on the upper deck to wear full uniform. He had based that decision on the grounds that many high-ranking visitors were coming and going for talks with Brock. Full uniforms meant the heavy, canvaslike whites, the hated #5s.

By 1030 the tropical sun in the cloudless sky had driven the temperature above eighty-five degrees Fahrenheit. The overpowering humidity, plus the heat generated from the steel decks, added to the discomfort. A group from the ship's Welfare Committee met with Parker to request a relaxation of his order. Parker refused.

At 1200 the pipe "hands to dinner" was made. At 1315 the pipe "hands fall in" was made. It was ignored by the seamen. Within a few minutes a chief petty officer appeared at the main door of the upper-after mess to enquire why no one had fallen in as ordered. He was told that no work would commence until Parker rescinded his dress rule. The CPO left after advising that the doors should remain unlocked, as locked doors would transfer the present status to one of mutiny.

After a few anxious minutes another pipe was made. This one changed the rig of the day from #5 whites to the cooler rig of the previous day. The crisis passed, but the crew's dislike for Parker grew. How much Brock had been involved in the incident is not recorded. It is unlikely he was even aware of the dress orders, as such matters were generally left in the domain of the first officer, the "Jimmy" in naval slang. Brock, however, would certainly have been informed when the crew refused the call to work. It seems likely he intervened to change the dress order, as the last thing he needed at that point was another incident on his record. It is equally unlikely that Parker would have changed the order on his own. Parker, a quiet man but given to outbursts of temper, was not popular with the crew at the best of times. The incident in Hawaii did nothing to offset that unpopularity. Nor would he, himself, do anything to lessen the tension felt by the men of the lower decks. The strained relations continued throughout the entire tour of duty.

Following the incident in Hawaii, the Welfare Committees became more active, and remained so for the duration of the Korean tours. These hard-working committees of elected representatives were instrumental in gaining a number of reforms which, though minor by today's standards, were great breakthroughs at the time. Most of the reforms have been carried over into the present forces, and serve as memorials of sorts to the members of those committees of long ago.

The Welfare Committees of the 1950s brought about changes in the daily rum ration by bringing Coca-Cola into the tradition as a substitute for the water previously mixed with the rum. They were responsible for the navy's agreement to issue baseball-style caps for use at sea, an issue still part of Canada's forces. They brought about daily issue of cold beer as an after-supper treat when the ship was at sea. These were the groundwork for important reforms made in future years.

* * *

The ships departed Hawaii during the morning of 15 July, on a direct course for Kwajalein, a minor atoll in the Marshalls Group. The uneventful trip took six days, and the stay at the tiny island was but twenty-four hours, just time for refuelling and a boat tour by some of the more curious to see the sunken remains of the *Prinz Eugen*, a German cruiser of World War II which had been scuttled there in 1947. Other than that the island had nothing to offer.

Early on 22 July, the three ships headed for Guam, arriving three days later only to be told they faced a two-day delay because of an error in resupply orders. It had been Brock's hope to stay only twelve hours, but all that could be done now was to wait until the USN could correct the mistakes it had made.

In 1950, (as it is still), Guam was a military base and had been since 1521 when the Spanish navy decided the island was an ideal staging area for their galleons. In 1898, Spain ceded the island to the United States following the Spanish-American War. It has remained an American possession ever since, except for a thirty-one-month period during World War II when it was occupied by the Japanese. The U.S. Marines retook the island in 1944.

Guam held no interest for the Canadian sailors. It had nothing to offer in the way of entertainment and all were happy to leave when the ships finally got underway on 27 July, to begin the final leg of the long trip.

Those aboard *Cayuga* would have forgotten Guam as quickly as did those aboard the other ships had it not been for a solitary walk taken by a thoroughly bored seaman. He was to make an interesting discovery.

* * *

Midway through the afternoon of 26 July, L/S George Johnson decided a walk along the beach might offer some relief from the heat and noise of the ship. The breeze from the ocean was cooling. He sauntered along, finding it easy to forget the crowded messdecks.

As he rounded a bend near an outcropping of rocks, he saw an islander not far ahead. The man appeared to be fishing with a net. Johnson drew near intending to watch a few minutes. To his dismay he realized the man was not fishing. He was drowning a large litter of pups in the ocean. By the time Johnson reached the spot only one puppy was left, and its future seemed a matter of a few seconds at best.

The islander, suddenly aware of the presence of a tall stranger, stopped his unpleasant task long enough for the drenched pup to free itself from the net. It tottered unsteadily to temporary freedom. The sailor scooped the dog from the gritty sand.

The islander, deciding the stranger meant no harm, asked for the return of the dog. He attempted to explain the necessity of ridding the island of unwanted animals to control a burgeoning population. The sailor, who could relate to the discomforts of over-crowding and confined spaces, could hardly disagree.

He could not, however, return the pup to certain death, so he made the islander a spot offer. The sailor would take the dog. No, the islander replied, that was not possible. The dog, once released, would merely go wild and compound the problem. Johnson countered with the proposal that he would take the dog away from the island. To the islander this seemed fair enough. Johnson gave the man a couple of dollars and headed back to the ship. He had not gone fifty feet when the realization of what he had done hit home. One simply did not bring mascots aboard a ship of the RCN without permission. He contemplated his self-imposed problem as he trudged along. He could not let the pup go free but he had his Good Conduct badge to consider. He needed a plan, one that would work.

The little dog, snuggled firmly as he was in the sailor's protective arms, seemed quiet enough. The problem of getting it aboard was not insurmountable, but the problem of keeping it from discovery might prove very different. Permission was needed to bring the dog aboard, but once in the ship it would be unthinkable that permission would be denied. The key? Of course! Have the ship at sea when the dog was discovered.

Almost as if in answer to his concerns he discovered a box with a lid. He placed the pup in the box, clamped on the lid, told the dog to remain quiet and walked boldly up the gangplank. In nervous haste he retrieved his station card, said a brief word to the quartermaster, then fled in the direction of his mess.

There he removed the dog from the box and, for the first time, took a good look at his acquisition. It stood on wobbly legs, a very small bundle of short brown and white fur. It had enormous brown eyes.

By now a small group had gathered. One, who had some experience with small animals, expressed fears the dog was unlikely to survive. He felt the pup, which he stated to be female, mongrel and about three weeks of age, was too young to have been removed from its mother. There was always the chance, he said, that a strict diet of evaporated milk might do the trick if feedings were hourly and around the clock. Another realist wondered how detection could be avoided. The pup would have to be concealed until the ship got underway.

Feeding proved no problem. Eager helpers came to the fore, each volunteering a few minutes of time to give the little stowaway her milk. Neither was a supply of milk a problem, as co-operative cooks happily donated an adequate supply of tinned milk.

Keeping her ahead of the officers as they made their daily rounds proved an interesting exercise in subterfuge. By the time the ship slipped her lines to depart Guam the pup, complete with bedding and saucer, had been moved by her guardians to no less than ten different locations before ending up in the "B" gun housing. There the tiny passenger was discovered when the ship was two hours out to sea. It was later revealed that at least two officers had been aware of the pup's presence, so that perhaps the constant moving about had not been entirely necessary. As things turned out the dog became as popular with the officers as she was with the crew.

The furry stowaway found, permission was sought to keep her. Brock concurred with the request on condition the dog be trained properly to clean habits, be cared for correctly, to have one official keeper, and to be kept out of the way during drills and action stations. Also the captain insisted, the pup must be trained to know which areas were out of bounds to her, including, presumably, his cabin and its surroundings.

The weeks passed. The pup, never lacking for care and getting more attention than it required, grew rapidly on her diet of tinned milk. In due course she was introduced to solid food. By popular consent she was named Alice, was given the rating of O.D. (Ordinary Dog) and began a rigorous course of basic training. She learned to climb stairways, learned where she could go and where she could not, and where she was to report when the action stations bell sounded. This was easier than anyone expected. She hated the roar of the 4-inch guns and eagerly sought a safe hiding place.

Alice became a familiar figure as she patrolled her ship. She eventually learned to climb the vertical ladders with some success. She managed this difficult feat by hoisting herself from rung to rung one leg up at a time. Of course, she could not descend ladders, but would patiently wait until someone came along to carry her down.

Alice had an affinity with people. She never doubted for one moment that she was human, and acted accordingly. She used charm and guile and could be coy or coquettish as the situation demanded. She sometimes nagged her way to what she wanted. She was known to have snarled on occasion to show displeasure.

She liked beer and had a particular liking for the dark ale sold in the Royal Navy canteens. She became a favourite with the RN sailors in Sasebo and took full advantage of their hospitality. She was allowed small rations of ale in a saucer. Only once did she imbibe too freely and, to her disgrace, staggered off the end of a table. This ended her evening ashore and the next day she seemed much the worse for wear. From that night she was limited to an amount of ale in keeping with her size. Also, she was watched very closely because she took to the devious habit of going from table to table in search of just a little more.

Canadian journalists who covered the initial stages of the fighting spent time aboard the three ships. Nearly all who visited *Cayuga* gave mention to Alice in their reports home. Because of the good press, the little dog gained some fame. When parcels eventually began to arrive for the sailors, not a few included a tin or two of dog food or a package of treats marked for Alice. Someone knitted a navy blue sweater, which she wore during the cold days at sea.

Alice, in her own way, did much to raise the ship's morale during trying times. She brought laughs to sailors grown weary of long, arduous patrols. She seemed able to pick out those who were down and blue. To them she would offer a minute or two of genuine affection, asking only in return a scratch behind the ears.

She caused problems now and then through carelessness. Twice she went over the side, once between two ships. On that occasion, it is said, the frantic cry "Alice overboard" brought a quicker response than the cry "man overboard" ever would.

Once, in Tokyo, she went adrift. The ship's departure was delayed several minutes in hopes she might reappear. When departure could be delayed no longer the order to slip was given with a certain sadness. *Cayuga* moved slowly astern and had already cleared the jetty when an officer on the bridge spied the dog running toward the end of the jetty. Brock, upon hearing the shout, gave the order which returned the ship to the jetty. A rescue was quickly made.

With Alice once more aboard, the ship made its second departure as a loud cheer went up, not from the ship but from a group of Japanese stevedores who had watched the drama with some interest. Obviously they were impressed by what they considered an act of great respect for one highly honoured. While all this was going on, Brock, no doubt wondering what he had done to deserve such a ship's mascot, was heard to mutter to no one in particular, "Well, that little caper just cost the taxpayers about twenty-five hundred bloody dollars."

As a result of this incident, a mock Captain's Report was convened. For her misconduct "prejudicial to good naval order and discipline" the red Good Conduct Badge was removed from her sweater. She earned it back in due course and, in fact, moved up the promotional ladder during her two years of Korean duty. Alice retired from the service as Leading Wren.

Alice left *Cayuga* in 1952 to live in Belmont Park, the navy's married personnel housing development. She remained there as the house pet of the Tyre family. It would be nice to report that she had died in her sleep at a ripe old age, but that was not to be. Always one to assume some duty, she designated herself garbage truck sentry. She would hop on a small step at the rear of the truck and ride the route as the truck made its daily rounds. One morning she slipped from her perch as the truck was backing, fell beneath a wheel and was killed at age ten.[10]

Of all the mascots with Korean service—Siouxsie (*Sioux*); Scoshi and Pom-pom (*Athabaskan*); Stokes (shared *Cayuga* with Alice for a few months in 1952); and Bubbly (later replaced by Swampy) of *Huron*—none logged more sea time, received more publicity or lived longer than did Alice. She is the only dog to be given an entire paragraph in any publication of the RCN. She had to share the page with a parrot named Tom and a coyote called Lestock, but all who had known her agreed she would not have minded in the least.[11] Alice was too much the lady to be subject to petty jealousies.

Chapter Four_____

INTO
THE FRAY

Our navy is addressed, our power collected.
Shakespeare, *King Henry IV, Part II*

───

His Majesty's Canadian Ships *Cayuga*, *Sioux* and *Athabaskan* sailed into the large harbour at Sasebo, Japan, on 30 July 1950 at 1530 local time.[1] The weather, as recorded in the ships' logs, was "hazy with a light, steady drizzle." The temperature was recorded as sixty-one degrees Fahrenheit. Leaden clouds hung low over the jagged peaks which protect the harbour on three sides. The greyness of the day, the chill rain and the low clouds gave the harbour a sombre appearance as if nature were attempting to cast a pall upon those assembling there. It seemed a grim reminder that war itself is dreadful and that the war in Korea was going badly for the defenders.

Sasebo's harbour, which would be home for the Canadians for months to come, teemed with ships that day. Warships rode at buoys in the stream, tied two and three together. Merchant vessels lay at anchor in solitary loneliness here and there. The few jetties were crowded with supply ships of both the Royal Navy and the United States Navy. All available space had been utilized.

The harbour, some five miles in length and very wide, had been zoned in a systematic manner by the USN in an effort to minimize the usually slow process of resupplying ships. The supply ships had been segregated in one zone, the repair ships in another. Fuel and ammunition ships were in other, distant zones away from the travelled paths.

While the USN had lessened the complications of resupply, it had also lengthened the travel for the boats' crews who had to do the running about in search of required goods. Unlike the more familiar system in use by Commonwealth navies, where a supply officer and his men could travel around for hours filling one requisition, the Americans had geared themselves to fill orders quickly. But it could not be done all in one area.

The USN kept the bulk of its supplies, including fresh and frozen foods, aboard huge depot ships. Warehouses ashore were strictly places serving as transfer points to the floating depots. Ships were thus highly mobile and on very short notice could be removed from Japan to any other operational zone.

This desire for rapid mobility had given the USN an inventory control system which could pinpoint any needed part, piece or parcel within a very short time. It effectively eliminated the need to journey, purchase order in hand, from place to place, only to be told the needed item was not in stock. This was a great weakness with most navies of that era, the RCN included. Canadian supply officers were pleased to learn their ships could be turned around quickly, often in record time.

Simply explained, the USN system enabled a supply officer of an inbound ship to signal his needs days in advance to the central supply depot in Sasebo. There the order was broken down by items and categorized. The items were then located and the appropriate depot ship notified which items were to be reserved. A signal was then sent to the inbound ship restating the entire order with each item listed as available or not available. Following each available notation was the name and location of the depot ship holding the item. From that final list the supply officer was able to pre-plan his schedule and route for the pickup. So successful was the system that a destroyer, even one almost totally depleted, could be fully restocked within seventy-two hours. In many cases, the time could be even further reduced if all boats were deployed and the crew worked around the clock.

The first order of business for the three ships upon arrival in Sasebo was that of resupply. This was carried out quickly. The next morning saw them all ready for immediate departure to the war zone in case they were needed. As they were not needed, however, they were told to stand by. The ships went into modified routine and leave was piped for those who wished to go ashore.

* * *

Sasebo, from a sailor's point of view, was not a good leave port. There were no night spots with the flavour of the western world. There was but one dining place of good quality—a large hotel some miles from the waterfront. There were no large department stores, but there were hundreds of tiny shops all peddling a vast array of souvenir-type articles of poor quality. Japan, still struggling to recover from its failed war, had not yet learned the secret of top-quality production.

There were brothels on every street. ("Hey, Canada boy-san! I take you to heaven, ni?") Some were operating with a large staff, others were one-girl operations. Although operating under license, these houses were under no medical supervision whatever. They became the bane of the medical officers, who could only issue stern warnings and treat the large numbers of sailors who would become infected over the next five years.

The *Reports of Proceeding* from all the ships lament over and over the ultra-high incidence and serious problem of venereal diseases, some of which were new to western doctors. But, in July of 1950, there was no inkling of how serious the problem would become. By the end of the year a pattern began to emerge. The so-called Butterfly Girls who inhabited the brothels were, by even conservative estimates, 98 percent infected. For the girls who worked the streets, the waterfront bars and the "skivvy parlours," the percentage was even higher.

Although Canadian ships were to spend five years in Japan, there were only two or three incidents in which Canadians were involved with Japanese nationals to a degree serious enough to warrant investigation. Of these incidents, only one was classified on a court-martial level.

The possibility of clashes between visitors and nationals had been foreseen by NHQ, so prior to arrival in Sasebo, each ship's captain issued warnings to his crew that Ottawa had no desire to become embroiled with the Japanese courts over questionable behaviour by Canadians. Neither did Ottawa wish to become involved over alleged violations against merchants or other civilians, no matter how minor the violation might be. Those in authority told the sailors that all bills must be paid, niceties must be observed and, above all, the Japanese social structure must be held in full respect. It was permissible to accept invitations to Japanese homes, but all customs were to be faithfully observed. Lectures were arranged which informed the sailors of the family structure of the Japanese and the customs of the society into which they were about to be thrust.

Few of the Canadians knew anything about the social mores of Japan, and this information was imparted to them in the days prior to arrival. The sessions were chaired by personnel of various rank who knew something of the country and its social structure. These sessions proved generally successful, doing much to anticipate problems and supply answers in advance. Unfortunately the sessions, for reasons never fully understood, soon deteriorated into lectures against the Red Menace. What had been interesting talks about a new adventure to an unknown land became almost overnight a series of old hat lectures which everyone had already heard. Attendance at these sessions dropped immediately, and they were soon abandoned.

The focal point for the Canadians while ashore remained throughout the years the USN's enlisted mens' club, the infamous Anchor Club. A noisy, crowded, smoke-filled canteen, it had available a variety of beer which sold for fifteen cents a can. Clean enough when it opened for business each day, by 1600 the arborite-topped tables were covered with ashtrays filled with half-smoked cigarettes. Often the floor was awash with spilled beer, and every so often a Japanese waiter was dispatched by the head bartender to go forth with a mop and dry the floor sufficiently that walking on it might be less hazardous.

The Anchor Club almost always had an adequate supply of the more popular brands of American beer. Miller's, Pabst, Schlitz and the ever-popular Budweiser were generally available, but occasional shortages forced the emergence of a woefully tasteless brew called Acme. The only beer the Americans would supply for shipboard sales (perhaps owing to its unsaleable status ashore), Acme became the *bête noire* of the Canadians. Even now Canadian sailors recall Acme with little enthusiasm.

Not far from the Anchor Club, along a narrow and twisting road, was an equally cheerless place which served as the Royal Navy canteen. A converted warehouse, it boasted long, wooden tables and hard plank benches. There were few chairs and these were also wood. The beer—Bass, Worthington, and several others—was, in British tradition, served warm. Dark and bitter, the British beer never found great favour with the Canadians. They preferred a cold Acme to a warm Worthington.

* * *

The ships were not long in Sasebo before they were assigned to duty. In the war zone things were faring badly, with the entire United Nations force bottled up within the confines of the Pusan Perimeter, unable to advance and unwilling to retreat. As success was dependent upon how quickly troops and supplies could be rushed to the front, it fell to the navy to see the convoys safely to Pusan. Most of the ships were kept engaged in escort duty in a busy and continuous series of arrivals and departures.

In the early hours of 31 July, *Athabaskan* left Sasebo on her first mission. *Sioux* remained in harbour as a rescue unit—not an enviable assignment as it meant the ship had to remain on full sailing alert. The ship was therefore kept in harbour until 12 August, except for one short outing on 5 August. *Cayuga*, because Brock was busy with a series of conferences with senior military officials, did not put to sea until 3 August.

There was really little need for warships along the coastal waters anyway. All the fighting was inland, beyond the range of even the biggest naval guns. The important work of the moment was convoy duty. *Cayuga* alone carried out five such assignments between 9 and 24 August.

The UN warships were designated their tasks according to nation and affiliation. British, Australian, New Zealand and Canadian ships were assigned to the west coast, while those of the USN were kept mainly along the east coast. The reasoning was a dictate of caution. It was thought that should a Commonwealth ship venture into China's coastal waters, the British ambassador in Peking might be able to settle the matter diplomatically, as Britain had recently established relations with Red China, while the United States still refused to recognize its existence. That was enough to negate even the remotest possibility of obtaining the release of any errant USN ship, should one be caught in Chinese waters. The east coast offered less chance of such violation. Great pains were taken to avoid any action which might draw China into the war.[2]

The organizational charts of the United Nations naval forces showed General MacArthur as supreme commander, with Vice Adm. C. Turner Joy, USN, as his designated commander. Admiral Joy had under his direct command one Task Group, four Task Elements and three Task Units.[3]

Commander in Chief
Gen. Douglas MacArthur, US Army

Commander Naval Forces Far East
Vice Adm. C. Turner Joy, US Navy

Task Grp. 96.5
USN

Task Element 96.50	Task Element 96.51
HMS *Black Swan*	Support Grp. #1

45

Task Element 96.52 USN		Task Element 96.53 RN
Task Unit 96.53.1 HMS *Triumph*	Task Unit 96.53.2 HMS *Jamaica*	Task Unit 96.53.3 HMS *Kenya*

The organizational charts were amended many times. In September 1950 several new task groups were added, one of which was the entire US 7th Fleet. In March 1951, the charts were once again amended to add Task Groups 95.10, 95.11, 95.12 and 95.13. One week later Task Force 77 joined the huge fleet as a highly mobile carrier force. By the end of 1951 the original UN Fleet had burgeoned to three task forces, five task groups, four task elements and several task units whose number changed constantly.[4]

The Canadian ships saw service with nearly all the groups over the thirty-seven months of fighting. They moved as required from one to the other as a group or as single units. Often a ship would be assigned to a unit only to be pulled out after an hour or two. Conversely, the stay could be for weeks. While it might be thought that this constant wandering would be annoying, the result was quite the opposite. The Canadians realized, and were pleased to know, that their gunnery, mine detection and radar expertise were much in demand. Rather than feeling like orphans, they took the sudden assignments as great compliments.

The only problem with that type of scuttling about was that only the ships' navigators and captains ever knew where the ship was in the maze of islands, or with whom they were working at the time. It also meant the Canadians were on their own much of the time. The experience gained in this type of solitary hunting was to prove invaluable during the so-called Island Campaign of 1951 and 1952.

TE 95.11, the Carrier Group, and TE 95.10, the Blockade Patrol, became familiar postings. The Canadians were to spend much time with each.[5]

The original intention had been to keep the Canadian ships together as a task unit, but the direction the war took changed that plan. While the original idea had been attractive to the Canadians, it was soon seen to be impractical, and the idea was quickly revised.

When the war took its unfortunate turn in December 1950, the RCN ships were quickly assigned to operational groups where their radar and gunnery skills could be best utilized. As a result, they found themselves only occasionally in each others' company. The months spent working with other navies proved beneficial in the long run. Much was learned and much was taught.

* * *

The delay the Canadians experienced in getting into action following their arrival, although unappreciated at the time, proved to be of some benefit. The days in harbour allowed time to study the situation ashore and at sea. There was time to study the maps of the rugged—and treacherous—coastline of the peninsula. The maps showed an inhospitable Yellow Sea, containing thousands of poorly charted islands and islets.

Korea hangs off China's eastern coastline like a downturned thumb. Its interior consists of high, brown hills and deep, craggy valleys. Vegetation is varied. In the south are sparse patches of stunted pine trees, but to the north are vast tracts of good timber. A rugged range of jagged mountains—the Taeback Range—extends the length of the east coast. Rugged peaks rise to heights exceeding 8,000 feet. The highest, Mount Paek'tu, rises to 9003 feet. Korea has an estimated 3400 offshore islands, mostly on the west coast, varying in size and importance. The Canadians were to become very familiar with many of these.[6]

The country has an extreme climate. Summers are hot and humid; winters are dreadfully cold. The north wind, which howls down from the great plains of China, intensifies the bitterness of the cold. In winter, snow lies deep in the valleys to clog the narrow roads for weeks on end. Snow squalls along the coasts are often of gale force, with snow blending with icy sleet which stings the face and exposed hands. The one single memory of Korea which all veterans of that war easily recall is the numbing cold of the Korean winters.

Summer is also unpleasant much of the time. September is the only month when the weather is more or less dependable. The summer weather is almost as unpredictable as that of winter. Heavy rains often precede or follow days of fog or heavy mist. Between the rain and the fog are sandwiched days of intense heat, made even hotter by an intense humidity. Each summer will see one to three typhoons which wreak havoc along the coastal areas, but only rarely as far north as Korea Bay.

The coastal geography is as diverse as the weather. The west coast is rugged, heavily indented by irregular fiords and shallow channels. All along the coast are uncharted islets, shoals and rocks.

The east coast has deeper water and very few islands. Except in the extreme north, the coastline is fairly even, with long stretches of high cliffs. During the war all the railways were on the east coast and, because they ran along the cliffs close to the sea, they proved vulnerable to the naval guns. This vulnerability was not overlooked by the task forces which prowled the coast.

The Sea of Japan, which comprises the east coast waters, is a far cry from the shallow depths of the Yellow Sea. However, the

Yellow Sea has much stronger tides, from lows of six inches to high tides of thirty feet. The gritty bottom is in constant turmoil caused by the tons of mud which flow daily into the shallow sea from dozen of rivers. Because the mud never settles, the water remains yellow. This condition gained the sea its name centuries ago. The yellow grit offered one benefit. It scoured the ships' bottoms to such a degree that they remained totally clear of barnacles.

Silt, as it pours forth from the rivers, forms bars and mud flats so quickly they cannot be charted. Harbours become clogged within weeks, and have to be dredged on an ongoing basis. Obviously, the war had an adverse effect on those operations.[7]

The problems which faced the UN fleet were as varied as the coasts themselves. The west coast provided shelter to small craft as they hopped from island to island in their attempts to escape the larger ships in pursuit. In many cases they escaped by hugging the shoreline, moving slowly through the shallow water and using the rocks for cover. The east coast denied them this tactic.

Mines were an ever-present concern on both coasts, but the lethal weapons were more easily spotted in the western waters. The mines planted by the Reds used rigid moorings, and during low tide appeared on the surface. These mines were called watchers because the detonation horns peered from the water like huge, bulging eyes. They were easily seen, and many fell prey to the 40mm Bofors, which proved ideal for the job.

* * *

Coasts, waters, geography and weather were not the only things the Canadians found to be different. They also found vast differences among the assembled Allies. Communications proved difficult as unfamiliar accents produced unexpected problems.

Surprisingly, the problems were not between English-speaking sailors trying to communicate with Korean, Dutch, French or Columbian ships, but between English sailors and Americans. Voice communication between a Yorkshire accent in a British destroyer and a Texan drawl in an American cruiser could produce some irritating moments and some irrational comments. More than a few insults were hurled from time to time across the ether.

Here the Canadians held a decided advantage, having been alerted to the probability of just such a problem through the circulation of a well-known story which had been making the rounds in the RCN since World War II.

A convoy, the story went, had departed Halifax for England during the early days of the war. The weather was poor, and worsened as the hours progressed until heavy fog had settled in. The following morning showed no signs of the fog clearing and two more days passed before a small break occurred. It was anticipated that the weather might clear, but the convoy was ordered by its senior officer to remain deployed for fog until further ordered. The convoy pressed on.

Suddenly a surface vessel was spotted by one of the corvettes on station, which moved quickly to intercept. If the intruder were German he would have to be sunk, hopefully before he could alert any nearby submarines of the position. The interloper proved to be Swedish, a neutral merchantman. As there was no threat, the corvette's captain moved close and called out a greeting over the loud-hailer. The greeting was returned. Could the merchantman, the corvette enquired, give an inkling of what the weather to the east had been? The Swedish captain replied he did not fully understand.

"Have you had any fog?" called the corvette's captain.

"Vat iss it you ask?" replied the Swedish skipper.

"I said," replied the corvette's captain, "have you had fog in the east?"

The Swedish captain, still unsure of the question, asked once again for a repeat. "I do not so good understand English," he called.

"Fog," yelled the Canadian over his loud-hailer." Fog. Have you had fog in the past two days?"

After a lengthy hesitation the reply came from the merchantman. "No. captain, none at all. Ve haff on board no vomen."

A Canadian communicator recalled the story as he told how he had listened to an American radioman trying to explain some message to his counterpart in a British cruiser. The British sailor was becoming more frustrated by the minute as he tried to fathom the American's drawl. "Finally," said the Canadian, he could take it no longer and called out, "Is there anyone out there who can tell me what this message is all about?"

The Canadian then broke in, "I am Canadian and I understand both your languages. It would be to your advantage to relay through me."

This type of relay service was used on several occasions which also included messages between ships and aircraft. Canadian communicators got along generally with their USN and RN counterparts. They used the same terminology as the British so difficulty was rarely encountered there, and they spoke almost the same version of English as did the Americans and so easily understood them.

The Canadians' main complaint was the American habit of asking repeatedly how the transmission was being received. The Canadian reply of the standard "I hear you loud and clear" was suitable to all others in the fleet. The Americans, however, wanted an actual rating on the volume and clarity of transmission. The standard "loud and clear" to an American had to be a "five by five" or a "three by three" depending on the reception. Why this was no one ever knew.

The Canadian communicators, because they could not understand the reasoning behind it, refused to comply. Eventually the word got around that RCN warships were not about to adopt the American method, and the "loud and clear" was accepted.

It is thought the final agreement came one dark night when an American voice crackled through the static-filled ether for the fifth time with the request, "How do you read me?" Plainly agitated, the Canadian replied for the fifth time, "I hear you loud and clear. I have been receiving you loud and clear for five minutes. There is no change."

"Is that 'loud and clear' a 'five by five'?" the Yank persisted.

"No! Gawdammit!" the Canadian snarled, "It's a two by two by two."

"I do not understand two by two by two," the confused Yank replied.

"It means," growled the Canuck, "that I hear you too loud, too clear and too gawdamn often."

From that time verbal communication became easier, but on occasion the air would be turned several shades of blue over annoying transmissions. The accents of Americans and British continued to grate on one anothers' nerves, while the Canadians continued in their role as interpreters.

This ability to understand both British English and American English aided them in their ultimate conquest of a far greater challenge. It took a few months, but they eventually learned Australian English—no easy feat.

* * *

While the first days in the theatre of operations had been spent either in harbour or on convoy duties, on 10 August all that changed. On that day the three ships were assigned to Task Element 95.53 for west coast duties. For four days they screened aircraft carriers, a boring duty, but by night, when the carriers were idle, the destroyers were released for island patrol.

As yet none of the three had engaged the enemy and, the situation being as it was in the Pusan Perimeter, there were times when it appeared the war might actually end before they would see any action at all.

This waiting ended on 15 August, when *Cayuga* and HMS *Mounts Bay*, a frigate, steamed away from the group on a course for the port city of Yosu. This minor port on the south coast had just been taken by Red forces and, though it could never be used by the invaders as a port, it did provide a strong base for the Reds in their expected push against the UN force's weak southern flank.

It was therefore considered prudent to destroy the existing dockyard facilities and the numerous storage sheds in order to deny their use to the enemy. Also, the Reds were known to have brought in heavy artillery which would be used in the forthcoming push, and these guns were known to be marshalled in the dock area.

The two ships arrived at mid-day. *Cayuga* anchored 7,000 yards offshore while the frigate moved in to 5,000 yards. An hour later an aircraft from HMS *Theseus* arrived, circling the port several times as its pilot radioed locations of targets.

At 1805 *Mounts Bay* commenced firing. The fall of shot indicated solid hits had been made. At 1815 *Cayuga* swung broadside to line up her three twin 4-inch gun mountings. For fully two hours the shelling continued without letup. Each broadside hurled six shells landward. When the shelling stopped at 2015, the entire dock area was a mass of flames. Not a single building remained intact. The jetties and piers were in shambles. Gasoline and oil tanks exploded to produce flames which added to the carnage. The aircraft then returned for a close look. The pilot reported twisted pieces of heavy artillery among the ruins. The reports, then, had indeed been correct. The North Koreans had brought in heavy guns.

Cayuga's action marked the first time since 1945 that a warship of the Royal Canadian Navy had fired its guns in anger. The casing from the first shell was set aside to be made later into an impressive ashtray. Suitably engraved, it was presented to Prime Minister Louis St. Laurent.

For *Cayuga* the action marked a personal milestone, as it was the first time she had ever engaged in a hostile action. Though her keel had been laid during 1945, she had not been commissioned until 1947. *Cayuga* had not known war, nor had the majority of her company. Only the senior petty officers and a few of the officers had seen wartime service.

That held true for a great many of those who saw service in Korea. These young men had not known the miseries and privations of World War II, so the experience of Korea was totally different from anything they had known before. Few had known how they would react and most were quite surprised at their thoughts about the shooting once they realized it was not another practice, but a hostile engagement in which men, many no doubt young like themselves, were being killed and maimed by the shells they were firing into the sheds and wharves. During those first two hours of action ninety-four HEDA (High Explosive Direct Action) 4-inch shells were expended.

* * *

Action stations became a way of life for the sailors. Once they got into action it seemed they were rarely out of it. Life changed drastically for them. Conditions, never comfortable in the ships at the best of times, worsened during the long periods on patrol. Extended periods at action stations brought about further discomforts. When the guns fired, their recoil and vibration loosened the insulating material from the deckheads. This material fell in showers of minute flakes to cover the decks, the tables and the lockers with a fine layer of snowlike powder which had to be swept up and removed. The powder got into clothing and foodstuff. In retrospect, the men who served in those ships can be thankful the insulation was not asbestos, but a less harmful material of the gypsum line.

Another annoyance was the smoke from the guns and the smell of the cordite. The living sections were permeated with both. The gunsmoke entered the ship through ventilation ports and could remain trapped for hours before dissipating. But as the days passed into weeks and months these annoyances came to be hardly noticed. Even the insulation showers became tolerable except during meal hours, when a randomly fired gun would dislodge the powder onto plates and into cups.

During lulls in action it was permissible to catch catnaps, and these short sojourns were greatly appreciated. Those who worked the magazines discovered that two ammunition boxes placed end to end made a more or less comfortable bunk. Some would nap in the flats directly adjacent to the magazine hatch. Thus situated they could quickly scramble below when the action resumed. This wandering got the *Cayuga*'s "X" magazine-loading crew into a spot of trouble.

One cold night in mid-December the action, which had been almost non-stop for several hours, saw a lull. In order to escape the coldness of the magazine itself, the loaders went up into the wardroom flats. This was the area in which the officers' cabins and the wardroom were located. Because the wardroom had a carpet, however threadbare it may have been, it seemed to offer some comfort. About ten sailors made themselves as comfortable as possible on the deck in the hopes of being able to nap on something a bit less uncomfortable than the hard deck outside. They were soon ordered out by the less-than-amused officer who saw no reason to share the wardroom with lower-deck personnel.

During the prolonged periods of action those in the depths of the ship, however cold they might have been, were spared the harsh winds which bedeviled those on the upper decks. Those on the bridge and at the guns were at the mercy of the often violent wind which swirled about them, often accompanied by sleet or rain. Ice formed on beards and eyelashes. Eyes watered in the lashing bite of the wind which caused the job of looking out a harsh chore. Uncomfortable enough when the ship rode at anchor, the discomfort increased accordingly when the ship was underway.

* * *

On 16 August, her crew unhappy at being beaten out of the first action by *Cayuga*, *Athabaskan* proceeded to Kunsan, another minor port on the west coast just south of the 38th parallel. There her guns put out of commission four batteries of 120mm artillery pieces recently installed by the North Koreans. During the attack she also destroyed important warehouses along the waterfront.

Athabaskan then steamed directly to the lesser port of Popsong'po a few miles further south. A garrison of NK infantrymen had been established there a day or two before, complete with several batteries of heavy artillery. The heavy guns and the infantry billets were all destroyed by forty-five HEDA shells. These shells were fused to explode on direct contact. Several intense explosions were recorded which indicated fuel and ammunition dumps had been hit. North Korean casualties, while no exact figures could be verified, were estimated as moderate to heavy.

Finally, on 20 August, *Sioux* got a break. Ordered to proceed to Popsong'po to evaluate the damage done by *Athabaskan*, she was greeted by fire from ashore. The North Koreans had replaced the guns destroyed the few days previously by *Athabaskan* and added four more. *Sioux*'s gunners fell to their task with deadly efficiency.[8]

Once again the batteries at Popsong'po were demolished, and *Sioux* left, her crew convinced the task was complete. They were somewhat dismayed when they learned some days later that an Australian destroyer had been dispatched to take out still more replacements hurriedly brought in by the Reds. Popsong'po was then code-named Tombstone, after the town in Arizona whose civic motto has been for many years "The town too tough to die."

The Popsong'po action was the only fighting *Sioux* was to be part of during August. She returned to carrier duty before heading back to Sasebo, where she would remain in harbour until September.

* * *

The ship which saw the most action during the first weeks of RCN involvement in Korea was *Athabaskan.* From 15 to 21 August, she plied the waters near Inchon, usually in company with HMS *Kenya**, a light cruiser. As a team, the two ships worked well together. Their combined firepower was considerable, with *Kenya*'s four turrets of 6-inch guns each having three barrels, plus her secondary armament of 4-inch guns and Bofors.[9] On 18 August, the two ships approached the island of Tokchok-To. The cruiser remained well offshore as *Athabaskan* sailed in to close range. In the darkness she anchored some 800 yards from the craggy shore.

Tokchok-To, a large island situated not far from Inchon, was deemed by the North Koreans to be vital for two reasons. First, only a few guns were needed to hinder any ships approaching from any direction and, second, it gave an excellent view of the entire area through which ships would have to pass enroute to Inchon. Tokchok-To was the Reds' first line of defence against any offshore attack against Inchon. The island, eight miles long and two miles wide, was very sparsely settled. It had only one small village—Supo—and there the Reds had established a small garrison.[10]

At 0700, *Athabaskan* began an intense bombardment against well-entrenched North Korean infantrymen occupying the village of Supo. Under cover of the shelling a platoon of ROK marines slipped ashore. At 0830 the marines signalled that the village was secured.

A volunteer landing party from the ship then went ashore to render whatever help they might offer to wounded civilians. Fortunately only a few had been hurt, all to minor degrees. These were taken to the ship for treatment. The marines reported that no prisoners had been taken.

This aspect of the war became unsettling to the Canadians. They had not been on the scene long enough to understand the ROK marines had no intention of taking prisoners unless there was a vital reason for so doing. If it were felt a prisoner might hold some information of importance, he would be taken to a point behind the line for questioning. Rarely did such prisoners survive the question

---

* HMS *Kenya* was commanded by Capt. Patrick W. Brock, RN. A native of Vancouver, B.C., he had spent his entire career in the Royal Navy, and was not related to Jeffry Brock of the RCN.

period. Eventually the Canadians became accustomed to the fact that few, if any, prisoners were ever reported.

Two days later *Athabaskan* moved to the island of Yonghung-Do in support of another group of ROK Marines. At 0630 all guns opened fire. The marines gained the beach with no difficulty and moved rapidly inland. This time, however, the North Koreans put up stiff resistance and, because there were five villages to secure, the island was not taken before 1800. The shelling had been continuous the entire day and the crew had a first taste of what continuous action would come to mean. Besides spending the entire day at the guns or in the magazines, they had to forego their usual hot meals. Because cooking was not possible during action stations, breakfast, lunch and dinner that day consisted of hastily concocted sandwiches with tinned fruit for dessert. Lulls in the action allowed brewing of coffee, which was eagerly received.

While the ROK Marines, as usual, reported no prisoners, there were in fact several taken when two motorized junks filled with North Korean soldiers attempted to flee the island. The ship's boats set out in pursuit as the Bofors gunners fired several shots across the junks' path of retreat. The junks stopped and those aboard surrendered without a fight. These soldiers were the only prisoners taken that day.

With Yonghung-Do now in UN hands, *Athabaskan* turned its attention to Palmi-do, a small, rocky islet a few yards off the larger island. Palmi-do was home to no one, but housed a small radio hut manned by two North Korean soldiers. They both were gathered up along with their radios and then the hut was destroyed.

The islands, now neutralized, were left occupied by ROK marines. *Athabaskan* departed for targets further afield, mainly in the north. Though not generally understood at the time, the August action had been carefully planned and timed. It had cleared the way for the invasion of Inchon.

The islands governing the approaches to Inchon were the main obstacles to an invasion of the city, and the heavy guns at Kunsan and Popsong'po were the completion of a tight ring of defence. By taking the islands and knocking out the guns so far in advance of an actual invasion the Reds were lulled into thinking the attacks had no other purpose than what they seemed. Certainly, there was no reason to believe there was a common purpose. Then, when the Inchon area fell once again into a period of quiet, the North Koreans gave no second thought to the possibility of invasion. Surprise was, of course, necessary for a successful invasion. *Athabaskan* and *Sioux* played a large part in gaining that much-needed commodity.

Chapter Five

ADVANCE

Strike up our drums, pursue the scattered stray.
Shakespeare, *King Henry IV, Part II*

War, in order to have any justification at all, must have as its sole purpose the retaking of lands lost to an aggressor and the liberation of the subject population. This liberation can be achieved only through the efforts of troops, mainly those who fight on the ground. Navies and air forces may soften the enemy or deny him the means of supplying his own forces, but only ground troops can secure the land successfully. This irrefutable fact has been known for centuries.

In Korea, in 1950, the United Nations held total, uncontested control of the sky and the sea. The land, however, was decidedly *not* under UN control. Even the few square miles of the Pusan Perimeter, all that stood between the North Koreans and their final victory, was a very precarious holding. The defenders, demoralized and weary from a series of savage maulings, were in danger of crumbling at any moment.

That the defenders, mostly American troops, were barely holding their own should not be considered surprising. Washington, having appointed itself the defender of Korea, had not considered a large force necessary for the task.

Equally unsurprising is the attitude held at the time by the Pentagon concerning numbers of troops. In all its history, except for the period of the war between its own states, the United States always kept its army relatively small, compared to those of European nations. The reasons for this are easy to understand. The

Americans, once Britain and France had withdrawn from North America, had little fear of attack from ground forces. As a result, the Americans decided their power should be at sea. Then, in 1937, their seapower was augmented by that of an air force which remains their dominant power to this day.

Because Washington felt, correctly, that any war in which Americans might become involved would be far away from North America, the American army was kept small. If, as in 1917 and again in 1941, American forces might be forced to fight, Washington reasoned their allies would be able to supply the holding power long enough for them to mobilize troops, to make ready a powerful war machine and enter the conflict at full strength. This philosophy worked well for Washington during two world conflicts, but when their troops were needed in Korea, there was no holding power upon which to rely. The South Korean army was not up to the task, and within hours all seemed lost. Worse, the only troops available to the Americans were in Japan and were, from a motivational viewpoint, not ready to fight. Thrust as they were into a war for which they were unprepared, they paid dearly from the moment they arrived in Pusan. Only when they came to realize their almost hopeless position as they huddled in the misery of impending total defeat within the confines of the Pusan Perimeter did they stiffen their resolve.[1]

So it was that in August General MacArthur found himself in command of a powerful fleet, an unchallenged air force and an army which might not last beyond the next day. MacArthur, while not the military genius his apologists would have the world believe, did know he could win only if some extreme action were quickly taken.

Douglas MacArthur was the type of general to whom Napoleon alluded when he made his oft-quoted statement that "Good generals are always able to explain in detail why they lost a battle, while lucky generals win and have no reason to make explanations."

MacArthur was a lucky general. He had, through a very effective public relations campaign begun in 1942, created for himself the image of a conquering hero. In truth, he conquered no one. His record in the Pacific campaign reveals a man usually unprepared and lacking in tactical imagination. He had himself been largely responsible for the loss of the Philippines because he had failed to follow any of the three feasible plans someone else had drawn up for the islands' defenses.

With the Philippines lost, MacArthur retreated to Australia, and it was there his public image was born. His first public appearance, in Canberra, was a classic example of promotional hype. He wore a uniform festooned with ribbons and decorations—thirty-six in all, along nine rows. His personal photographer moved the general through a series of poses, all presenting the best profile. From that day his every move was carefully planed with nothing left to chance. Even his celebrated return to the newly-liberated Philippines was orchestrated with as much care and management as any Hollywood movie. Fortunately he managed to make his return in only one take.

MacArthur carried his image with him to Japan when that nation surrendered in 1945. As supreme commander, his presence was only slightly less opulent than that of the emperor. The general's arrivals and departures to and from his HQ were carefully staged to assure the most favourable impression.

When the Korean War began, all eyes turned to MacArthur. As commander in chief of UN forces the responsibility for a successful conclusion to the fighting fell on his shoulders. There were, even at that time, many who held serious doubts about his abilities, but the majority had faith in him. He had carved out his image very well.

His ultimate failure in Korea was to be delayed by circumstance. Like General Burnside at Antietam, MacArthur would "snatch defeat from the jaws of victory."[2] But that was still to come.

MacArthur was convinced that victory could be achieved only by launching one overwhelming attack. There was no way Korea could be won through grinding infantry and artillery duels across its rugged, cruel terrain. He envisioned a two-pronged attack—one of which would be a thrust at the enemy's back. In a meeting with his commanders in early September, MacArthur outlined his plan for an attack from the sea upon the city of Inchon. At that same time he told them the army bottled up in the Pusan Perimeter would engage in a great push, a massive counterattack which would add to the enemy's surprise and confusion. He would utilize both the navy and the air force in the Inchon operation, along with the newly arrived 5th Marine Division and the 10th Corps.

The landing at Inchon was opposed by both the marine and the naval commanders for a variety of reasons. To a man they favoured landing at Osan, a small city a few miles south of Inchon. At Osan the landing facilities were good and the area only lightly defended. Inchon, a major port, was considered to be heavily defended.

Equally sound were the navy's objections. The target date of 15 September was the one day in the month when the tides would be at the extreme ends of ebb and flow. High tide would be in excess of thirty feet before ebbing to a low tide of only six inches. The canals leading to the city (coded Flying Fish and South Channel) were filled with mud flats and sand bars, largely uncharted. The low tide would prohibit navigation in either the channels or the approaches for the entire day except for a two-hour period. Because of the long ebbing period, an invasion would have to be made in two phases. Should the soldiers in the first phase fail or even meet heavy resistance, all would be lost. "The operation is not impossible, but I do not recommend it," Admiral Doyle of the USN told MacArthur at that meeting. His sentiments were echoed by most of those present.[3]

The marines were also concerned that intelligence reports, which placed enemy strength at 4,000 infantrymen, could well be underestimated. The marines had grown sceptical of such reports during their island fighting in the Pacific only six years before. They were concerned the 4,000 might easily prove to be 10,000, and that with their forces split into two groups, they could find themselves in deep trouble. The warships, forced to stay well out in deeper water, would be of no use to them. Indeed, as it turned out, the warships were of very limited use. With their guns working at the longest of ranges their accuracy was limited. Their boats' crews were unable to offer any assistance. It was well the marines managed to take early control of the situation.

Whatever reservations the marine and naval commanders may have held about the Inchon landing, the plan went ahead successfully. At the press conference following the landing, MacArthur made the statement that he had estimated the chances for success at five thousand to one. He was, of course, indulging in his penchant for exaggeration. Like most generals MacArthur kept himself going on a great ego. The odds of success at Inchon were indeed long but hardly five thousand to one. They would have been less had the landing been made at Osan, but MacArthur could not bring himself to change a plan at the suggestion of someone of lower rank. Inchon was a success because of the combined effort of 265 ships and their crews, the men of the 5th Marine Division and the 10th Corps, plus the strength of the carrier and land-based aircraft and those who flew them.

The RCN was at Inchon not in an offensive role, but as escorts to the supply and troop carriers. This less-than-exciting duty was carried out with efficiency, and its contribution to the landing's success was no less than had they been in the bombardment flotilla.

* * *

The Inchon invasion began at 0600 on 15 September,[4] with a heavy bombardment from naval guns and a series of raids by carrier-based fighters. At 0630 the 3rd Battalion of the 5th Marine Division went ashore on the island of Walmi-Do. Their primary objective was the long causeway leading to the docks. Its capture and retention was the key to the operation's success. The marines took but ninety minutes to secure their objectives. By then the tide had begun its ebb toward the lowest point in months.

At 0800 the naval bombardment intensified. All day long the marines, more or less secure on the island, were covered by a virtual blanket of shells. So continuous was the shelling that no counterattack from the land was possible. The shelling was cut back at 1600 when the tide once again turned. The water rapidly filled the channels, and small ships now began to move into the area.

At 1705, the main force from the 5th Marine Division proceeded ashore. By 1730 they were scaling the sixteen-foot walls of the Inchon breakwater and had begun to fan out through the rubble of the city. As the main force went over the walls, the 3rd Battalion swept across the causeway from Walmi-Do. As all this was going on, marines of the 1st Marine Division landed unopposed some miles to the south.

Time now became the greater enemy. The gathering dusk offered more problems than did the enemy, who had been overwhelmed by the assault. Fighting went on sporadically throughout the night but opposition was never heavy. During the early hours of 16 September the invading marines linked up on all sectors. Inchon was fully encircled. All primary and secondary objectives had been secured.

Within a few hours confused North Korean soldiers, unable to believe their recent victories had been for nothing, were formed into long lines to begin the journey to prisoner-of-war camps far to the south on the island of Koje-Do. Inchon had been taken back at relatively low cost. The marines had lost twenty men and had a further 150 on the injured list. One was listed missing in action.

With Inchon in UN hands the counterattack in the Pusan Perimeter was launched. Within days the North Koreans were in full retreat on both the eastern and western flanks. Within a few more days much of South Korea had been regained. Seoul was retaken two days after the victory at Inchon.

* * *

Following the success at Inchon, life aboard the three ships returned, at least for a few days, to near normal. Much remained to be done in the way of mopping-up, but there was respite from the all-night action stations which had plagued the crews for weeks.

For those few days the ships lay at anchor in the stream not far off Inchon. Those were lazy days, spent mainly in watching supply boats which moved in a continuous flow to and from the city with tons of supplies for the troops ashore. The troops, now in complete control, had to be supplied and the harbour was crowded with boats and lighters going about their business.[5]

The Canadians were amazed, amused and sometimes perplexed by the type of supplies they saw being ferried to the depots ashore. Besides the necessary items—food, ammunition, spare parts and fuel—they also saw vast quantities of Coca-Cola, Hershey Bars, typewriters and barber chairs passing by the holds of the lighters. All this passing by and unobtainable, while their own canteens were empty! The barber chairs brought forth mirth, and not a few one-line jokes: "MacArthur has decided to type out invitations to any gook[6] who wants to surrender so that he can get a free haircut and a Coke before he heads off for the POW camp"; "MacArthur insists his troops be neat and well-trimmed in case a *LIFE* photographer drops by."

Their attitude toward the American overabundance of frivolous material was not a charitable one. Their own supplies of razor blades, boot polish and candy were depleted. Rationing of cigarettes was being considered seriously. There had been no mail from Canada for weeks. The cooks were having to consider the feasibility of using powdered eggs and dehydrated potatoes. The Welfare Committees had managed to negotiate the substitution of Coke for water in the daily rum, but there was no Coke in the canteen. On the more serious side of the shortages, star shells and 4-inch shells were hard to obtain because the USN didn't use that calibre (they used 5-inch shells) and the RN had not had the foresight to realize that they would be required to supply themselves and the ships of other Commonwealth navies. So, rationing of ammunition was imposed.

The Canadians had problems like that while the Americans were worrying about typewriters and barber chairs. It showed the sailors their own navy had some very serious flaws, not the least of which was an inability to plan along logistic lines. There they were, halfway around the world in a war zone with three destroyers, being forced to scamper about in search of supplies. They began to refer to themselves as the orphans of the Yellow Sea; and that was said more in angry frustration than in jest.

* * *

With Inchon now behind them and the North Koreans in flight, the navy went back to regular patrol duty. *Sioux* resumed shelling the installations along the north coast, while *Cayuga* and *Athabaskan* teamed up for a series of skirmishes near the Yalu River.

61

On 22 September, the two ships were sent to Beijaa Bay. [7] Two long bridges were their intended targets. The bridges were considered of importance since they were being used by the North Koreans in their retreat. As each prisoner meant one less rifle to face later, the UN was most anxious to contain as many of the enemy as possible within the confines of South Korea. This could be accomplished by denying the enemy the means of crossing the Han River. The bridges at Beijaa Bay were slated for destruction.

As the destroyers approached the bay, they were met by a ROKN gunboat. Its captain reported a battery of heavy guns emplaced near the bridges. He lamented his inability to engage them, since he was both out-ranged and out-gunned. He was happy to see the larger ships because he knew they were more than a match for the shore pieces.

Forewarned being forearmed, the two destroyers sailed into the bay at full alert. They were greatly disappointed to see that the bridges had already been brought down by heavy bombers, so they turned their full attention to the shore batteries. It was not long before the guns were knocked out. To complete the good hunting, the pair took an extra two hours to maul a large group of North Korean troops spotted milling about searching for an alternate escape route. They unwisely chose to seek shelter in some sheds near the waterfront. These sheds were brought down in quick order.

Their work done, the two Tribals departed. *Athabaskan* headed north while *Cayuga* returned to Sasebo for a few days to have some repairs made on her desalinization equipment.

* * *

Athabaskan was not long without action. Before she even neared the Yalu River, orders were received rerouting her to the Haeju-Man, an area just south of the 38th parallel. Teeming with islands as it was, the Man became a prime hunting ground for the ships.

Within a couple of hours of her arrival, she was sent to Paryon-po, [8] a town not far from Taech'on-ni. There in support of USS *Bass* and a group of ROK Marines, she levelled ten large buildings and destroyed a number of ammunition and fuel dumps. A gun battery was also destroyed. The marines landed shortly after to light resistance. Within twenty minutes they had secured all objectives.

The North Koreans had decided to offset the possibility of attacks from offshore by fortifying the ports as heavily as possible. Several of these smaller ports fairly bristled with guns. Large camps of infantry had been sent in to repel any such attacks. No doubt the troops sent to those places considered themselves fortunate in drawing easy duty, considering the heavy fighting was being done far to the south.

Despite the defeats and wholesale surrenders by their fellows at Inchon and along the eastern and southern fronts, those in the port cities and on the islands decided to fight on. The navy was called on to dislodge these holdouts, and the destroyers were ideal for this type of operation. *Athabaskan* was one of the ships most active in this work during those days. Her guns proved deadly as the ship moved quickly from one target area to another. Because her guns had greater range than those ashore, she was able to stand off with impunity while picking off her targets.

By 25 September the Haeju-Man was deemed clear of enemy activity, and parties of volunteers began to go ashore on the various islands to check out conditions and give some aid to the villagers. The volunteers, though heavily armed, were not raiders. They were under strict orders to avoid fighting if at all possible and, as things turned out, few saw action of a serious nature.

In the early morning hours of 25 September, a heavily armed party of thirty left *Athabaskan* in two boats for the island of Piun-to.[9] On landing they found only islanders among the demolished buildings which had, only hours before, held a large detachment of soldiers. Already small boys were playing on the shattered guns. The North Koreans, taking their dead and wounded with them, had pulled out the day before. Arrangements were made to supply the villagers with rice and flour before the sailors left.

The war to this point had been new and exciting to most of the sailors. Few had ever been witness to the misery and tragedy they saw that morning on Piun-to. Now the plight of the islanders began to bring misgivings. Those who had been in the landing party were noticeably subdued when they returned to the ship. To those who had remained on board the impact of war would come a few hours later.

* * *

Athabaskan left Piun-to and proceeded to Osik-to where its guns were wanted as support for a group of ROK Marines about to engage the enemy. The invasion did not go well. The marines ran into opposition much heavier than had been expected. Though they made some gains, heavy fire from well-fortified positions pinned them down. Because the landing party was small, and not prepared for a long fight, the attack was called off. Under covering fire from the ship, the marines withdrew to the beach carrying several wounded.

63

It was during this retreat that one of the marines stumbled across a little girl, perhaps three years of age, who lay, bleeding from bullet wounds, among the boulders. He scooped the tiny victim into his arms and headed for his boat. Knowing no medical help could be obtained in any of the ROKN ships, the boat's coxswain headed for the *Athabaskan.* There the child was taken aboard and carried immediately to the sickbay. She lived only two hours, just long enough for the ship's company to form a few thoughts on her misfortune. Her death came to them as a personal loss.

In what was probably the final irony, no one knew to whom she belonged, and there was no way of gaining that knowledge without a return to the island—a definite impossibility. The sailors did the only thing they could have done under the circumstances. They named the child Scoshi girl-san which means "little honoured girl," and as such she was entered into the ship's log as having come aboard.

A few hours later Scoshi girl-san was buried at sea in the tradition of seafarers. The tiny body was placed in a large square of canvas which was then weighted and sewn tightly. She was carried to the quarterdeck where a short prayer was read. The quartermaster piped the "still" and the too-young victim of an incomprehensible war was committed to the sea.[10]

* * *

Meanwhile, in Tokyo, General MacArthur celebrated his victory at Inchon. He was already thinking of his next great move. The war was now going well, with the enemy well above the 38th parallel. He would, he decided, stage another Inchon, this time on the east coast. He chose Wonsan, a major port city many miles north of the 38th parallel. This time, however, the opposition to his plan was even more vocal than it had been to Inchon. Everyone except MacArthur's staff raised objections, but once again these were overruled.

The entire operation proved to be a study in futility and a comedy of errors. *Athabaskan* was selected as the Canadian contribution over the objections of Brock, who wanted nothing to do with what he considered an ill-advised scheme. However, as every nation was to be represented (this was the express order of MacArthur) Brock assigned *Athabaskan* to the exercise.

MacArthur's plan was to combine a two-prong move behind the fleeing Reds. With this in mind, he deployed an airborne force which was to parachute to an area some miles inland from Wonsan. This force would advance southeast toward Wonsan. There they would link up with the marines which were to land from offshore. The Reds would be caught in a vise from which there would be no escape.

The paratroopers landed on schedule and began their movement south and east. A huge fleet and many troopships proceeded into the Sea of Japan with the marines. It was then that things began to go wrong. Two ships on minesweeping duty struck mines on their way to Wonsan. Both, USS *Pirate* and USS *Pledge*, were sunk. That delayed the clearing of mines from Wonsan harbour. While replacement sweepers were located, the ships containing the marines were forced to stay at sea. For several days the armada sailed slowly up and down along the coast. Soon, the whole exercise was dubbed "Operation Yo-Yo" by the unhappy soldiers.

When at last they finally landed, they found the city had already been occupied by an ROK division. Also, they had to endure the wrath of angry airborne troops, who had fought their way to a rendezvous only to find no one there to meet them.

MacArthur, in his own inimitable way, managed to turn the entire farce into a victory by staging a press conference and handing out heavily censored accounts of the operation. It was not until some time had passed that the truth became known. By that time MacArthur was gone.[11]

Chapter Six

LONG DAYS; LONGER NIGHTS

The days run together and few know the date off hand.
Report of Proceedings, HMCS Sioux, November 1950.

While *Athabaskan* was participating in the Wonsan fiasco, *Cayuga* and *Sioux* were working along the west coast on blockade patrol and carrier screening respectively. *Sioux* had no relief whatever from the tedious task, but *Cayuga* had been able to break away for a three-day visit to Tokyo. There her crew welcomed the chief of naval staff, Vice Adm. H. T. Grant, CBE, RCN. Grant had flown from Ottawa on an inspection tour of the ships. He stayed two weeks, visiting each ship, as well as taking side trips to Inchon, Sasebo and the Royal Navy base at Kure, a port which would also become familiar to the Canadians. On 12 October, Grant returned to Tokyo and visited with MacArthur.[1] The following day he returned to Canada.

Grant's visit coincided with visits to Korea by observers from other nations. Reports had begun to filter back to the various capitals of the contributing nations that all was not well within the UN command itself. Korea, the reports read, had become the scene of some dreadful crimes by ROK authorities against civilians, of botched military operations and rampant black-marketeering by corrupt military and civilian officials. Many nations hastened to send investigative teams for a look at the situation on a firsthand basis.

The concerns over what may or may not have been happening in Korea had been fuelled originally by correspondents covering the fighting. These men and women were voicing concern over obvious corruption within the UN command. They were also beginning to report their doubts about MacArthur himself. As Reginald Thompson, a British reporter, was later to state in his book, *Cry Korea*, "It was clear there was something profoundly disturbing about this campaign and something profoundly disturbing about its Commander-in-Chief."[2]

Correspondents, in the early months of the war, were reporting the truth and their stories were indeed disturbing. Surprisingly, there had been no censorship during those early days, but that oversight was cleared up suddenly by Tokyo HQ when readers in Canada, Britain, United States and elsewhere began asking questions of their elected officials about the news of panic retreats, poor leadership, lack of equipment and "general desperation, horror and lack of purpose."[3] Censorship was invoked on the grounds that the reporters were "giving aid and comfort to the enemy" and "had been guilty of disclosing information [that affected morale]."[4] Suddenly the reports from Korea took on almost neutral tones, and the about-face caused an increase in the questions being raised. Those asking the questions wanted answers.

In Ottawa questions were also being raised by concerned Members of Parliament. Reports of low morale among the Canadian sailors had begun to sift back to Canada, prompting embarrassing questions. What, the opposition members asked, was happening aboard the RCN destroyers to cause low morale and unrest. The Defence Department shuddered. Visions of 1948 raced headlong into their thoughts. Prime Minister St. Laurent, well aware of the navy's penchant for incidents, ordered immediate action. Admiral Grant, appointed as a one-man fact-finding committee, joined the parade of investigators heading toward the war-torn nation.

Grant, upon his arrival in Japan, threw himself into his task. Meeting with sailors from all three ships singly and in groups, he heard the complaints about mail shortages and saw for himself the empty shelves in the ships' canteens. He learned of the shortage of ammunition and shared with the sailors the long nights at action stations. By the time he left he was convinced, for the most part at least, of the validity of the complaints. He also knew, for he had read well the sailors' attitude to the war, that there would be no incidents of the 1948 variety. Yet he was deeply concerned. He returned home to write a lengthy report outlining the problems the sailors were facing, and made a long list of recommendations which, he obviously felt, would lead to a remedy.[5] Grant's report (which was presumably read by someone) was then filed away. Mute testimony to a caring man, it remains to this day in the RCN Collection of the National Archives. No action was ever taken on any of the recommendations.

Meanwhile, in Korea, the sailors soon realized that Grant, however good his intentions, had not brought about changes so badly needed. By November, the problems had intensified. There was still no mail, the canteens were still empty, and to make matters worse the sailors were also becoming victims of censorship. Now, they were being denied news of the proceedings ashore. Worse, they knew little of their own operations. Aboard the three ships a steady erosion of morale began to take its toll. Still, perhaps surprisingly, the low state of morale had no effect on the fighting efficiency of the ships' companies. When the bells for action stations sounded the men leapt to the task. In reality, they were anxious for any break from the monotony of shipboard life with no mail to read and no treats to purchase from the canteens.

* * *

While Admiral Grant's visit was to prove futile, his presence in Korea indirectly provided a boost to the morale of *Cayuga's* sailors. As Captain "D" Brock was required to transport Grant from Tokyo and return him to that city. This, of course, meant the crew would have an opportunity for shore leave. The sailors enjoyed Tokyo. The Japanese welcomed them with city tours and other diversions. They were given free passage on the city's buses and trams. And they visited the Ginza.

The Ginza, at the time, was the world's largest midway. Neither Hong Kong nor Tijuana, Mexico, could rival the Ginza for noise, revelry and variety of entertainment. It had none of the shabby ambience of Sasebo, nor did the denizens of the nightlife make themselves total nuisances as did those of lesser ports. Hawkers, pimps and hookers there were, certainly, but they kept a low profile, giving their occupations almost a respectable mien.

The Canadians were treated royally. They took full advantage of the hospitality offered, and they responded by behaving themselves. When the ship eventually left, they felt they had not been cheated nor did they feel anyone could have accused them of acting like boors. As proof, no one got into even the slightest trouble with the authorities. Only one sailor was counted as adrift, and he had a story to offer.

The sailor's story, as related to Brock by the young man as he stood to rigid attention before the unsmiling captain at Captain's Report, had him returning to the ship well before the 2359 curfew. However, as it was dark, he became lost among the stacks of boxes and crates piled high on the docks. He could, the sailor related, sometimes see the ship's mast, but the mazelike aisles of crates so totally overwhelmed him he gave up in his efforts to find his way. He had never, he stated, felt so lost since leaving his home in Newfoundland the previous year.

"You sees sar," he said to Brock, "I was lookin' and lookin', but it were some dark and I was always after goin' into the deadends. It weren't until the marnin' sar, that I finds the ship." Lard Jayzus, sar, I just didn't know where the ship was to." Brock, in keeping with his policy that he would dismiss any minor charge if the excuse he heard was one he had not heard before, kept as straight a face as possible as he muttered "case dismissed."

* * *

Cayuga, having said goodbye to Admiral Grant, left Tokyo to return to the patrols off the west coast. (It was on this departure that Alice had to be rescued when she returned late.) Assigned to blockade patrol, *Cayuga* spent several uneventful days cruising in search of ships in places they should not have been.[6] It was on this patrol she intercepted a tramp steamer whose heading was a direct route to the Yalu River.

The tramp, rusty and weatherbeaten, and flying a tattered Panamanian flag, made no reply to *Cayuga*'s signal. It proceeded along its course as if unaware of the destroyer's presence. If its captain intended to run, he had made an unwise decision. Brock was in no mood to be ignored by a merchantman. He sent a messenger to fetch Lt. Harry Shergold, the gunnery officer. Shergold reported within minutes.

"Guns," said Brock to Shergold, "I would like you to direct your 4-inchers fully broadside at that rusty old bucket. We'll see how brave he really is."

Brock brought his ship to within five hundred feet of the freighter and drew parallel as the three guns were levelled directly at its side. Once again the signal was flashed across ordering the tramp to stop. This time, impressed no doubt by uneven odds, the freighter's master stopped the engines, listened to Brock's instructions to clear the area, then turned about on a southerly course to less troubled waters.

The excitement over, the patrol resumed. For four more days the ship plied the murky waters seeing nothing and doing nothing. There was a sigh of relief when, on 19 October, Brock gave the order to leave the area and head north for a rendezvous with HMS *Kenya*.

Early the following morning the two joined up. A quick conference followed. Then the two ships, *Cayuga* leading, swung northward on course to the Yalu River. As the two ships steamed at half speed, the bridge lookouts kept a sharp watch both to the sky and to the water. Although the North Korean air force was almost non-existent, they had still a few planes available. Mines of course, were a constant threat.

Below the bridge, in *Cayuga*'s operation room, L/S W. R. "Robbie" Roberts, gave his full attention to his ASDIC set. The regular echoes of the sonar device sounded out in unbroken repetition. The sea ahead was clear. Suddenly the echoes intensified, their duration became shorter, the pings closed their gaps of silence. Something lay dead ahead. The gaps of silence between the pings grew shorter and shorter. Roberts knew he had picked up the echoes of many stationary objects, the dreaded mines. At once he called the alarm to the bridge and felt immediate relief as he felt the ship heel sharply to starboard. The pings began to recede into distance astern. At the moment the destroyer was swung "hard-a-starboard" an Aldis lamp flashed a message to *Kenya* astern. She, too, was turned to starboard.

The miss had been close. Too close. Lt. Andrew Collier, *Cayuga*'s navigator, later reconstructed the situation and determined the ship had missed entering the minefield by less than forty-five feet. *Kenya*, with the more timely warning, had missed by a much wider margin. Had Roberts delayed his warning to the bridge by even one more second, *Cayuga* would have steamed into the minefield and certain disaster, perhaps destruction. *Kenya* would probably have followed her in.

L/S William R. Roberts, RCN, was subsequently Mentioned-in-Dispatches.

* * *

The advance of the UN forces ashore proceeded unabated. The pressure being exerted on the Red army was so intense that only token resistance was being put forth. The Red troops in the west were in full flight, their line collapsed. The U.S. 8th Army surged northward almost unhindered. The collapse of the North Korean western line removed the security upon which their central line depended, and it also cracked wide open. On 19 October, units of the 8th Army entered Pyongyang. The city was devoid of government officials. Kim Il Sung and his advisors, along with all the civil servants, had fled to China. Three days later the ROK 6th Division reached the banks of the Yalu River. The end of the war was now in full view. The final mopping-up began.

Much of the mopping-up fell to the navy. The Canadian ships became very active among the islands. *Athabaskan* saw much of the action. She generally travelled with other ships, and it is said she was often sought out by others to assist with the gunnery assignments which proved difficult. It was also said she knew where to find the war and thus was in on many of the plum kills.

Cayuga, on the other hand, had become a lonely hunter. She prowled the islands, keeping neither to a set route nor a rigid routine. She had no definite schedule. As in *Harry Black and the Tiger*, she "travelled in solitude and to her all places were the same." Because of her ramblings, which seemed to put her in several places at the same time, she was dubbed "The Galloping Ghost of the Korean Coast."

Lest anyone ever dispute this, a permanent record was noted on the wall of a dry dock in Kure. During the spring of 1951, while the ship was in for repairs to her ASDIC dome, some seamen went to work with wide brushes and black paint. Using the entire right side of the giant dry dock as their signboard they painted in letters seven feet high the message:

H.M.C.S. CAYUGA—218

THE GALLOPING GHOST OF THE KOREAN COAST

1950-1951

The paint used was the thick, waterproof paint used on ships' bottoms, and one wonders if the unknown artists' work has survived the continuous exposure to nearly four decades of salt water as it flowed in and out of that huge dry dock. The painters hoped it might last fifty years.

While her sisters roamed as free agents, *Sioux* had been caught in the monotonous duty of carrier screening. Her crew, dissatisfied with their lot, complained to anyone who would listen. One such was Ross Monroe, a Canadian correspondent covering the war for the Southam newspaper chain. He had arranged for time on each ship and had boarded *Sioux* the day she began her carrier-screening duty. He, too, missed the action he had enjoyed while with the other ships.

Monroe championed *Sioux*'s cause in his reports. Whether those stories actually had any influence is difficult to state with certainty, but it is a fact that within two weeks of his first dispatch[7] *Sioux* was suddenly replaced by a U.S. destroyer and told to report to the group on the island patrols. By year's end *Sioux* had more than made up for the time she had lost following the carriers.

* * *

As mentioned previously, morale aboard the three ships was at a low ebb. Admiral Grant had come and gone, armed with facts and statements to submit his report, leaving the sailors with some hope for the future. More weeks passed with no changes. Morale slipped even lower.

The entire situation could have been easily avoided had the RCN been able to keep the mail flowing. Lack of mail was the root cause of the sailors' unhappiness. Mail supply was hardly a new problem to the navy. During World War II the RCN had encountered similar problems, but seemingly had learned no lessons. Those with direct responsibility for mail delivery had not approached the challenge with foresight, intelligence or common sense. Logic had never been the RCN's strongest suit. As a result of this traditional weakness, the navy had opted to move the mail via an unworkable system.

When the ships sailed toward Korea the RCN set about to find a way to get mail to and from Korea. There were several options, one of which would have utilized the RCAF. It was dismissed out of hand. The system the navy settled on was a complicated deal with the USN. The Canadian mail would be sent through the Canadian post office with a special address which would dispatch it to the fleet mail office in Esquimalt. From there it would be forwarded to the United States naval post office in San Francisco. From there the USN would send it via military air transport to Japan. At that point it would be turned over to the Royal Navy for furtherance to HMS Ladybird, the administrative unit docked permanently in Sasebo. The RN would then send it out to the Canadian ships.

The RCN had, unfortunately, overlooked three important factors in their haste to deal with the forwarding of mail. First, the USN was willing to help, but considered its own mail a priority, so the Canadian mail was relegated to a priority little better than "space available." Second, the Royal Navy in Japan had problems of its own, and the extra load on the less-than-adequate facilities availed to the RN was soon felt. But the most important factor was the one which the RCN had either overlooked, or worse, had ignored. That was the availability—and willingness—of the RCAF to carry the mail. The RCAF's 426 "Thunderbird" Squadron was running flights into Tokyo on a weekly basis.

Using North Star freighter aircraft, the RCAF flew personnel and materiel to Japan on their regular flights from Lachine, Quebec, via

Vancouver. During the Korean War 426 Squadron flew 599 round trips, and ferried many thousands of tons of materiel and 13,000 passengers without losing a single piece of freight or suffering a single casualty despite two crashes.

However, the RCN disregarded the obvious, chose the USN/RN combined service, and saw the troubles begin almost at once. Letters and parcels were sent to remote outposts in error. Letters took anywhere from three weeks to six months to reach their destinations. (*Cayuga* received the bulk of her crew's Christmas parcels and letters in March of 1951. That shipment, having been discovered in a warehouse on one of the USN's bases in the South Pacific, was delivered in fairly good condition two days prior to the ship's departure for home.)

Ross Monroe, who was proving to be a true champion of lost causes, once more took up the banner and entered the fray. In several of his November reports he blasted the RCN for its ridiculous mail arrangements. He stopped short of suggesting that inter-service rivalry, which had often led to a lack of co-operation within the military, was at fault, but he made much of the effect the lack of mail was having on morale.

The day before Monroe's final story on the mail problem was published, the RCN and the RCAF issued a joint communique which stated that an agreement had been reached which would ensure quick and efficient mail delivery to the warships in Korea.[8] From that day forward, except for the mail already in the USN system, there were only minor problems with mail delivery.

* * *

During the autumn of 1950 the ships remained on long and arduous patrols, performing tasks of a varying nature. Sleepless nights and long hours closed up at action ran days and nights together. Commander Taylor of *Sioux* lamented in a *Report of Proceedings* that "days run together and few know the date off hand." Not knowing what day it was had its disadvantages, but no one knew where they were either, so everyone felt a little lost most of the time.

Sioux and *Cayuga* set a shared record among UN ships of thirty days on a single patrol, but that record soon became redundant. *Cayuga* eventually set the UN record with a single patrol which stretched from November 1950 to January 1951, a total of fifty-one days.

During those long stretches at sea the ingenuity of various crew members came to the fore. In their efforts to alleviate boredom, individuals joined forces to produce news bulletins, chess and checker tournaments, bridge and whist matches. Individuals took up hobbies ranging from wood carving to learning how to play musical instruments, with varying degrees of success. One young seaman took up the violin, but was banished from his messdeck. He found temporary refuge on the galley fiddley—the area just above the galley under the forward mast—and practiced until the cooks complained. His practice sessions were thereafter limited to the hours when the galley was idle.

The *Athebulletin* became a popular newsletter aboard *Athabaskan*. Originated, written and printed by three seamen, Richard Griffon, Kenneth Perry and Ronald Emmerson, who was also the cartoonist, the paper was one of the few bright spots during the long weeks at sea. A great deal of hard work went into the twenty-eight editions eventually completed.

Aboard *Cayuga*, CPO M. Richard, the chief steward, set about to organize a chess club. Richard, who had been a provincial champion in his native Quebec, found eager students. Some became quite expert as the weeks of playing increased their interest and skills.

For those not inclined to such pursuits, the ships' entertainment officers did their best to supply movies. These movies were shown every afternoon in the petty officers' mess. The length of the patrols, however, was such that replacement movies proved difficult to obtain. As a result, the three or four films with which each ship would begin its patrol would be shown over and over again. Trading with other ships was not always possible for a variety of reasons, and eventually there always came the day when only the operator was in attendance.

In a war where records were kept as a matter of course, movies were included. Some of the films set show records which were never broken. *Tarzan's New York Adventure* ran for twenty-one continuous showings aboard *Athabaskan*; and *It Came From Outer Space* ran for forty-three days aboard *Cayuga*.

The game of Uckers, a version of Parcheesi, was very popular. Single games were carried into marathon matches. The call of "uckers stations" would send the players scurrying to the tables to continue a game which may well have started two mornings before.

The ubiquitous—and highly illegal—poker games were never hard to find. Large pots were not uncommon. Some players became legends in the tiny fleet, earning such nicknames as "Red Dog," because that version of three-card poker became his specialty. Some still talk with awe of "Old Bet-a-Nickel," who had a habit of suckering his opposition into large pots through his patented way of raising minimal amounts, which gave the impression that he was holding a hand full of nothing. Once the pot was at a size he deemed worthwhile, "Old Bet-a-Nickel" would show a hand of four aces or a straight flush or a combination of cards which would have had anyone else betting to the limit. It is believed by some this sailor made a modest fortune during his tour of duty.

* * *

The boredom was not helped by the lack of variety in the type of action the war afforded. When the ships first arrived the men looked upon the immediate future as an adventure into unknown areas. Constant awareness of possible aircraft attack made the first few weeks interesting. To add to the interest, the rumour that North Korea had submarines caused the Canadians to look forward to an encounter with one or two.

The submarines soon proved to be only a figment of someone's imagination. North Korea had no submarines, had no navy for that matter, so the dreams of sinking a few subs soon died away. Eventually the threat of aircraft died also, leaving only surface-to-shore action, which soon palled.

In his book, *The Dark Broad Seas*, Jeffry Brock wrote that General MacArthur was of the opinion North Korea had submarines and had prepared a rather elaborate defence against the threat. Brock, in one of his first meetings with the general, pointed out to him that submarines could be of no use in the Yellow Sea for a variety of reasons including the fact the water was too shallow. The general seemed surprised by this revelation, which caused Brock to ask himself what kind of staff the man had in his employ, as any sailor could have told him the same thing.[9]

On 19 August, *Cayuga*'s ASDIC did make contact with what was thought at the time to be a submarine. Three passes were made in which depth charges were used. After the third pass, despite a fairly sizeable oilslick which rose to the surface, the contact was declared to be a sunken freighter, probably of World War II vintage or the victim of some tragedy at sea. Its location was recorded on the ship's log.

The incident, however, did raise the question of what was to be reportable as a threat and what could be ignored. On one occasion a sub-lieutenant aboard *Cayuga* roundly admonished one of the bridge lookouts for failing to report a large mass of seaweed some distance off the port bow. The seaweed, "Subbie" declared, was without doubt "easily capable of concealing a periscope." The lookout, who knew more about such things than did the newly appointed officer, tried to explain that a submarine at such short distance would already have been picked up by the ASDIC operators. "Subbie," feeling a little embarrassed, reacted with a severe scolding and a lecture on what was reportable and what was not.

Within minutes the lookout, smarting from the unwarranted reprimand, loudly reported to the sub-lieutenant, "Bearing Red 045 and closing fast, a flock of sea gulls." Subbie, now very angry, demanded the reason for such a report. With a straight face the sailor replied solemnly that such a large flock of birds could very easily be concealing a "Gook" fighter plane. Subbie, not in the least amused, was about to place the seaman on report when the First Officer of the Watch, who had been listening to the exchange from its onset, told them both to "Knock off all that crap and act your ages."*

---

* This story is well remembered by many who served aboard *Cayuga* and was related, with variations of colour and language, by several who offered information and stories to me during my research for this book.—Author.

_____

Chapter Seven

THE WAR
ENDS —
ALMOST

_____

During the latter part of October and all of November the United
Nations forces pushed the battered enemy relentlessly
northward, destroying entire regiments and brigades as they advanced. The survivors of the once powerful army Kim had unleashed
on South Korea only weeks before were now surrendering en masse.
The war, it seemed, was in its final weeks.

The offshore islands remained havens for many of the enemy
and, as previously mentioned, the navy was charged with the
mopping-up. It was during this phase of the action that the plight
of the villagers became truly appreciated. Whenever possible, emergency supplies were given to these people by the destroyers' crews.
Such offerings were never sufficient and this gave rise to a unique
proposal.

Brock submitted to HQ his opinion that restoration of law and
order was needed, as was the issuance of food and the basic staples
necessary for survival. Only if helped, his submission read, could
the villagers return quickly to some semblance of normal living. His
idea was looked upon favourably by the UN.

Code-named Operation Comeback, plans were quickly laid.
Sioux and *Cayuga* were delegated as the principal ships for the

operation. These two, in company with ROKN vessels, soon were moving about the islands carrying out the work necessary for successful implementation of the plan. Comeback would have been completed quickly, had the war not taken an unexpected turn in late November. The expertise of the Supply and Administration personnel within the RCN ships would have achieved the transferring and distribution of goods with a minimum of problems.

It was unfortunate indeed that the two ships had been only a few weeks at their work before the war took its change of course. Nonetheless, much was accomplished before the ships were recalled to active patrol. With some reluctance they turned the remainder of the project over to the South Korean navy.

* * *

By the first week of November the enemy was considered whipped, the war all but over, and thoughts turned to the possibility of going home. The various participating nations considered the feasibility of reducing their forces. The Royal Navy was particularly anxious to return the bulk of its fleet to the China Sea, where pirates had begun to venture into waters hitherto denied them.

The developments in Korea were also welcomed by the Canadian government. Ottawa had, with great reluctance, finally authorized formation of a contingent of troops for voluntary service in Korea, but had managed to stall long enough that the troops were not yet ready for deployment overseas. Ottawa welcomed the possibility of not having to follow through on its commitment. However, Brooke Claxton, Minister of National Defence, refrained from making any quick moves toward disbanding the force. For a change his wait-and-see policy was to pay off. Claxton ordered the fledgling army to continue training and recruiting. There was no difficulty in attracting recruits to the force.

In Korea the easing of the fighting became more obvious each day, and soon there were more ships idling away their days in harbour than there were on patrol. It was deemed as good a time as any to allow the three destroyers a few days' leave in Hong Kong. Besides, the ships all needed repairs of varying importance and Hong Kong had the facilities.

On 5 November, *Cayuga* and *Athabaskan* sailed out of Sasebo on course for the China Sea. *Sioux*, one of the few ships still on patrol, would follow in two days. The weather that Sunday morning was pleasant, with blue skies and a smooth sea. By early afternoon clouds began to obscure the sky and a freshening wind began to churn the sea into choppy waves. The barometer began a rapid decline at the same time, and by nightfall stood at 96.25 and falling rapidly. The warning was clear that a typhoon was on the way—and that the two ships were sailing into its teeth.

Typhoon Clara had not been unexpected, but her ferocity had been very much underestimated by the forecasters. She hammered the coast of China before crossing the Formosa Straits to Taiwan (Formosa) where she flattened entire villages and swamped fishing fleets. Then, free of the land, Clara swept across the open water with winds in excess of 90 miles per hour. Huge waves rose to towering crests and dipped into cavernous valleys.

The two ships sailed headlong into the storm, receiving maulings which neither had ever before known. Day and night through 5-8 November the battle between ships and Clara persisted. The odds lay with the storm, but the spirits of the ships were also strong. In times of such stress ships and crews seem to join together in a bond which transcends the common link of normal times. There was a great bond between the men and the ships of the RCN all during the war in Korea, and it was prevalent that night in the East China Sea.

The spirit which seems present in a good ship is not easy to explain because a ship is, after all, a hollow vessel. How can it have a spirit? Only those who have sailed in such a ship can understand this feeling, but none can fully explain it. It is not something known to those who have lived their lives on land. Not all ships have this spirit. While it is not confined to warships, it is those ships which most often exude the feeling. Like people, some ships seem to possess a certain courage or determination missing in others. Some quit easily in heavy going, while others press doggedly onward, refusing to concede defeat. No one can ever fully understand this, but a sailor will readily testify to it.

The contest between Clara and the two ships continued without let-up until the morning of 8 November. During those two-and-one-half days the typhoon ripped motor boats and cutters from the davits, tore carley floats from their mountings and warped one of *Cayuga's* main doors to such an extent that it could not be closed.

Athabaskan suffered one casualty when Chaplain(P) Harold Todd was seized by a great wave which broke across the starboard railing. Todd was carried some thirty feet before being hurled into the housing just aft of the torpedo tubes. He suffered severe bruising, and for several hours it was feared he had sustained broken ribs. Fortunately this was not the case, but on arrival in Hong Kong, Todd was transferred to the RN hospital where he was kept for two days.[1]

An even more serious drama had played itself out just prior to Clara's assault on the chaplain. A combination of superb seamanship and almost unbelievably good luck prevented the loss of a crew member. When O/S Robert Elvidge came up to the forward funnel area in search of some fresh air he had no idea of the terrible ordeal he was about to endure. Certainly, he had not intended to go to the quarterdeck, but that is where he ended up, courtesy of Clara.

Elvidge had joined a group of seamen near the funnel*, but had stood apart a few feet as he watched the huge waves assault the ship. Suddenly a great wall of water crashed across the bows to engulf the entire front section of the ship. Unable to react, the young seaman found himself in the grip of the wave as it pulled him relentlessly toward the railing. He was washed over the side in an instant. When the initial shock wore off a few seconds later he realized he was alone in the sea. In panic he watched the ship as it steamed away. Elvidge was not a swimmer. Indeed, he had failed the swimming test during basic training. He knew he could stay afloat for only a few minutes. He began to tread water, but the ship continued to open the gap.

The moment Elvidge had been swept over the side the cry of "man overboard" went up. Before a full minute had passed the cry had been relayed to the bridge, where the 1st OOW gave the order that turned the ship about.[2] While the ship was being turned, a squad trained for just such an emergency rushed to the upper deck. The signalman on the bridge flashed a message to *Cayuga*, who immediately hove to and prepared her own squad for action, should assistance be needed. Commander Welland, who had rushed to the bridge to take personal charge, saw at once the impossibility of launching a boat as part of a rescue. His only option was to bring the ship alongside the swimmer in hopes that he might be pulled aboard.

All personnel except the rescuers were ordered off the upper deck and those remaining lined the rail. As the ship moved closer to the tiring swimmer, all knew his chances were slim. Seamanship and luck would determine the outcome. The waves could move him away from the ship or pull him into the churning screws. With the final scene set, Welland moved the ship toward the frantic swimmer as he gave crisp orders to the helmsman. As if deliberately timed, the ship slid alongside the swimmer just as the wave crested. Elvidge

---

* The Funnel Watch was the name given those who suffered from seasickness. There were two ways to alleviate the rigours of *mal de mer*, neither very effective. One way was to keep busy to occupy the mind and the second was to sit quietly in a breezy area of the upper deck. The best place was near the funnel because the wind swirled about and seemed cooler.

was brought level with—and within inches of—the upper deck. At that precise instant O/S Joseph Adamson reached out, grabbed Elvidge by the belt and hauled him onto the deck.[3] Clara had lost her victim.

The rescued sailor, cold and in a state of shock, was hustled quickly away to the sick bay for a check over, a hot drink and some dry clothing. For all his ordeal, he proved none the worse for wear. In all, he had spent about fifteen minutes in the water— a remarkably short time considering all that had transpired in effecting the rescue. The following morning he submitted an official request to have noted on his record that he had passed the RCN basic swimming test. The request was granted.[4]

* * *

Following the dramatic rescue of O/S Elvidge the ship proceeded on course after a short delay in which a damaged cutter was cut loose from its davit and sunk by Bofors gunfire. *Athabaskan* quickly caught up with *Cayuga* and together they pressed once again into the storm.

Within a few hours the winds began to ease and the waves decreased in height. With happiness the crews realized they were sailing out of the typhoon. Clara, however, had one parting shot. Midway through the Middle Watch a towering wall of water struck *Cayuga* directly on the starboard side with such force that the ship slewed wildly to port. This placed the ship directly parallel to the huge mountain of water which towered above her, and meant she was attempting to climb up the wave sideways.

In the wheelhouse L/S William Bethel instinctively knew his ship was in deep trouble. He swung the wheel hard over to starboard in a frantic effort to head the ship into the wave. If the ship remained in her sideways position she would roll over. *Cayuga* was top-heavy and this knowledge was uppermost in Bethel's mind as he fought to turn the ship. The sudden lurching of the ship caused turmoil below decks. In the messdecks, tables and lockers came loose from their moorings. Boots, books, utensils, anything loose, hurtled like missiles across the confined spaces from starboard to port. Lights went out. Pumps stopped dead. The soundest sleepers were awakened, more by the eerie silence and the unusual darkness than by the clatter of the objects as they fell from their racks.

Cayuga was now at fifty degrees of roll, a degree no Tribal had ever exceeded, and was still heeling. The port side was now parallel to the surface of the water. The starboard propeller was completely out of the water, flailing the air. The ship continued to heel. *Cayuga* ultimately reached 52 degrees of roll before she gave an agonized shudder and hung momentarily in a long pause. Then, as if in no great hurry, she began a slow, almost leisurely, return to an upright position. The entire ordeal had lasted a little more than sixty seconds. The ship's log records the event in one terse notation: "08 0200. Ship broached by huge wave. 52° roll."

Clara, having lost the final skirmish, conceded defeat and did not molest the ships again. By 0500 the ships were into much calmer waters. The crews began to check for damage and make assessments. Boats and carley floats dangled from davits and racks. Many of the floats were gone completely. Doors were twisted and warped. On both ships all the 4-inch guns had snapped their locking restraints and the barrels pointed directly skyward, almost ninety degrees to the deck. The seamen fell to and began a long day of cleaning up.

Far to the north *Sioux*, who had departed Japan just in time to run headlong into the storm, took a severe mauling. Despite much material damage, she suffered no casualties and arrived in Hong Kong on schedule.

* * *

Hong Kong in 1950 was a sailor's port. The city held an aura of mystery and an allure unequalled by any other city in the world. The shoreline was a fantastic stretch of tall, white buildings which gleamed in the morning sunlight. The waterfront, a bustling, hustling hubbub of confusion, played host to the ships of all sizes, all flags and all manner of endeavour, legal and otherwise. Hong Kong was, and still is, the port to which all ships come at one time or another. It is the crossroads of the world.

The morning *Athabaskan* and *Cayuga* sailed into the harbour, the jetties were crowded with ships. Dozens rode at anchor or were tied to buoys in the stream, awaiting their turn to go alongside. Many, in a hurry for a variety of reasons, unloaded where they were by means of barges and lighters which journeyed back and forth in a continuous parade.

Boats, sampans and junks, some small, some large, some of wooden hulls and some of steel, plied their way to and from the harbour entrance. Freighters, some clean and gleaming, others dirty and rusting, vied for room in the crowded harbour with warships and police patrol boats. All gave way to the green and white ferries making their regular runs between Hong Kong and Kowloon, the mainland city.

Piers and jetties thronged with cranes, trucks, tractors and the men who operated them. Gangs of stevedores went about their work. Sailors and merchants made their way among piles of boxes to their ships or places of business.

The Canadian ships spent their first two days moored to buoys in the stream. They spent the entire time under constant siege from hawkers, dealers and merchants who arrived in sampans and small boats laden with wares. All had a common mission, to separate the sailors from their dollars. There was seemingly nothing which could not be bought, and some of the merchandise was of very good value. Tailors did a brisk trade by offering custom-made suits of top quality cloth (gabardine was very much in style at the time) for as little as twenty dollars in either Canadian or American currency. The same suit made in Canada would bear a price tag of ninety dollars or more. The only flaw was the sewing, so most suits were purchased with the intention of having them resewn by a Canada tailor. This would add a few dollars to the initial price, but the value was well worth the extra.

Not all who arrived in their boats had selling on their minds, and a special alertness had to be kept against them. These were the thieves, all fellows of enterprise and certain courage. They would glide their craft along the ship's length until an open port hole was seen. As the heat kept the temperatures below decks high, most portholes were left open. The boat would be positioned below the opening while one of its occupants would peer into the ship to determine if the compartment was empty. If so, he would reach in as far as possible and scoop up everything within reach. Some of these enterprising fellows were caught, whereupon the groping hand would be rapped smartly across the knuckles with a blunt instrument, as often as not a heavy wrench or the heel of a boot.

Arriving also in boats were the "pom-pom girls," sea-going hookers who seemed surprised when refused permission to venture aboard. The world, the madams would loudly call, revolved on the services their girls were able and willing to provide for a most reasonable fee. Good, old-fashioned "pom-pom" was beneficial for all, as it reduced tensions which had built up over weeks at sea. A business arrangement could be easily negotiated, the madam would call from her place in the sampan's bow, and would work to mutual benefit. The sailors would be made happy and the girls would be able to afford to buy some supper that night.

"Come on, Canada boys," the madam would call loudly, "do not be so cold to girls with such warm hearts."

"Sorry, gals," the officer of the day would shout back. "You'll just have to go somewhere else. You're wasting your time here."

After a few more minutes of cajoling the madam would head for a more hospitable ship, shaking her head in disbelief that anyone would refuse the convenience of a house call.

The sailors enjoyed Hong Kong. Most of them took full advantage of the many fine hotels, staying a night or two in the comfort of large rooms with beds having crisp, clean sheets. An added treat was the privacy not available at any time aboard the crowded ships. Some stayed at the Royal Navy's Enlisted Men's Club. This well-run establishment boasted a very good restaurant, clean single rooms and a well-stocked bar. The prices at the club were much lower than those in the hotels, but that advantage was offset to some degree by the many regulations under which the club operated. It was, after all, a naval establishment and therefore subject to the stringency of naval discipline.

Whether the sailors stayed at the RN club or elsewhere, the time ashore was considered pleasant and of quality. After many weeks in crowded ships and stifling confinement, the openness of the city was bliss indeed.

Hong Kong was special to the many Canadian sailors who were to visit during the years of the Korean fighting. Many had the good fortune to make two or more visits, and few ever turned down the opportunity of spending their allotted days ashore.

International in flavour, the city was a horn of plenty, a cornucopia of all known pleasures. Taverns all stocked the world's most famous ales, including Canada's famous Black Horse Ale, long a favourite of Canadian sailors. Surprisingly, perhaps the only food not easily available was the western version of Chinese food. To the Pacific Coast sailors (who could envision Chinese fare only as that served by Don Mee's Chop Suey House on Victoria's Fisgard Street) this seemed a sort of oversight. To those who came later in the Halifax-based ships there seemed a certain irony when they discovered chop suey and chow mein could be had only at a dingy, out-of-the-way place called The Yankee Cafe.*

To the sailors' delight they found the Canadian dollar to be in high demand by street vendors and the money traders who operated from kiosks on nearly every corner. Money could, of course, be traded at the banks, but the official rate of HK$5 to CDN$1 was far short of the rate on the street. The street rate varied from HK$6 to $10 per CDN$1, depending on the denomination involved. The

---

* The Yankee Cafe in Halifax, no longer in business, was a place of dubious repute. Frequented by sailors, it was a trysting place for lonely sailors and girls of easy virtue. In Victoria, The Liberty Cafe, now also long gone, located at Douglas and Yates Streets—and better known as Pusser's Corners—was the west coast equivalent.

larger the bill, the higher the exchange. Some kiosks were offering HK$200 for CDN$20. The rush on twenty-dollar bills began.

Naval tradition interfered to some extent with the free trade plans to which many aspired. Ratings were traditionally paid in fives and tens; only officers were offered twenties. No one seems to know how this had come about, or why, but it was part of naval life and no one had ever questioned it. Hong Kong changed the acquiescence of years' standing. Now the seamen wanted twenties, but the only recourse was to approach an officer and try to make an exchange. However, the officers were also changing their dollars at the street kiosks, so very few could see any advantage in exchanging their twenties for tens. Still, some deals were made which enabled some of the wealth at least to be shared equitably. It was rumoured the supply ratings were paid by their paymasters in twenties.

None who visited Hong Kong fail to recall the ubiquitous shoe-shine boys who dogged the tourists' every step. From five to twenty of these street urchins would encircle the potential customer, all clamouring for the opportunity to shine and polish the shoes of the "rich American." (To these street waifs anyone with money was American unless he spoke with an English accent. In those cases he became the "rich English gentleman," a sobriquet which infuriated the Australians). These youngsters had to be watched very carefully at all times, as most were expert pickpockets.

The ricksha became the favourite mode of transport, not only because they were inexpensive, but because the ricksha boys lacked the surliness of the taxi drivers. Rickshas were limited in their speed while taxis had no limits. Taxi drivers were inclined to aim for any opening in the road and, with one hand on the wheel and the other on the horn, surge ahead at top speed, scattering pedestrians before them.

Hong Kong traffic did not leave the Canadians without casualties. While *Sioux* was there for repairs in 1951, A/Bs R. J. Moore and F. R. Laker were killed when their jeep overturned as they were making a routine duty run to an RN establishment. They were buried in the Saiwon Military Cemetery with many other fallen warriors from Canada.[5]

Saiwon Cemetery is located in the beautiful hills which overlook the area. Like all other Commonwealth cemeteries, it is well tended. Row after row of white markers, all in precise formation, dot the neatly manicured lawns. In this peaceful setting are the graves of Canadians who died while serving in Hong Kong.

Here are situated the graves of the valiant soldiers of the Royal Rifles of Canada and the Winnipeg Grenadiers, whose heroic stand in defense of Hong Kong in 1941 against the Japanese invaders is part of Canada's history. No ship of the RCN has ever visited Hong Kong without sending to Saiwon an Honour Guard and Colour Party as part of a memorial service in memory of the 249 gallant men who fell in that battle.

On 15 November 1950, the first of many such services by those who served in the ships in Korea, was held at Saiwon. A selected guard from all three ships journeyed to the cemetery, heard the prayers and fired the ceremonial shots over the graves. The "Last Post" was played by A/B William Patterson of Lethbridge, Alberta.[6]

* * *

On the morning of Thursday 16 November, the three ships left Hong Kong for Sasebo. The sailors would never forget the crowded streets, the opulence and the poverty, the rats and the cockroaches, the pom-pom girls and the ten-cents-a-dance girls, the shoe-shine boys and the ricksha boys, the friendly merchants and the surly taxi drivers. As the years passed, one memory might blend into another and names and dates fade. But memories of Hong Kong fade more slowly than do those of the other ports. So those who knew the legendary, almost mythical, city during those years find recollections come easily and quickly to mind.

The city, for many forever and for others temporarily, was now well astern. Serious business lay ahead. For two or three weeks reports had been making the rounds about Chinese troops having been found among the dead and prisoners from the Korean army. As the days passed the numbers of those wearing the quilted uniforms of the Peoples' Liberation Army of China increased.[7]

In response to the news release in western papers about the numbers of Chinese soldiers present in Korea, Radio Peking claimed them to be "volunteers" who had chosen to assist their Korean comrades against the aggressions of the "Imperialists" and their "running dogs." These so-called volunteers were bad news and everyone knew it. Volunteers or otherwise, China had decided to enter the war.

On 18 November, as the three ships neared the Japanese coast, Rear Adm. W. G. Andrewes, RN, the commander of the Commonwealth arm of the UN fleet—Task Group 95.1—sent Ottawa an urgent message requesting that plans to recall the RCN ships be reconsidered.[8]

Ottawa replied in the affirmative, and the ships' companies, as they sailed into Sasebo, were greeted with the news that Christmas at home was no longer a possibility. Instead, they were to resupply their ships as quickly as possible, then make at full speed for the

Yalu River zone to await further orders. With urgency the crews complied. By nightfall the trio was outward bound, heading north. The following morning the ships joined Task Element 95.12, Brock took immediate command, then divided his force into smaller groups. These he deployed along the entire patrol area.

TE 95.12, consisting of six destroyers and several minesweepers, prowled the waters between Inchon and the Yalu River. The destroyers worked singly, moving among the islands in search of junks and sampans which might be transporting Chinese soldiers from the mainland of China to points along the Korean peninsula. During a search of three days, only a few suspicious vessels had been spotted and boarded. None had been carrying soldiers. If China was about to enter the war on a grand scale, she was not going to do so with a sea attack in mind. The UN still controlled the Yellow Sea.

The situation at sea was a sharp contrast to that on land. There the entire picture was about to take a dramatic and fateful turnabout. On 23 November, the U.S. 8th Army, having advanced to a point far north of Pyongyang, had the remnants of the North Korean army at its mercy. With the Yalu River at their backs and the UN forces bearing down on them from several directions, the Koreans prepared for their final battle.

On 24 November, the U.S. 8th launched what most felt would be the last fight of the war. The full-scale attack was stopped dead in its tracks. The U.S. 8th found itself facing an army of tremendous size—not Korean but Chinese. No volunteers, these. The army was composed of entire regiments of regulars, well-disciplined, highly trained troops skilled in fighting and seemingly unafraid. They swarmed en masse into the awesome fire-power of the Americans.

The first wave of Chinese met with stiff resistance, and faltered, but before long a second wave attacked. By nightfall the entire 8th Army cracked and fell back along a wide front. Within a few hours the entire 8th was in retreat. Many of the Americans deserted their vehicles, dropped their rifles and fled headlong across the frozen terrain. They left behind their equipment, their artillery pieces and, for most, their honour. The entire west flank opened up to the Chinese advance, and the Red Army moved relentlessly forward.

Forty-eight hours later, a massive attack was launched against the U.S. Marines, 1st Division, which was dug in near Yudam-ni. The city fell in a few hours.

By 28 November, the situation had swung full circle. The Reds were once again in full control of the land. In the west the U.S. 8th was still in full flight, so rapid that the Chinese could not keep up. Soon the distance between the two lines was vast. The Reds, perhaps fearing a trap, slowed their advance thereby opening the distance further. The disgraceful retreat by the U.S. 8th was to plague that army for years after. The marines in particular never forgave the men of the 8th, whom they blamed for their defeat at Yudam-ni. The marines felt the 1st Division could have held their positions, had they not had to face the overwhelming numbers sent against them—numbers which should have been contained, or at least hindered, by the U.S. 8th.

Farther to the east the 10th Corps also fell back. Their retreat was orderly, as they had the marines' 1st and 5th Divisions on the flanks. The 10th Corps fell back to Hungnam, and there made preparations to hold the sector.

Chapter Eight _____

CHINNAMPO

Bend to the charts, in the extinguished night.
Mariners! Make way slowly; stay from sleep.
Louise Bogan, *Putting to Sea*

The collapse of the western sector caused much concern (the military historians Cagle and Manson call it panic) in General MacArthur's headquarters. The general, confidently expecting total collapse of the North Koreans, was not prepared for the unexpected turn of events. He appeared confused, without a plan, for he had never thought the Chinese would enter the war, although he had been warned weeks before by various authorities that such intervention was highly probable.

Jeffry Brock relates in his personal memoirs a meeting he attended with the general only a few weeks prior to the Chinese intervention. Brock, who had sailed *Cayuga* far into the Yalu River, had seen massive buildups of Chinese troops all along the river on the north shore. So had others from a series of ships which had gone into the Yalu. Thus the sightings were neither isolated nor the product of one person's imagination.[1]

MacArthur, who refused good advice at the best of times, once again failed to heed timely warnings. According to Brock, the general could not believe China would dare intervene, because such action would pit her against the United Nations, the very body China wished to join. Further, he felt the Chinese leaders would not wish to enter a situation without sea or air power. He also felt the communications problems facing them would be overwhelming, and that problems of logistics—given the traditional mistrust and dislike between Koreans and Chinese—would hinder their efforts.

Now the impossible had happened. The Chinese swept headlong into Korea and took complete charge. The North Koreans, finished anyway, were swiftly relegated to support units, rarely used. Because the Chinese had pushed the Koreans to the sidelines, they had no need to converse with their allies. Thus ended the problem of communications. Logistics proved no great problem as each Chinese soldier carried his meagre rations with him. If he ran short he was expected to live off the land. The Chinese soldier had no need of Coca-Cola, Hershey Bars or barber chairs. He did not live from payday to payday because he received no regular pay. Whatever he earned would be paid to him at some point in the future (if he lived to collect it), so he gave the subject little thought. The Chinese infantryman was tuned into following his officers' orders on cue. He might have preferred to fight a sort of guerrilla war, but if ordered to charge headlong into battle he did so. He lived by and for the teachings of Chairman Mao Tse-tung and understood those teachings very well. General MacArthur had never studied Mao, knew little of the Chinese army and its battle tactics, and this lack of enlightenment would cost the UN effort dearly.

Now, faced with a grave crisis, MacArthur turned to the navy. Orders went out to intensify naval operations along both coasts. The ships went into action all along the northern patrol routes at once. Brock must have felt a sense of irony when, as commander of TE95.12, he received the order to assist by all means in his power the evacuation of the US 8th Army. Perhaps he thought how different things might have been, had his warnings to MacArthur not been dismissed so quickly.

Brock drew his plans carefully. He was faced with long odds, not the least of which involved the feasibility of taking his ships into Chinnampo and bringing them out again safely. He would, he decided, make full use of his larger ships, even to the extent of using them as evacuation vessels. Accordingly, he called for a fleet of attack transports which were dispatched at once from Inchon. Under the protection of USS *Forrest B. Royal*, a destroyer, the transports arrived a few hours later at Cho-Do and anchored in a safe area while the *Forrest B. Royal* sailed north in search of *Cayuga*.

TE95.12, when the first frantic signals from HQ began to arrive, was scattered far and wide along the coast. *Sioux* was just north of Inchon with the oil tanker, *Wave Laird*. *Athabaskan* and HMAS *Warramunga* were cruising near the Yalu. *Cayuga* and HMAS *Bataan*, also a Tribal Class destroyer, were well into the river, shelling Chinese troops in rubber rafts. These two ships, two nights

90

previously, had run up a particularly large score of the rubber boats which were ferrying the Chinese across the river to the south shore. *Cayuga*, with her HDWS radar, could spot these rafts easily even though they rode so low in the water as to be undetectable with ordinary radar. In the hopes that good hunting lay ahead for the night the ships had made their way a good distance up the river.

The incoming signals told the gloomiest of tales with each being more pessimistic than its predecessor. While the plight of the 8th Army was well enough known, the full picture along the front, and in the various sectors, was hazy. Pyongyang had fallen to the Chinese, and it appeared likely they would swing a sizeable force westward to secure Chinnampo. The port itself would be of little use to them because of the naval blockade, but Chinnampo held huge reserves of supplies, including large storage tanks filled with oil and gasoline. The Chinese, it was felt, would certainly move quickly in an attempt to forestall destruction of these vital commodities.

Brock's concern was not for the materiel, but for the hundreds of soldiers who were in Chinnampo. It was of the utmost importance that they be saved. There was, however, one great problem. Chinnampo was too far inland for naval guns to provide covering fire from the sea. The distance—in excess of twenty miles—was far beyond the range of the guns available to him. He realized his only option was to sail into the port with the ATAs and offer cover at point-blank range, with the distinct possibility of losing one or more ships.

Possible consequences notwithstanding, Brock had been ordered to do all he could to assist in the evacuation of the troops, so he made his plans and called his ships together. They converged in the lee of the island of Cho-Do, refuelled from *Wave Laird* and lay at anchor awaiting the arrival of *Cayuga* and *Bataan*.

Darkness had already settled in when the two ships arrived to join the little armada. A north wind, blowing very cold, was making the water choppy, and leaden skies warned of worsening weather. The air temperature was recorded at forty-two degrees fahrenheit, but with the wind-chill factor, the effective temperature was close to thirteen degrees below zero. To make matters worse, a steady drizzle had begun. As it hit the steel decks it froze, and movement along the upper decks became a treacherous adventure.

On arrival in Area Shelter, the code name for the zone in which the ships were anchored, *Cayuga* moved directly alongside *Wave Laird* and began refuelling. The pumps had barely started when *Bataan*, approaching to join *Cayuga*, was caught by a sudden gust of wind and pushed into *Cayuga*'s side. Before those on *Bataan*'s bridge could react, her port anchor had crushed *Cayuga*'s starboard motor cutter. The hook then caught the break of *Cayuga*'s forecastle

91

and tore open her side, allowing light from a compartment to flood out into the darkness. The light shone like a beacon in the blackout under which the ships were operating. Frantic scurrying ensued when it was discovered the door to the compartment was locked. The duty storesman who held the key could not be found for several minutes, during which the three ships stood in great danger from any shore batteries the Chinese may have emplaced. The Chinese advance had been so rapid that several units had already entered that sector of the mainland. Fortunately, they had not advanced their artillery at the same pace as their infantry.

Subsequent assessment of the damage showed the ship's side could be repaired on a temporary basis using materials at hand. The boat was not repaired until the following month, when *Cayuga* finally returned to Japan.

* * *

If life on the upper deck was miserable because of the cold, it was even worse below for the opposite reason. All the ships were crowded and, because of the blacked-out conditions, very hot inside. Fresh air was greatly reduced despite efforts to pipe it through ventilation systems which forced cool air into the compartments from long, rectangular ducts which ran along the deckheads. This air was released through small, round openings called punkaloos. Under normal routine the system was adequate, but under prevailing conditions its system was sadly lacking.

Cayuga was having more than the normal problems associated with the ventilation system. Her heating system was overworking because of a malfunctioning thermostat. The lower deck, as a result, was in the grip of a heat wave. This heat, added to the already overwhelming stuffiness, became worse when the ventilation system quit.

At about 1830, a young seaman descended the ladder into the forelower messdeck. A/B Vince Liska, a member of the Radar Control section, was only two hours away from becoming the RCN's first fatality of the Korean War. At that moment, however, his thoughts were only on a poker game in progress. Liska entered the game about 1845, played a few hands and lost a few dollars. Deciding that luck was not with him that evening, he gave up his place, joined a small group in the background and continued to watch the players. As he stood there someone, perhaps he himself, mentioned he was celebrating his birthday. A jug of rum was produced and presented to him. He drank the rum as he watched the game. No one paid any attention to him, and no one noticed when he left.

At approximately 2035 he was seen climbing the vertical ladder from the upper deck to the platform housing the midships Bofors gun (S2—just aft of the forward funnel). A few minutes later he was seen leaning against the outboard railing, looking down at a group of Australian sailors aboard *Bataan*. The Australians later recalled that he was having a bit of trouble keeping his balance.[2]

The ships, tied together as they were, rose and fell in the choppy sea. As they rose a gap would open to a width of some three feet. When they fell the gap would decrease to about six inches. Only the woven rope fenders which were hung over the sides kept the ships from grinding together.

At 2040, the groggy seaman leaned too far over the railing, lost his balance and, without a sound, plunged downward between the two ships. As he fell the gap widened to its farthest point, and he disappeared into the narrow chasm between the ships. The cry "man overboard" sounded on both ships at the same time. Men rushed to the rail. Stout poles were obtained from *Wave Laird* and jammed between the ships to keep them apart as far as possible. A strong light was beamed into the inky blackness below, but Liska had disappeared completely.

Meanwhile, on *Bataan*, a boat's crew was quickly assembled for the already-lowered starboard cutter. These seamen began a wide sweep of the vicinity. Because the sound of a motor would drown out any call for help they were forced to use oars. Within a short time, however, the search had to be called off. The fierce tide had swept the cutter beyond a safe distance, they had found no trace of the missing seaman and the darkness was putting the searchers in some jeopardy. Eventually the Australians, exhausted, got back to their ship and were quickly hauled inboard.

Vince Liska was never seen again. In keeping with naval tradition, his personal effects were sent home to his widow. His clothing and mess kit were auctioned by his shipmates and the money thus raised also sent to his widow.

There have been inconsistencies in several publications concerning this particular incident. In the RCN's official account of the navy's operational role during the Korean War no mention whatever is made of the mishap, giving the impression the RCN had wished it could be forgotten. Then, in his book, *The Dark Broad Seas*, Brock refers to the sailor as a leading seaman.[3] This can be considered an honest mistake, as a ship's captain cannot possibly know every man aboard, but Brock then goes on to describe Liska as being his personal motorboat and jeep driver. He had, wrote Brock, "made

himself not only a useful but likeable and trustworthy companion."
It seems surprising, therefore, the captain did not know his rank.
Equally surprising is his contention that Liska was placing fenders
between the ships when he fell over the side. Brock must have been
aware the fenders had been in place from the moment *Cayuga* came
alongside *Wave Laird*. Small lapses of memory can be justified, but
total disregard of a sad occurrence aboard a warship in the RCN's
official accounting is difficult to understand.

Following the loss of A/B Liska, the collision with *Bataan* began
to take on a more ominous meaning. Sailors, notoriously superstitious, can read omens into almost anything. Believing as they did
that troubles always come in threes, crew members felt increasingly
uneasy about the intended journey up the river to Chinnampo.

* * *

In 1950 Chinnampo had a population of about 75,000. An industrial
city, it had for hundreds of years been the link with the sea for the
larger city of Pyongyang. Situated near the mouth of the Taedong
River, its roomy harbour boasted good facilities.

The Taedong directly connects the two cities but is not large or
important. As a travelway it is of no use whatever, as neither boats
or barges can navigate its shallow water, and all goods were
transported to and from Pyongyang by road. Chinnampo thus plays
an important part in Pyongyang's commerce. The Taedong River,
once it reaches Chinnampo, widens as it rushes to the Yellow Sea.
Here the river meets the estuary of the Daido-Ko, a thirty-five-
kilometre stretch of narrow, shallow, thoroughly unpleasant water
that winds along in a series of sharp bends and tortuous curves.
Filled with mudbanks and shoals which shift and change so rapidly
they cannot be charted, the Daido-Ko is a navigator's worst
nightmare.

During the night of 4 December, the Daido-Ko held another,
more serious hazard. The waterway had been heavily mined by the
North Koreans, and the ships would have to work their way through,
sweeping as they went. The proposition was not pleasant. Brock
called in his minesweepers, briefed their captains on the job at hand,
then set the little ships into the channel to sweep a wide path
through which the destroyers might safely travel.[4] This the
'sweepers did, marking their progress as they went with buoys. The
buoys proved none too effective, as they were painted black and were
hardly visible in the dark. Further, their cables were unable to
withstand the pull of the current and the buoys pulled loose to drift
from their original positions. Fortunately, the problems were known

94

before the ships went forth, so other means were utilized, including the ASDIC readings which told of a mine's presence in plenty of time.

Brock, his fleet at anchor in Area Shelter, had initially decided to wait for morning before making the run. There had seemed no hurry to get to Chinnampo. USS *Bayfield*, *Foss* and *Bexar* had been in the harbour for several days and *Bayfield*'s CO,* in overall charge of that group, had not indicated any need for a night journey.

Brock, hoping to get a reasonable night's sleep, retired to his sea cabin, but was only there a few minutes when Communications Officer Lieutenant Peter May informed him that an urgent message had been received from USS *Foss*. The message, "EMERGENCY. WE ARE UNCOVERED. TAKE NECESSARY ACTION IMMEDIATELY" gave the distinct impression that things had taken a turn for the worse. The fact that *Foss* had originated the signal rather than *Bayfield* suggested that the latter may have become incapacitated, perhaps sunk.[5]

Then a signal from *Bayfield* arrived. Although it had none of the urgent overtones of the one from *Foss*, it did give the impression that the picture in Chinnampo could easily be serious by sunrise: "LOCAL SITUATION MAY REACH EMERGENCY BASIS TUESDAY 5 DECEMBER FORENOON. PRESENCE OF DESTROYERS RE-QUIRED."

Brock now decided the run into Chinnampo must be made at once. He ordered his flotilla to make ready for immediate departure, signalled his intent to HQ, then headed his ships into the Daido-Ko after once more sending the minesweepers ahead for another sweep of the channel. They were then to position themselves in the channel at pre-arranged places.

HMAS *Warramunga*, already a mile into the channel, was told to stay with the 'sweepers. She had weighed anchor a half hour after the three little ships had moved upriver, getting underway at 2200. At 2230, the five other ships began to move out, *Cayuga* leading. *Athabaskan*, *Bataan*, *Forrest B. Royal* and *Sioux* followed at close intervals in that order. Each ship was guided by a blue stern light from the preceding ship. With engines at "dead slow ahead" the line moved through the darkness toward the port of Chinnampo. What has often been called the most important, and the most dangerous, naval mission of the Korean War was underway.

As if the darkness and the natural hazards of the Daido-Ko were not enough to contend with, the tide had ebbed to its shallowest depth. At times the ships' keels had less than twenty inches of water

---

* Capt. S. G. Kelly, USN. He and Brock had been in constant touch since the emergency first came to light. Kelly had not seemed to think a night journey was necessary and Brock had happily agreed with him.

below them. As might be expected the shallow water claimed the first casualty. Shortly after midnight *Warramunga* ran aground. Her captain managed to take her off the shoal unassisted, but he suspected damage to the keel and made the decision to return to Area Shelter for a closer inspection. She played no further role in the operation.

Just prior to *Warramunga*'s grounding, *Sioux* had fallen off the pace. As the gap between *Sioux* and *Forrest B.Royal* widened, the radar operator in *Cayuga* advised Brock that something seemed wrong with *Sioux*. Brock told the operator to keep close check on the ship. A few minutes later radar informed Brock that *Sioux* was dead in the water, hard aground with thirty feet of keel on a sandbar. The ship's log reveals:

0016½ Echo sounder not marking. Slight vibration. Speed 5 knots.

0027 Stopped both engines. Suspect grounding.

0028 Commenced putting main engines astern to free ship. Estimate only first thirty feet on bottom.

0032 Ship has considerable sternway on. Pointed to 025° and proceeded at 5 knots.

The following are excerpts from the *Official Enquiry Into the Grounding of His Majesty's Canadian Ship Sioux* held some days later as required by naval regulations.

Narrative Of Grounding[6]

The echo sounder was operated continuously from the time of proceeding from Cho-Do anchorage[7] and soundings were reported to the bridge for each change of one fathom.[8]

At 0026 depth shallowed very rapidly and echo traces disappeared. This was reported to the bridge and main engines were immediately put to slow and then stopped. Shortly after that at 0027 it was evident that the ship had touched bottom. It is estimated that only the first thirty feet of keel was aground.

It is interesting to note that the passage southward near 'buoy Charlie' [sic] at 0742 1/2 the echo sounder again stopped marking. Charted depth at this point is 4 3/4 fathoms and the height of the tide at the time was 7-8 feet [on Sok-To] making six fathoms in all. It is estimated that in fact depth at this point was barely 3 fathoms at this time. [sic]

Owing to the darkness of the night it was not possible to sight any of the channel buoys these being spherical, about 3 feet in diameter and painted black. [sic]

Shortly after grounding an object was heard to pass down the starboard side of the ship. Owing to excessive vibrations it became evident that the starboard propeller had been fouled. [sic]

The presence of the buoy, for such it later proved to be, is still unexplained.

Included in the *Narrative of Grounding* is a further appendix, *The Report of Grounding*[9], which summed up the narrative to the naval secretary's satisfaction, for he signed it with no comment. Excerpts from this report read:

It is noted that the estuary[10] is characterized by salient points drying mud flats between them. . . .

In view of the above [Narrative of Grounding] [it is understood] the strong tidal streams in the area and the numerous fixes [by the various navigators] it is assumed that the shoal to the eastward of the channel must have extended into the channel whereupon HMCS *Sioux* grounded.

(signed) R. Bidwell, RCN, Naval Secretary,
Ottawa, January 1951.

As recorded in both the narrative and the report, the vibrations had been caused by wires from an errant marker buoy. Despite all efforts to free the propeller shaft, the wires remained tightly wound about it. *Sioux*'s captain, Commander Taylor, had no choice but to retire at once to Cho-Do. There *Sioux* joined *Warramunga*, and the two spent the remainder of the night repairing their damages.

The four who remained, continued the tortuous journey through the twisting channels. While the blackness of the night had not lessened, visibility had improved slightly as the mist began to clear. The mist, however, was shortly replaced by wind-driven sleet which made the going even tougher. More lookouts were placed in the bows to keep wary eyes on the water ahead. The fear of mines was uppermost in their minds.

The ship's company remained extra alert. The stokers and engineers remained close to their stations, their attention never drifting from the valves and gauges and switches. In the magazines, hoists were filled with ammunition. Shells were stockpiled on deck beside the hoists to save precious steps should the shooting start in earnest.

In the crowded plot rooms there was almost frantic activity as the navigators scurried between chart table and radar screens. During that night each navigator was to make dozens of fixes in his efforts to keep his ship in the deepest water possible. The navigators had no chance to relax for even a moment. Any delay on their part in announcing the latest fix could result in the ship taking ground. Each navigator would complete over one hundred markings by the time the journey ended, a remarkable number for a relatively short distance.

Because she was the leading ship, *Cayuga* saw the most intense activity. Without doubt her navigator, Lt. Andrew Collier, was the busiest man aboard. Collier, a gifted navigator, set a total of 132 precise fixes over the distance. He spent the entire night on a virtual run. His superb work won him a Distinguished Service Cross. His efforts helped guide the ships which were trailing.

The run up the Daido-Ko was a team effort. The busiest team was probably that of Collier, A/B William Kobes, who manned the Sperry Radar, and CPO Douglas Pearson, the helmsman. Kobes, whose precise readings from his screen contributed greatly to the exactness of Collier's fixes, also helped Pearson to hold the ship on course. The close work from these three went far to ensure ultimate success in the operation. Pearson was later awarded a medal for his work that night, as was Brock. Kobes, for reasons unknown, was overlooked.

For many weeks after the run up the Daido-Ko, praises were heaped upon Collier for his work. An American navigator, when he saw the charts, was astounded, and recommended the entire record be published in the *Mariners' Manual* for study by others.

* * *

At 0300 the four ships steamed cautiously into the spacious harbour at Chinnampo. The entire waterfront and much of the city was ablaze, not with flames but with electric lights powered by special equipment aboard *Foss. Foss*, the originator of the emergency signal which had put the six destroyers into needless jeopardy, lay still and quiet at a jetty, serenely churning out electricity.

Chinnampo was at peace. There was no disaster. *Bayfield* was still afloat, as was *Bexar*. Activity ashore did not include fighting. The Reds, however close they might be, were not hammering at the city's gates. There being no emergency, the ships' crews, with the exception of the main guns' crews, were released from red alert.

At 0800, Brock and the other commanders attended a conference with Kelly aboard *Bayfield*. Kelly, his hands already filled with the problems of troop evacuation, turned responsibility of the harbour's defenses over to Brock. As this included the protection of the demolition teams who were preparing the wharves and jetties for destruction, all guns were once again returned to red alert.

It soon became clear the demolition teams were not working. They could be seen near and under the wharves but there was no activity. An enquiry brought forth the answer that work was slow because there was no air cover. Brock asked what air cover had to do with the task at hand. The American replied that U.S. army policy insisted on air cover for such work. As the air force had not provided the promised cover the work could not go on.[11]

Brock, anxious to get things moving, signalled HMS *Theseus*, requesting a fighter plane. Within minutes a plane arrived to cavort about in a series of loops and rolls. Thus comforted, the demolition squads which had been under cover by platoons and sections in compliance with U.S. army directives came out to resume the work. Engrossed in their work, they seemed not to notice the plane leave or to realize it was not replaced.

By noon it was clear the demolition preparedness was far behind schedule and would not be completed on time. Brock decided his ships must complete the destruction of the harbourfront after the evacuation had been completed. The U.S. commander, happy with the suggestions, ordered his squads to join the general withdrawal. Much of their work had been completed anyway.

At about 1300, reports began to come in that the Chinese had overrun areas defended by rearguards of the U.S. 8th Army. The reports, as was so often the case in those hectic days, proved to be exaggerations, but at the time had to be considered authentic. The overall action was hurried up as a result of the reports.

To add to the immediate concerns, the CO of HMS *Ceylon* signalled his intention to bring the cruiser to Chinnampo. He felt his 6-inch guns would be of considerable help. Brock, as diplomatically as possible, told *Ceylon* to stay put. He suggested the 6-inch guns would be of little use to anyone if the ship to which they were attached were stranded on a sandbar. He mentioned also the great danger to the others, should the cruiser run aground in a place which would deny the open sea to the destroyers.[12]

At 1430, the first ATA, loaded to capacity, moved toward the harbour exit. For the next five hours a continuous line of ATAs and LSVPs headed into the dubious safety of the Daido-Ko.

At 1700, *Foss*, *Bexar* (which ran aground almost immediately), and *Bayfield* departed. *Bexar* remained aground for several hours, but was floated free on the high tide. The other two made open water without incident.

By 1730, the harbour was clear of military traffic. Only the four destroyers remained. They picked their way gingerly among the scores of civilian sampans and small boats heading for pre-arranged positions. The civilian traffic caused concern, not only as hazards to navigation, but because they could well be harbouring Korean agents bent on laying a few more mines. Previous experience with armadas of fleeing civilians had caused the sailors to adopt a wary— cynical—attitude toward these fleets. On several occasions civilian junks and sampans had been found harbouring those who would lay mines along the way.

As a precaution *Athabaskan* was sent back into the channel to a point some five miles distant. There she established a checkpoint from which she could scrutinize the parade of boats passing by. Special crews in motor cutters moved among them. Every so often a squad of heavily armed sailors would board a boat and check it carefully. None were found which carried anything more lethal than the usual pot of fish stew simmering on the hibachis. These stews, a concoction of fish (complete with heads and entrails), spices and vegetables, reeked so foully that searches below decks were often only cursory. Besides finding no mines, the searchers also failed to turn up any suspicious persons. There were no incidents of resistance. The closest any of the sailors came to firing his weapon occurred when a cow, tethered in a dark corner below decks, thrust its wet nose against the man's exposed neck. The sailor, startled, whirled about and came face to nose with his equally alarmed assailant. Fortune smiled on the cow that night. The sailor was not trigger-happy. "Besides," he was to state later, "the bloody Lanchester* would have more than likely jammed. I was tempted though, to put a few shots into those stew pots. That brew those people cooked was enough to turn a dog away. I don't know how they could eat it."

Athabaskan remained busy all night. While her boats patrolled, her gunners scanned the north shoreline. They were rewarded in their efforts by the spotting of several newly emplaced artillery pieces. These were destroyed by the 4-inch guns.[13]

In the choppy water of Chinnampo's harbour, *Cayuga, Bataan* and *Forrest B. Royal* moved into their positions. The American, with 5-inch guns, had been assigned the concrete and brick buildings of

---

* The Lanchester machine gun, unlike the trusted Bren, had one dreaded flaw. While capable of firing in rapid bursts, it would usually jam after a few rounds, and precious time would be wasted correcting the jammed mechanism. If given a choice between a rifle and a Lanchester, most sailors assigned to landing parties would choose the rifle. The RCN used the dependable and accurate .303 Lee Enfield.

a sprawling complex which had, in more peaceful days, produced most of North Korea's cement. *Bataan* would use her 4.7-inch armament against the railway yards, the gasoline storage tanks and the western section of the harbour, which included two ship-building yards with two ships under construction.

Cayuga had drawn the eastern sector. This gave her the large oil tanks, long rows of wooden sheds, numerous warehouses and a marshalling yard used by a local railroad. It was crammed with wooden railway cars.

At 1735, on a signal from *Cayuga*, all guns opened fire. Within seconds explosions were heard, followed by the brightening of the dark sky as great flames swept high into the air. At about the same time as the first shots were fired, the demolition charges set by the U.S. army teams erupted. The jetties and wharves shuddered and crashed into the water. The final hours of Chinnampo had begun.

Those who witnessed the scene were to later describe it as sight of spectacular fury. Not unlike a Wagnerian scenario without music, Chinnampo met its *Gotterdammerung*. The three ships, swung broadside, laid on with all armament plus whatever Bofors could be brought to bear. Within minutes the entire dockside was a mass of flames. Huge fireballs rose skyward before dissipating into black, acrid smoke. The increasing winds, which fanned the flames, carried the smoke inland as a message to the advancing Chinese that Chinnampo would serve them no useful purpose.

The abundance of gasoline and oil storage tanks meant there would be no shortage of fuel for the fires. The tanks, ripped open by the HEDA shells, spilled their contents onto the ground where rivers of the volatile liquid formed. Because Chinnampo, like most Korean coastal towns and villages, sloped toward the water, the burning fuels flowed into the warehouses and sheds along the docks.

Forrest B. Royal had good gunners. Unlike many American ships, she had seen much action on the west coast where most of the gunnery warfare took place. Laying their shots carefully, the Americans were hitting the buildings near the foundations, weakening the structures sufficiently to cause the walls to fall in on themselves. Fires were started which fed on wooden framework and whatever flammable material was within. The huge complex lay in total ruin within an hour. Only one tall smokestack, like a huge tombstone marking the site, remained upright.

So widespread had the fires become that the entire city seemed engulfed. With no firefighters or civil defence workers in the city the flames moved with the wind. The flimsy buildings of which the city was mainly constructed burned quickly. The fires were still burning late in the afternoon of 6 December.[14]

Official assessment of the destroyers' work was listed as "total." All the oil and gasoline tanks were wiped out. A large radio station building had been destroyed. *Bataan's* shipyard targets had been hit hard. The two ships under construction—one almost completed, and the other half finished —were totally destroyed. The completed vessel had taken hits from one hundred 4.7-inch shells; the other had taken forty. All the shipyard buildings were flattened, all cranes and derricks toppled, and the gates of the dry docks holed. It was doubted at the time if the dockyard facilities could be made service-able again within months or even years. The last explosion from within the stricken city was reported and logged at 0616, 6 Decem-ber.[15]

* * *

Prior to the bombardment, the greatest concern had been felt for the civilians attempting to flee the city. These unfortunate people crowded the docks and the beaches in the hope of gaining access to a boat capable of transporting them to the Yellow Sea or, at least, to the south shore. There was no way of knowing how many remained in the city itself.

Brock, in order to clear as many civilians as possible from the area of immediate danger, sent ROKN personnel out in boats.[16] Equipped with loudhailers, these sailors warned the refugees to leave the area at once, but with little effect. Finally, as a last resort, Brock had his gunners place several shots into a vacant warehouse. The shots scattered the crowds, most of whom fled to the safety of the beaches. Brock also declined to destroy the boats which lay along the beaches, despite orders from HQ to disable all craft. As a result of this gesture many hundreds of refugees were able to get away. He was later commended by the UN for his refusal to destroy the boats.

The bombardment itself lasted only one hour and fifteen minutes, but during that time the three ships hurled out hundreds of HEDA shells, many thousands of Bofors shells and a lesser number of Oerlikon rounds.[17]

The action at an end, the ships prepared for their own departure. *Forrest B. Royal* and *Bataan* cleared the harbour without incident. *Cayuga* was delayed somewhat by the necessity of having to chase down and convince the captains of the ROKN minesweepers that they, too, must leave. Although he understood their desire to stay and fight, Brock told them to obey his orders or he would sink their ships where they stood. He had no intention of allowing three serviceable ships to fall into the hands of the Chinese. Sullenly, but without further discussion, the three ships fell into line astern of *Bataan* and made their way into the Daido-Ko. *Cayuga*, once the Koreans had cleared the harbour, moved toward the harbour exit just a step ahead of a huge patch of flaming oil which had pursued the ship across the harbour.[18]

Those on the bridge and in the operations room once more prepared for troubles. The tide had ebbed to its lowest point and darkness was complete. It looked as if the trip down the estuary might well be as hairy as the trip up had been. Once again extra lookouts were sent to the sharpest point of the ship and into the crow's nest to scan the north shore for gun emplacements. *Athabaskan* had taken out four batteries some hours before, but the possibility that more existed could not be overlooked. The last thing anyone wanted at the moment was a gun battle against fixed guns ashore. Such a duel fought in water where manoeuvring was impossible was not in the ship's best interest. Because she was many minutes behind the other two, *Cayuga* would not be able to depend on them for assistance.

The ship had barely cleared the harbour when, as if by some special order, an extremely heavy fall of snow began. The wind had suddenly died, so the fall was gentle but so heavy that visibility was reduced to near-zero. It was exactly what was needed. No shore-based gunners could see the ship now, and concentration was shifted to the search for mines.

The curtain of snow lifted as suddenly as it had started, just as *Cayuga* entered the defended area. With all ships at anchor the fleet settled in for the night. Special crews, guns' crews and special sea-dutymen remained on full alert, but most of the ships' companies were able to retire for the night. For most it was the first decent rest in seventy-two hours.

*   *   *

Because sailors are a superstitious lot, the snowstorm, coming as it did in such timely fashion, caused no amount of small talk throughout the ship. As might be expected, the chaplain took credit for it on behalf of "the Boss," as he often referred to God, and no one argued the point.

The tiny fleet's RC chaplain at the time was one Father R. M. Ward, RCN; the protestant chaplain was Rev. H. Todd. The two shared their duties, each staying a week or two in turn on each of the ships. During the Chinnampo operation, Todd was aboard *Athabaskan*, Ward in *Cayuga*.

Ward was a respected, well-liked man. His humour, tolerance and understanding of young sailors set him apart from many of his colleagues. A pianist of some talent, he could often be found aboard *Cayuga* coaxing tunes out of a reluctant piano bolted to the deck in the fore-upper mess. It had been there since the ship's first commission in 1948, but had never been tuned. But Ward could get music from it; and as he played a small crowd would gather about him. When there were enough assembled to form a small glee club, Ward would launch into the "North Atlantic Squadron" and the fun would start. He did not mind the sailors' ribald songs, but he had made it known that no blasphemy would be tolerated, and this order was never disobeyed.

Stories abound about Ward. Those who knew him never fail to recall a story or two in which he was the central figure. A tireless fighter for the ordinary sailor, he cared not which religion he might or might not espouse. Atheists, he would say, are also "my Boss's children," and as such deserved his care. He was instrumental in gaining lenient sentences for several who had committed serious crimes against "good order and naval discipline." He had quickly arranged the return home of a sailor whose wife had deserted their home and child. He could arrange compassionate leave faster than any of the other padres, so it was natural that when times got a little tough it was to Father Ward that people turned.

Father Ward died in 1957, the victim of a RCAF jet fighter crash. The jet, on a routine training mission, crashed into a convent near Bagotville, Quebec, to which Ward had been posted by his church as resident chaplain after leaving the naval service about 1955. None felt more badly than did those who had known him during the early months of the Korean fighting. To the sailors of the original three destroyers he had been a special friend.

* * *

As dawn broke over the Daido-Ko on Wednesday 6 December, it cast a feeble light upon a scene of turmoil and confusion. Strewn along the channel in varying degrees of distress or indecision were LSVPs and ATAs by the dozen. Some were hard aground. Some, having suffered engine failure, lay dead in the water. Others, their coxswains having become confused by the darkness or lost sight of their leader's blue light, had simply dropped anchor where they were, their occupants hoping mightily that some larger vessel would not run them down.

Once repaired or refloated, they were quickly assembled into a long line, and the journey resumed. *Cayuga*, because Brock wished to keep his eye on the ROKN minesweepers, kept its trailing position. The entire morning was spent in keeping the boats from lagging or wandering too close to the shoals and mud flats.

The Daido-Ko by daylight was not the fearsome stretch it had been by night. At 0940, in bone-chilling sleet driven by brisk winds, the line of little ships and their larger escorts sailed out of the channel to the safer waters of the Yellow Sea. Quickly formed into short columns, within an hour they were headed toward Inchon.

TE95.12, its work completed for the moment, turned northward on a course for the Yalu River area. The Chinnampo adventure was ended, but a new one was about to begin.

* * *

TE95.12, having given over their charges to the UN at Inchon, steamed at full speed for the Yalu. Upon reaching the area, the ships once again split into teams of two and went their separate ways. The war along the west coast was heating up as the Chinese, now in full control, surged headlong toward South Korea. They had also begun to think in terms of taking the Chorusan Islands off the coast, an ideal base for attacks on the more southerly islands.

The Chorusans had been occupied by UN forces, mainly ROK Marines, during the great advance northward. The main island, Taewha-Do, had become HQ for one Lt. A. N. Allan of the U.S. army, who commanded the Leopards, a large group of which more will be heard. Allan felt sure the Chinese would make a move against the island, and made plans to defend it, including a request for UN naval support. The Canadians were assigned a major role in this undertaking. Within a week following Chinnampo, Allan met with the Canadian commanders to determine the best means of defense.

It was agreed the best defense should be an ongoing program of harassment against the Chinese depots and garrisons on the mainland. This, it was felt, would deter the Chinese from attempting a full-scale invasion and risk tangling with the naval guns. From 7 December until the middle of January 1951, the ships prowled the area, hitting hard at the Chinese encampments. Their efforts were rewarded in that they enjoyed complete control of the waterways leading to Taewha-Do and the lesser islands. The Chinese made no move until well into 1951, even though they had retaken all of North Korea by early spring. Exploratory assaults against some of the small islands had been easily repulsed by the ever-present ships, which did much to discourage the Chinese from launching full-scale attacks.

This phase of the war, which became known as the Island Campaign, was still some distance in the future. The campaign, however, had its beginnings during December 1950.

During the waning days of 1950 the future looked bleak indeed for the UN forces. Even the success at Chinnampo did little to lift the spirits of the troops, although those who had contributed felt justifiably proud of their achievement. Now 1951 was fast approaching and Chinese troops were running rampant over the terrain so recently held by the UN. The navy looked somewhat gloomily into the future and prepared for what would prove to be a very interesting year.

Chapter Nine _____

THE LONG
WAY BACK

Past and to come seems best, things present worst.
Shakespeare, *King Henry IV, Part II*

The retreat of the UN forces—the 8th Army in particular— became a source of pessimism and bleak outlook for those in charge of the conduct of the war. Each passing hour saw the issuance of new orders, many in direct contrast to their predecessors.[1] During the first crucial days of the Chinese advance, once again the rumours of a great sea-lift to Japan made the rounds. The rumours, combined with MacArthur's inertia, caused the entire system to waver. Only the naval and air forces seemed to be fighting with any purpose or direction; the land forces were being mauled severely. The U.S. Marines in the central sector were holding but weakening by the day. Within a few days they also cracked, and the Chinese broke through.

In contrast to the UN troops' lack of direction, the Chinese were very well disciplined. They attacked again and again in shouting, bugle-blowing hordes. They never seemed to stop for regrouping, never appeared to slacken the attacks long enough to allow a counterthrust. This strategy saw them win back all of North Korea without ever having to fight a major battle. By 30 December, the Chinese armies were poised along the 38th parallel. South Korea lay before them, theirs for the taking.

Surprisingly, they called a halt to their advance. This unexpected move raised several questions. What was China's intention? Would they cross the line into the south? Did they intend another push on Pusan? Were they waiting for the UN to put out peace feelers? These questions troubled the governments of the participating nations who, while willing to supply men and materiel to the effort against North Korea, were not anxious to cross swords with China. They were also deeply worried that Russia might decide to take an active role. If both the Red superpowers were to enter the war on the side of North Korea, a local war could easily cross borders into other Asian countries. These concerns were causing uneasy feelings in capitals around the world.

To the credit of those involved, the spirit of the UN resolution prevailed. In the weeks following the initial Chinese intervention, there arrived in Pusan troops from Greece, Turkey, Australia, Britain, Canada and France. Other nations sent units which varied in size from a small company of Luxembourg militiamen to a frigate from Columbia. More warships arrived from France and Holland to reinforce the dozens already there. Denmark sent a modern, fully equipped hospital ship with its complete staff. Supplies of all kinds arrived daily in Japanese ports for transshipment to Pusan and the front lines farther north.

The Chinese delay along the 38th parallel gave the UN the breather required. By the time the Chinese crossed the parallel during the first month of the New Year, resistance had stiffened against them. The Chinese did recapture Seoul, but from that point onward made only limited advances.

Meanwhile, in Washington, President Truman was taking a long, hard look at his uneasy relationship with MacArthur. For the time being he did nothing about replacing him, but in what was seen as a significant move, Truman ordered General Matthew B. Ridgeway to take command of the shattered 8th Army. Under Ridgeway's leadership the 8th regrouped and once again took up the fight.

By March, Ridgeway had whipped his troops into shape.[2] He then felt ready to make a series of major attacks against the Chinese lines in the western sector. Later that month the 8th Army retook Seoul and surged across the 38th parallel. By April the UN troops were once again in control of the border and had pushed some distance into North Korea.

Truman, with Seoul firmly in UN hands, made his long-planned move. He recalled MacArthur and fired him. Ridgeway was named as the new overall commander and immediately announced as his primary objective a push against the Chinese which would drive them as far north as possible in the shortest possible time.

Ridgeway took charge with a firm hand and made a clean sweep of his HQ. He fired most of MacArthur's staff; those he could not fire outright he transferred to postings far removed from Korea. He deployed his available troops to areas where their skills and talents could be put to the best possible use. Mountain fighters were sent to the Taeback Range. British Commandos and Ghurkas went to the western sector for work along the coastal inlets and fiords. Such deployment of specialized troops had not been considered by Mac-Arthur. He had been too busy garnishing his image to give thought to such things.

Under Ridgeway the UN forces commenced a relentless offensive. The Chinese fell back steadily. Their counterattacks were repulsed and their lines were split by multi-pronged thrusts. Divided by these innovative tactics, Chinese divisions found themselves fighting as smaller groups in which they could not use their human-wave assaults. The fighting became more hand-to-hand, and the Chinese infantrymen fared poorly in close combat. Chinese losses became heavy.

UN losses, however, were also heavy. Long, bloody skirmishes were fought in valleys and on hills, many of which changed owners several times in a matter of days and sometimes hours. There seemed no end to the fighting. Moreover, neither side appeared willing to make the first move which might lead to peace talks.

* * *

In December and January, however, the recapture of Seoul and the firing of MacArthur were still weeks away, and the patrols along the Koreans coasts remained long and arduous. Very little harbour time was logged during those months.

The patrols, seemingly endless, were days and nights of search-and-destroy missions, the boredom of carrier screening and investigation of hundreds of sampans and junks. The nights during those patrols were generally sleepless because of the almost continuous action. The lack of proper sleep took its toll as each wearying day passed into yet another wearying night. Tempers grew short as the sailors, forced by circumstance to spend the nights in the close confinement of their various action stations found the mornings offered no change. The overcrowded messdecks seemed like prisons to them.

To further antagonize the men, the colossal mail snafu was still having its adverse effects. The deal struck between the RCN and the RCAF could do nothing to alleviate the backlog still held within the USN FPO system. That mail was still arriving in trickles. Morale aboard the ships, never high, began to sink once again. Each new day saw further signs of discontent.

109

Messdeck arguments and disagreements increased. A remark which would normally bring a good-natured retort[3] was now more than likely to produce a sharp rebuke. Personal feuds erupted, some of which lasted for weeks and even months. Captains' Reports saw increasingly long lines of defaulters at each session. Many of the charges were for fighting. The loss of Good Conduct badges and periods of detention increased.

Aboard *Sioux* a young seaman was roughed up by two of his mates for using what they considered an excessive amount of jam on his toast. Jam was not strictly rationed but was in somewhat short supply. Timely intervention by others cooled the situation, and little of consequence was recorded, as the Divisional Officer handled the charges at a low level.

Cayuga, however, had an incident which could have proved very serious. A seaman on sentry duty one dark night thrust the muzzle of his revolver into the ear of a contrary cook as the latter, seated quietly on a bollard, looked out over the silent water. The cook had been engaged for weeks in a running feud with the seaman over a continuing request for two scoops of potatoes. The request, made every supper, was refused each time. The seaman began to brood over what he had come to consider a grave insult. The more he thought about the affront the more it rankled. He crept up behind the unsuspecting cook with drawn gun and stuck the muzzle into his right ear. Then, in a quiet voice, he suggested the cook might wish to reconsider his attitude toward the issuance of potatoes.

The feel of cool metal in his ear was enough to convince the cook that two scoops of mashed potatoes were hardly a valid reason to continue a policy which might well prove fatal. He quickly agreed to show more generosity in future. The seaman, obviously satisfied, padded away into the darkness, leaving the shaken cook alone to ponder his next move. He soon decided he had no next move. He did discuss the incident with a couple of his mates, but they were of the opinion that he should forget the incident. They also reminded him that he had no witnesses. To make an issue of his personal moment of terror would only cause more problems. Discretion, he decided, was the wisest course. A destroyer which spent its nights knifing through the cold waters of the Yellow Sea was hardly the place to test the seriousness of a threat.

Incidents, major and minor, plagued all three ships during those weeks. The problems recorded in the various reports on file in the RCN Collection and the ships' logs show the extent to which morale had tumbled. So it went to close out the old year and usher in the new—at least until mid-January when the first of the long patrols came to their ends.

Chapter Ten _____

HAPPY
HOLIDAY

Do nothing but eat, and make good cheer,
And praise God for the merry year.
Shakespeare, *King Henry IV, Part II*

The final six months of 1950 had not been merry, and the three months just past had been the least merry of all. Korea, both halves, lay ravaged, devoid of productive life. Rice paddies, which in June had been laden with promise, now were shattered; the terraced layers pocked with shell craters; the diked troughs flattened by tank treads and truck tires. Entire villages had been obliterated beyond recovery or repair. Small towns, once bustling with the commerce of an agricultural society, stood deserted, only a few burned-out buildings standing like mute guards amidst the rubble. The bitter Korean winter had settled in to make life even harder for the unfortunate citizens of the war-torn peninsula. For the mainly Bhuddist Koreans it was just as well they did not recognize Christmas as one of their feast days.

Aboard the destroyers, however, Christmas was very much a part of life. The sailors, determined to make most of the day, made their plans accordingly. *Athabaskan*, in Sasebo, made different plans than the other two, both of whom were still on patrol.

Christmas Day fell on a Monday. The weather, bitterly cold, was made worse by a strong wind from the northeast which whipped the Yellow Sea into choppy waves. The ships rose and fell in short rolls as they cut through the murky turbulence. The sky, heavy with leaden clouds, threatened continuance of the cold rain which had been falling for days. Those on the bridge and those who manned the guns found it difficult to stave off the numbing cold, as the ships cruised at half speed among the bleak, unfriendly islands of the Sojoson-Man. Many of the small islands had already been occupied by Chinese troops. There was no doubt they were assembling in preparation for all-out invasions of the western islands.

In contrast to the unpleasant weather outside, the atmosphere within the ships was cheerful. Fresh supplies had been obtained from a USN provisions ship sent out for that specific purpose. It had also brought some mail and a few parcels. The mail lifted the spirits a bit and the thoughts of fresh apples, oranges and grapefruit increased the prospects for a happy Christmas. There had been no fresh fruit for weeks, so the shipment was greeted with more than usual enthusiasm.

On 23 December, a small landing party from *Cayuga* had ventured out to one of the small islands on a routine search mission. While they had found no enemy troops, they discovered some spindly pine trees. Poor things though they were, they represented Christmas and were deemed adequate. Some were cut down and distributed between the two ships to decorate messdecks and wardrooms. Each ship also ran a tree up the halyards to the top of the mainmast. Even in war, traditions must be upheld.

Christmas in the RCN had always been celebrated in the traditional way, regardless of whether the ship was at sea or in harbour, or whether the ship was large or small. The tradition had been upheld even during the harrowing days of World War II, so there was no reason for not keeping tradition during the less dangerous Korean War.

Christmas for *Athabaskan* was routine. Turkey dinner was served at noon and leave was piped shortly after. The morning had been spent traditionally, the youngest member of the ship's company being appointed captain for the day. He made his rounds, ordered the usual double tot of rum for the crew, had his dinner in the wardroom along with the officers. Perhaps he had a drink from the bar despite being underage. He then signed the ship's log in an undecipherable scrawl and his day was over. Perhaps he went ashore with his buddies to carry on the celebrations. It is assumed his stint as ship's captain was uneventful, as nothing in the record indicates otherwise.

Cayuga and *Sioux* also spent the day in relative quiet. The necessity of remaining on full alert negated the usual great merriment, so there was no problem with alcohol-generated exuberance. *Sioux*'s log shows her captain for the day as having been eighteen-year-old O/S Stephen Matthews, while *Cayuga*'s log names O/S Kenneth Crooker, also eighteen, as her captain. These two commanded their respective ships for the allotted hours, ordered the ships' supply officers to "splice the main brace,"[1] signed the ships' logs and eventually returned to their normal duties after the ceremonial dinner in the wardroom.

The menus for dinner were similar aboard all ships. Breakfast included fresh fruit plus freshly baked cinnamon rolls, hot cakes and French toast along with maple syrup. There were no eggs served that morning, which was considered by all to be an act of mercy.

Fresh eggs were unobtainable during the early months of the conflict. The USN had eggs which they had brought out of cold storage from depots in the States and elsewhere. These eggs had been in storage for many months and in some cases for more than a year. They had been stored in refrigerators not quite at the freezing level, and because they were still in the shell they were considered fresh. They were not.

Because of their age all eggs were carefully selected for use. Of any ten selected at random, at least four were totally rotten while the remainder could be used but had to be thoroughly checked. Every morning the cooks cracked each egg into a saucer and, if not too offensive to sight and smell, proclaimed it fit for use. Within minutes of the selection procedure, the malodorous stench of sulpher permeated the entire ship. None who served in the ships will likely forget the eggs of Korean days. Their absence from the Christmas breakfast menu was considered the best treat of all.

Dinner was strictly traditional. The turkeys were stuffed with a dressing of bread and nuts. Peas, carrots, brussels sprouts, mashed potatoes and gravy topped it all off. There were olives, pickles and other condiments. The dessert, called duff by sailors, was steamed plum pudding, reported to have been made especially for the three ships as a gift from Edmonton's Home for Ex-Servicemen's Children and flown to Korea by special arrangement.[2]

To emphasize the serenity of the day the ships' guns remained silent. The ships extended the limits of the patrol in order to stay at the extreme edges so as not to invite enemy fire. Christmas Day 1950 was a day in which many gave some thought to the reasons for their presence in that strange arena in which two forces, each with radically differing philosophies, faced each other. Some found a reason or two; others found none at all.

In this the Canadian sailors had common ground with the Koreans. The Koreans, whose land this was, understood the war no better than did the sailors. The terrified peasants, unfortunate victims, could only watch helplessly as the assorted armies shelled

113

their villages from far at sea or marched through their rice paddies and killed their livestock. To the Canadians the war was as much a mystery as it was to the poor Korean peasants. The sailors had no interest in Korea. Few could understand why anyone would want to fight over the place at all and would have been pleased to call off the entire venture. On that Christmas day they were tired of the crowded messdecks, the sameness of routine that bored them to a distraction few had ever known. Worse, they could see no positive results from the destruction they themselves had helped impose.

What they could see was 1951 looming before them, looking no better than the final months of 1950. The defeats were memories, to be sure, but could the future promise better? No one saw much reason for optimism. So, they refused to curtail their celebrations, limited as they were, and they made the most of it—*Cayuga* and *Sioux* soberly at sea, *Athabaskan* quite the opposite in harbour.[3]

A fourth ship also celebrated Christmas away from Canada. HMCS *Nootka* had departed Halifax on 25 November bound for Korea. Under the command of Cdr. A. B. Fraser-Harris, RCN, she sailed westward through the Panama Canal, stopped at Pearl Harbour and, with stops at Kwajalein and Guam, would arrive in Sasebo on 14 January 1951. *Nootka* arrived on schedule to a tumultuous welcome. Those who gave her the most enthusiastic greeting were the men of *Sioux*. *Sioux* was going home.

Chapter Eleven _____

OLD WARRIORS; NEW WARRIORS

And more such days as these to us befall.
Shakespeare, *King Henry VI, Part II*

_____

During the first hours of 1951, *Cayuga* and *Sioux* moved quietly together among the rugged islands of the Sojoson-Man. There was no moon to break the blackness of the night. The stars twinkled in the black velvet of the northern sky. The land, visible off the ships' starboard beams, lay in wintry solitude under a fresh blanket of snow. The Sojoson-Man was still free of ice, but only a few miles to the north the ice packs had begun to form. The two hunters, on a seek-and-destroy mission, were starting the forty-first day of patrol.

What had proved to be a successful partnership was about to be dissolved. At 0600 *Sioux* turned southward, gave three whoops from her siren and headed toward Sasebo. The time had come for her return to Canada. She was overdue for some major repairs, and her tired crew were looking forward to some time at home. Some, they knew, would be asked to return to Korea, but most hoped there would be replacements waiting in Esquimalt.

Sioux had served well. During her 168 days in the Korean theatre of operations, despite her slow start, she had seen a full share of action, had known the tedium, had been part of the Inchon invasion and had at least started the Chinnampo adventure. She had earned her rest. On 15 January, having been officially relieved by *Nootka*, *Sioux* steamed from the teeming harbour that had been home port for so many months and set her course for Canada.

On 10 January, *Cayuga* returned to Sasebo just in time to say "sayonara" to *Sioux* and "konichiwa" to *Nootka** who, still resplendent in fresh paint, appeared in shining contrast to the faded blues of her sisters. She was yet to experience the rigors of the Yellow Sea patrols and the deteriorating effects of its water. She was a perky young lass among jaded harridans. *Nootka*, like other Tribals, carried a full complement of 4-inch guns and 75mm Bofors, as well as depth charges and Squid bombs. But she sported brand new radar tracking devices for her guns which the others lacked. This would give her an advantage which she would put to good use.

Her captain, Cdr. Alexander Beaufort Fraser-Harris, a former Royal Navy officer who had transferred to the RCN some years before, was a flamboyant individual with a flair for showmanship which he would, perhaps unintentionally, show during approaches to mooring buoys. *Nootka* became almost legendary for her harbour entrances, many of which were adventures in themselves.

Nootka's initial entry into Sasebo had been no exception. Approaching the mooring too fast, her prow struck the buoy head-on. Dragging its anchor and bobbing wildly, the buoy was pushed several feet from its proper position as the forecastle crew tried to get it under enough control to finalize the ship's arrival. Over the next months *Nootka*'s erratic approaches were watched with unbounded glee by all who were in harbour at the time.

Nootka's welcoming ceremonies were subdued. She had lost one of her crew two days out of Guam. During the waning hours of 11 January, O/S L. A. Gauthier disappeared over the side. It is believed he was swept over by a wave, but as he was not missed for at least two hours no one can be certain. The ship retraced her route and carried out an extensive search but the seaman was not found.[1]

Nootka's crew had barely enough time to provision ship before she was ordered to sea. Accompanied by *Cayuga*, she sailed to the west coast. There was some grumbling as shore leave had been denied, but the thought of some action quieted the moans. The two ships headed out late at night for Inchon.

* * *

---

* Good-bye and Good Morning, respectively, in Japanese.

Inchon had fallen to the Chinese on 5 January, but the occupying troops had been given no peace whatever. Each day various ships had gone into the area for the single purpose of intense bombardment. The continuous harassment had kept the Chinese off balance and in a state of constant alert. As the Inchon garrison was fairly small, the constant shelling had forced them to move from one shelter to another. They spent most of their time in flight.

Inchon, therefore, was deemed a suitable place for *Nootka* to learn the fundamentals of this unusual war. The two ships spent two days in the spacious harbour picking out targets and honing the newcomer's gunnery skills. Then the ships headed north. *Nootka* was shown the points of interest, the places to avoid, the hot spots and the islands which held Chinese troops. The locations of Korean guerrilla units were pointed out. Sandbars and shoals which remained unmarked on the maps were detailed. In three days *Nootka*'s sailors learned the ins and outs of the entire operational area, knowledge which had taken months for the three original ships to compile.

Nootka stayed with *Cayuga* for two full weeks. Finally the time came for her to go out on her own, but the ships' parting was delayed at the last minute when some Chinese gunners on Walmi-Do decided to fight. The day was 25 January, and as the ships steamed slowly past the island on their final run as partners, shore batteries opened up against them. The Chinese gunners, however anxious they may have been to fight, were woefully inefficient. Their fall of shot was short by many yards.

The ships' gunners, on the other hand, were coldly professional. The main armament on *Nootka* opened up in full fury, the opening rounds on their way even before the waterspouts from the Chinese shells had been reclaimed by the sea. Within minutes the Chinese guns had been silenced. *Nootka* had accepted her first challenge and had slain her adversary. With *Cayuga* lying back in covering position, *Nootka* then moved in for a closer look, but drew no fire. Using her Bofors at close range, she hammered at the wooden sheds, buildings and other fortifications. Within a few minutes the threat from Walmi-Do had ended. The island was to pose no threat for several weeks.

* * *

Inchon continued to be of interest to the naval forces throughout the early weeks of the New Year. The port, abandoned to the advancing Chinese with little resistance, had been given up almost intact. The city had not been destroyed as had Chinnampo, although it could have easily been. Indeed, there had been many who advocated such a tactic.

The sparing of Inchon proved a wise decision. Indeed, there had been no sound reason for destroying the port. The UN forces had left the city in orderly fashion. They had not deserted their equipment, nor had they left anything of value for the Chinese. Long lines of ATAs and barges had toiled for days plying back and forth to waiting ships, loaded with the supplies and equipment they had only so recently brought in. One may assume the Coca-Cola, Hershey Bars, typewriters and barbers' chairs were among the rescued material. Inchon was considered recapturable, and once recaptured the dockyard facilities would be of prime importance to the UN war effort.

By 4 January, the city had been evacuated. The long rows of warehouses lay empty. The last barge had made its way out of the harbour late that afternoon. *Cayuga*, alone in the vast harbour, rode at anchor. Those aboard the ship looked out at the quiet city. High in the director and below on the bridge officers and men contemplated the deserted jetties and piers. There were some who yearned for a second Chinnampo. As darkness descended, the anchor was weighed, and *Cayuga* moved slowly toward the harbour exit, the last UN ship to leave Inchon.

When the Chinese entered the city the next day they brought with them many pieces of heavy artillery. These they set up along the waterfront, on the island of Walmi-Do and along the coastal approaches. Fearing an offshore invasion, they set up most of their defensive artillery in positions facing the sea. This proved a serious error. When Inchon was again invaded the attack came from the landward side. With most of their heavy guns pointing seaward, the Chinese robbed themselves of firepower they needed.

The Chinese had actually fallen into a trap. Until General Ridgeway was ready to attack Inchon he had used the naval forces as his bait. For weeks prior to his assault against Inchon, Ridgeway had depended on the navy to convince the Chinese that a second invasion from offshore was imminent. *Nootka* and *Cayuga* were the chief players in this drama. For several weeks these two ships, often together, moved into Inchon's harbour on a daily basis to shell the Chinese gun emplacements. As the weeks passed the activity increased, until by the middle of February as many as seven ships, including cruisers, would daily enter the harbour. This intensified activity convinced the Chinese an attack was indeed about to be launched. They based their conclusions on the fact that naval activity of the same sort had preceded the first invasion to almost the same degree. Hurriedly, they moved even more guns to positions which would give the best protection from offshore assault.

During the first days of March, Ridgeway's assaults began on a broad front. The rejuvenated 8th Army began an encircling move against Seoul and Inchon. The ROK 1st Division, as part of the 8th Army, attacked Seoul, taking it on 5 March. Inchon fell to the UN troops the same day. The Chinese heavy guns, all pointing westward, looked out over an empty harbour. Not a single ship was in sight.

* * *

During the early weeks of 1951, the ships were once again in the grip of a morale crisis. The problems were the same as those which had caused the situation the previous autumn. Once again the lack of mail was the culprit. While the grumblings were not as pronounced as in the previous instance, they were loud enough that some captains gave the situation priority mention in their monthly reports. "Morale is at a low ebb," wrote one, "the situation is not at a serious level but could easily grow worse."[2]

Morale, particularly aboard ships with confined space, can be a very volatile thing. It can be very low one day only to soar within twenty-four hours. The smallest incident can be the trigger. Some commanders instinctively know a morale booster when they see it, while others let things go too far, then wonder why they have a mutiny on their hands.

Cdr. Paul Taylor of *Sioux* was one who knew how to raise morale. It was he who initiated the first of several contests held among the ships of all nations. Taylor, perhaps by design, started the Refuelling Championship Challenge.* Contested by many, it was ultimately held by one.

Because of the long patrols all ships refuelled at sea. Both the RN and the USN had tankers on continuous station for that purpose. The Tribal Class destroyers proved to be the tankers' best customers, fuel consumption being the major flaw in that class of ship. The procedures for refuelling at sea were essentially the same in all navies, so few problems were ever encountered. Because the RCN was at the time working mainly in the Yellow Sea, RN tankers were being used. It was the RN procedure which spawned the contest.

Refuelling at sea was an exercise in basics. Co-operation between crews was essential, the officer of the watch had to know the

---

* This was the contest's official title. The sailors called it the Oiling-at-Sea Contest.

drills, the helmsman required a steady hand on the wheel, and the oiling parties on the upper deck had to move about smartly under the direction of the officer in charge. Over the years many changes have been made, and today the entire operation is automated. In 1951, however, it was still a matter of wires, ropes, Coston guns and a lot of running. Brute strength was also needed at times.

Once the receiving ship had closed with the tanker, a signal was given which told the tanker all was ready. The firing of the Coston gun[3] hurled the gun line across the gap. Attached to the gun line were two lines called messengers: one the light messenger, the other the heavy messenger. Once received, these lines were secured firmly. Then, from the receiving ship, the span line was tossed across to the tanker and secured. These lines were kept taut throughout the operation by the united efforts of a team of seamen deployed along the upper deck. With the span line in place, the tanker released the large oil line, a rubber hose some six inches in diameter. This hose was hauled the distance between the ships along the heavy messenger by a second team of seamen. The faster these men moved, the faster the hose could be hauled inboard.

Once inboard, the hose was fitted to a receiver pipe and screwed down tightly, at which point a signal was given the tanker, whose crew started the pumps. At the same time a white pennant was run up the tanker's halyards to warn others of "oiling in progress" so they could keep a safe distance. Oiling at sea was not generally a hurried effort. The RN, years before, had decided a period of eight minutes to be fast enough, and this standard had been adopted by all the Commonwealth fleets.

One cold winter morning *Sioux* glided into position alongside RFA *Wave Knight.* Perhaps it was the cold or perhaps it was boredom—or a combination of both—but the oiling party wheeled through the drill in a very short time of four minutes and forty-five seconds. Someone remarked that the time had to be some sort of record, and Taylor ordered a signal sent out, proclaiming to the UN fleet that HMCS *Sioux* was the Oiling-at-Sea Champion.

Three weeks later, following a period of intensive drilling, *Cayuga* set a new record of three minutes and forty seconds. She was the new champion, and a signal went out accordingly.

It was at this point that the contest began in earnest. For days after, many ships tried without success to best the new record. Confident her record would stand, *Cayuga* sailed for home. Her crew talked of posting a better time on their return in a few months.

Cayuga had no sooner cleared the area when *Nootka*, her crew showing patience, skill and teamwork, tore the record to shreds with an almost unbelievable time of three minutes and ten seconds. Her communicators wasted no time in announcing the fact.

What those in *Nootka* had failed to notice was the quiet indifference to the contest shown by the sailors in *Athabaskan*. They had shown no interest when *Sioux* set the initial record, had yawned loudly when told of *Cayuga's* feat, had watched with total disinterest the USN, RN and RAN efforts to play the new game, and made no comment at all when *Nootka* told the fleet of her new status as champion.

Athabaskan's company, far from being disinterested, had been watching the proceedings with unusual attention. All the while they had been drilling, waiting for the ideal moment to have a go at the record. *Athabaskan* approached the challenge scientifically. Her crew had not grown impatient as new records were being set. They had stood aside, had remained on the sidelines until all others had either quit their attempts or had left the area. They had time. There was no hurry.

Then, in early March, they felt their time had come. *Sioux* and *Cayuga* were well out of the picture, the USN, RN and RAN had quit the contest and the newly arrived *Huron* was not ready to attempt such a challenge anyway. So it was that during the second week of March, on a gently rolling sea, *Athabaskan* refuelled in the incredible time of two minutes and fifty seconds. *Nootka's* people recoiled in shock. They had believed the record they held to be unbeatable. But they said nothing. Instead they began a series of exercises and dry-run drills.

At this point the matter of safety was raised in high places. To prepare a ship for refuelling in a time of less than three minutes, many thought, meant that needless risks were being taken. The eight minutes allotted originally, these adherents felt, had been set with safety in mind and should not be altered. The Canadians agreed, but felt the issue should be decided by those involved. It was therefore agreed that *Nootka* and *Athabaskan* be allowed one last contest, whereupon the matter would be forever closed. *Nootka*, as challenger, would be allowed one run. Should she fail to better the record, it would belong for all the time to *Athabaskan*, but if she did set a new record, *Athabaskan* would have one final run. Then the end of the contest would be announced and no further challenges would be entertained.

The meeting was set for 28 March, the one day both ships would be refuelling from *Wave Knight*. HMS *Theseus*, who would be refuelling from the port side of the tanker at the same time, was selected as official timekeeper. The commander of *Wave Knight* was duly informed of the contest and, in keeping with the spirit of the contest, told his deckhands to move sharply and give their fullest co-operation to the destroyer men. The day, a Wednesday, dawned bright under a cloudless sky. The sea was extremely calm, the temperature warm. Both ships arrived on schedule at 0800. *Theseus* was already in position her oiling well under way. With the stage set, Cdr. Fraser-Harris guided his ship toward the tanker.

Those in *Nootka* had made up their minds. They were determined to win. The adrenalin flowed from the first signal and became a flood at the report of the Coston gun. The lines fairly flew as the sailors working them raced fore and aft along the upper deck. All worked in perfect harmony. Then suddenly the white pennant ran up the halyard. The pumps had started. Aboard *Theseus* the astonished timekeeper could hardly believe the reading on his stopwatch. But he announced the elapsed time to be an incredible two minutes and six seconds. The time was verified by watches on the tanker and the destroyers. *Nootka* erupted in wild cheers.

Aboard *Athabaskan* there was dismay. An immediate meeting was called, at which it was agreed that only superhuman effort could best the time. There could be no attempts to shave seconds. The record would have to be shattered and that meant the effort had to be all or nothing. With that attitude the oiling party turned to the task. Commander Welland took personal charge of the bridge. He called down to his coxswain to have a more than steady hand, as he intended to bring the ship so close to *Wave Knight* that the Coston gun would not be needed. That he did. He brought the ship so close that CPO John Rodgers was easily able to toss a line onto the tanker's deck. By so doing he enabled the messengers, span line and oiling hose to be sent over as a single unit. The team then ran the hose to the filler, screwed down the coupler and gave the signal to start the pumps. The white pennant was run up.

If the timekeeper aboard *Theseus* had been astonished by *Nootka*'s time, he was dumbfounded at what he now saw on his watch. He obviously spent a moment checking with others because his signal was delayed for some time. But when it was officially made, *Athabaskan* had set the final record of one minute and forty seconds.[4] At that the contest officially ended. Those in *Athabaskan* rejoiced, while those in *Nootka* lamented. But all agreed that the ultimate time had been reached. The combination of sea conditions, weather and training would likely never be duplicated. They were happy to let the matter rest. The Oiling-at-Sea Championship was held by a Canadian ship, and that was enough.

A few days later the captain of *Wave Knight*, with ceremony befitting an epic contest, presented *Athabaskan* with an attractive scroll in commemoration of the ship's company's tremendous effort.

Chapter Twelve _____

THE
CHANGING
OF THE
GUARD

Spring of 1951 saw the first of many changes in the RCN contingent. *Sioux* and *Cayuga* returned to Canada, following relief by *Nootka* and *Huron* in that order. *Athabaskan*, while still on the scene, had a crew which was beginning to look in near-desperation for a departure date.

The arrival of the two Atlantic Command vessels marked the end of an era, as it were, and in the process caused many problems in administration. The three original ships, all Pacific Command, had made their reports to Flag Officer Pacific Coast. The newcomers were required to report to Flag Officer Atlantic Coast. This caused complications in the paying of bills for ammunition and the use of Local Purchase Orders. The RCN solved this problem by appointing a liaison officer from the Supply Branch. He worked ashore, paid the bills from a central fund and did the paper work. The ships' supply officers worked through him and were spared the frustrations of dealing directly with two separate commands.

Huron's arrival also caused a change which had profound effects on the tiny fleet. With *Cayuga's* departure, the title of CANCOM-DESFE was assumed by Commander Fraser-Harris when Brock left with his ship. Brock had attempted to keep the RCN contingent together as much as possible, but was only partially successful in this, because the ships had to be deployed where they were most needed. Usually these deployments were for single units so the ships rarely worked together. After the Chinese intervention they very rarely saw each other.

Brock's initial insistence in keeping his ships together had produced vehement objections from Rear Adm. W. G. Andrewes, RN. As commander of the Commonwealth Fleet, Andrewes assumed the Canadians to be under his direct command. He was, he thought, supported in this assumption by the British Commonwealth Act under the Visiting Navies section. Brock objected on the grounds that the RCN destroyers were engaged in hostilities against a hostile nation and were in no way visiting.

Brock's interpretation, upheld by both Ottawa *and* London, forced Andrewes to back down. Not without reluctance, he acknowledged Brock as being commander of the RCN ships as part of the Commonwealth Fleet. Brock had won the day, but Andrewes made it clear at every opportunity that he did not appreciate the attitude of the upstart Canadians.

Once Brock departed, Andrewes immediately moved to restore matters to his original design. Following a meeting with Fraser-Harris on 17 March the rear admiral announced that henceforth the Canadian ships would "work closely" with those of the Royal Navy. For "work closely" one was to read "do as bidden." Fraser-Harris, in his newly attained capacity as CANCOMDESFE, set about undoing most of what Brock had accomplished. While Fraser-Harris could not give up all authority without running afoul of Ottawa, he danced to the Royal Navy's fiddle most of the time.

He had his reasons. First, he was generally disinterested in the new wave of Canadianism which was coming into prominence within the RCN. Fraser-Harris, a former RN officer, could not understand the average Canadian sailor's dislike of the RN and its style of discipline, which many officers wanted for the RCN. Second, Brock was a captain and as such had more prestige and clout than did a commander, whose rank made it imprudent to challenge a rear admiral. Third, Brock was a thoroughly political animal who enjoyed a good bout of infighting. While he had sometimes emerged with minor abrasions, he had never been bloodied, and certainly had never known defeat. (That would not come until he tangled with the issue of unification of the Armed Forces. See Chapter 20.) Fraser-

Harris was not inclined to engage in such tussles, preferring instead to ride out storms in the safe waters of acquiescence.

The "safe water" policies of Fraser-Harris meant that RCN ships would work mainly with—in reality under—the RN. Much damage was done to the emerging spirit of Canadianism, but there was nothing anyone could do to alleviate the situation. Ottawa seemed disinclined to challenge the new policy—if, for that matter, the Minister of Defence was even fully aware of it—so a reluctant acceptance set in and compliance adopted.

Fraser-Harris continued his appeasement policy until 20 July, when he gave over his title to Cdr. James Plomer on the return of *Cayuga*. *Nootka* had barely cleared the harbour on her departure for home when Plomer reinstated the stance abandoned by his timid predecessor. Plomer, as if to make some atonement to his sailors for Fraser-Harris' lack of understanding, abolished the hated #5 white uniform in favour of the comfortable #2A rig (actually #2 blues minus jackets, silks and lanyards). This single move endeared Plomer to the entire contingent.

Plomer was unable, however, to attain more than partial success, as the war took yet another turn which necessitated operational changes. The Island Campaign was beginning in deadly earnest, which meant the ships would be mainly on solitary patrol. The Island Campaign became the final stroke against the idea of a single RCN group. Until the end of the fighting the Canadians rarely worked together, and when they did it was only for a matter of a few hours or a day or two at most.

* * *

Huron, under the command of Cdr. E. T. Madgwick, DSC, CD, RCN, entered Sasebo harbour during the afternoon of 15 March 1951 to a warm welcome from *Cayuga*. Slated to arrive days earlier, *Huron* had been delayed in her departure from Halifax and had faced another delay in Hawaii. As a result, *Cayuga* had been forced into another patrol, and retaliated by preparing for *Huron*—and presenting to her in a greatly exaggerated ceremony— The Right and Royal Order of the Turtle. Then, before the crew of the tardy ship could fully absorb the meaning of the gift, *Cayuga* sailed out of Sasebo for Esquimalt.

Huron spent only a few hours in Sasebo before sailing for the east coast. There, in company with *Athabaskan*, she prowled the length of the coast on a sort of training cruise. The targets available allowed the gunners considerable practice on gun emplacements, railway lines and troop staging areas.[1]

On 8 April, the two destroyers became part of Task Element 95.11 for some time, as they roamed the coast seeking out the Chinese communications system.[2] The area assigned, code-named Tail-light, was a long stretch which ranged from Wonsan south to Yangyang. The two ships enjoyed extensive work during this period, as their guns were often called on against elusive targets. They were used mainly in areas where enemy guns were hard to get at. *Huron* developed some of the finest gunners in the fleet. Their reputation as such was much envied. They added much to the record compiled by the RCN in the field of gunnery. Korea was mainly a war for gunners and the RCN took full advantage. By long hours of drill and a desire to be the best, the Canadian gunners soon learned they could lay and train their guns so well that only one or two salvos would be needed to take out a target which had foiled the best of other navies. The RCN ratio of shell usage per target destroyed was far below that of any other navy involved in the Korean fighting.

* * *

Because of the intense activity along both coasts and a buildup of UN troops in the central sector of the interior, the Chinese were well aware that a full push was only a matter of time. Their forces in the west were already falling back steadily, and those on the eastern flank were wavering. They knew a general retreat could be avoided only if their troops in the central region could advance in a series of attacks to consolidate lines farther south.

On 22 April the Chinese attacked in full force near Kap'yong. They moved in waves of thousands against two regiments of the ROK 6th Division, which fled en masse.

Meanwhile, troops of the newly arrived Princess Patricia's Canadian Light Infantry (PPCLI) had moved to Hill 677 along the ridge which was part of it. At the same time, the 3rd Royal Australian Regiment was digging in on Hill 504 to the west of the PPCLI. The Australians were the first line of defence.

When the first wave of fleeing Koreans was spotted, the Canadians knew they were in for a battle. After making quick changes which put their platoons into better positions they waited and watched the long lines of Koreans moving rapidly southward.

The following morning the Chinese army swarmed into view, hurling the full force of their assault against the Australians on Hill 504. In wave after wave they assaulted the hill, only to be beaten back each time. By 1730 on 24 April, after nineteen hours of fierce fighting, the Australians were ordered to pull back to positions to the rear.

126

While the Australians were holding the Chinese, the Canadians were busy making more changes. The official history of the Canadian Army tells how the Canadians deployed their forces. Col. J. R. Stone, M.C., D.S.O., in overall charge, placed his troops along the north edge of the hill on a mile-long ridge. "A" Company was to the right with "B" Company on a salient forward of "D" Company holding the left. "C" Company was in the centre. Then the men of the PPCLI waited and watched the battle between the Australians and the Chinese, wishing they could help, but knowing they could not.

Now that the Australians were gone, the Canadians became the front line, and just after sunset the Chinese threw their forces against Hill 677. They came blowing bugles and beating drums in their usual style. Wave upon wave of infantry crashed through the brush shouting and blowing whistles. Throughout the dark night the battle raged, the chatter of machine guns and the sharp reports of rifles rending the darkness. The drums, the bugles and the whistles mingled with the groans and screams of wounded men. The curses and shouted orders of platoon commanders could be heard above the din. Most of the fighting was hand to hand.

At 0400 the Chinese, beaten, retired from Hill 677, leaving behind dead and wounded numbering in the hundreds. The PPCLI had suffered ten dead and twenty-three wounded, an amazingly low casualty list considering the intensity of the battle. In this, their first taste of the war, they had beaten an army outnumbering them by many hundreds.

The PPCLI stand at Kap'yong is considered a turning point in the war. Had the Canadians broken, the UN line would have been breached and would more than likely have collapsed totally. In recognition of its heroic stand, the PPCLI was awarded the U.S. Presidential Citation. This was the first time a Canadian force had been so honoured. Several soldiers were awarded decorations for valour ranging from the Military Medal to the Military Cross. Both are but a degree below the Victoria Cross, the ultimate award for valour in battle.

The Chinese, stung by the defeat, retreated to lick their wounds. They stayed quiet a full three weeks before hurling their regrouped forces against Korean troops at Hwachon, many miles from Kap'yong. As at Kap'yong the Koreans fled in panic. The Chinese, in full pursuit, surged through the breached line, but were stopped by determined U.S. Marines. Though outnumbered, the marines held until reserves were able to arrive. Once again the Chinese retreated in defeat and disarray.

On 21 May, UN troops launched a full attack against the Chinese on the right flank. After twenty-five days of heavy fighting, the Chinese line cracked wide open on 15 June. The Iron Triangle, as the area had been coded, was completely breached. The UN took total control of the entire front, pursuing the retreating Chinese in a relentless advance.

Then, to the amazement of nearly everyone, the advance was halted. There were two reasons for the halt: first, the line of the west had surged ahead too fast, and in so doing had placed the central line at a distinct disadvantage in case of counterattack. Second, the Chinese were now showing a willingness to discuss a cease-fire. On 10 July preliminary talks began at Kaesong.

During the discussion period, the armies in the field spent the time solidifying their respective positions, resupplying and strengthening their forces. Fighting continued on a reduced basis, but only small gains or losses were reported. On 23 August, negotiations broke down completely and the war was on once more.

Fighting resumed on all fronts, but it was soon obvious that neither side was capable of making any great headway. Thus the fighting ground down to a steady, draining routine of attack and fall back and attack again, each side taking turns. Little was gained and little was lost in terms of territory, but much was lost in terms of life.

* * *

The talks at Kaesong had no effect on naval operations. The UN fleet, continuing its long-range assaults on coastal positions, moved unmolested among the islands. There were continuous skirmishes along the east coast in which *Huron* drew fire from shore batteries on several occasions. These attacks merely forced her to withdraw to deeper water from whence she returned the fire. In all instances she destroyed her tormentors.[3]

Along the west coast there was less activity, owing mainly to the earlier neutralization of the islands. The ships continued their patrols, showing the flag and preventing the Chinese from undertaking any serious adventures against the larger islands.

During this period *Nootka* was sole representative of the RCN on the west coast. *Athabaskan* had left for home at last, having been relieved by *Sioux* who had returned on 30 April to join *Huron* on the east coast. The Chinese walkout at Kaesong, however, was followed by renewed activity along the west coast. The two Canadian ships working the east coast patrols were called to the west in late July, joining *Nootka* for a rare period of work together.

The Yellow Sea was, of course, clear of enemy shipping, but in the Yalu River there was increasing activity by small craft. The three destroyers spent nearly all their time in the river hunting these.

During this period the Chinese air force also entered the fray, but was no match for that of the UN. The Chinese pilots lacked the verve and daring of the UN flyers, and their planes, Russian-built MIGs and YAKs, were inferior to the Sabres flown by the UN. The Chinese had a brief interlude as part of the air war and were only rarely seen. No RCN ship was ever attacked by the Chinese planes, but sightings were reported from time to time.[4]

The three RCN ships worked together about two weeks before being re-assigned to RN units. They would not see each other again for many weeks, and never did work together again as a unit. Although Rear Adm. Andrewes had left in April, his successor, Rear Adm. A. K. Scott-Montcrief continued Andrewes' policy toward the RCN. As mentioned previously, Commander Fraser-Harris made no attempt to persuade the new commander to change the policies.

* * *

ESTHER WAS A LADY

Sioux steamed into the oil slick that was Sasebo's harbour during the early hours of 30 April. She had returned for her second tour of duty with many of her original crew, including her commander. The ship's company had enjoyed the short stay in Canada and had been very much thrilled by the reception they received on their return to Esquimalt. A huge crowd (the *Victoria Colonist* in its 5 February edition estimated it at 25,000) had gathered to cheer the ship home.

Of particular concern to *Sioux*'s officers was the whereabouts of Esther, a plastic-encased photo of the beautiful, leggy swimming star and Hollywood actress Esther Williams. A pinup from World War II days, it had long been a prized possession of Lt. Lindsay B. Brand, RAN. Lieutenant Brand had acquired the pinup in 1943 while serving in HMAS *Nepal*. The picture had hung in the wardrooms of whatever ships he served in, and had come to be a mascot of sorts. When Brand went to *Bataan* bound for Korea, Esther went with him to take her usual place in *Bataan*'s wardroom.

It was while in *Bataan* that she came to the notice of visiting officers and, as frequently happened, a game was conceived. Esther, it was decided, would become the prize in a game of stealth and trickery. She would become the temporary property of any wardroom whose members could capture her by fair means or foul.

The only stipulation was that she be returned to Brand upon the final departure of either her captor or *Bataan*.

Esther visited many ships. Most capture attempts ended in failure, but some were successful. A frigate officer swam nearly a mile in the oily water of Sasebo's harbour one dark night, shinnied up the mooring cable, stole the picture and, with his prize in a waterproof container, re-swam his route to the safety of his own ship. Three days later Esther was again stolen, this time by a team from an American cruiser. So it went until December of 1950, when *Sioux*'s officers decided to enter the game.

A group of these men conspired to kidnap Esther when they learned she had returned to *Bataan* a few days previously. They also had learned she was under close watch by the Aussies, who had decided to call a halt to the game, but didn't quite know how to get the word out. The Canadians decided they would have to strike quickly, so they laid their plans and awaited an opportune moment.

Chinnampo provided the opportunity. Following the action *Sioux* met with *Bataan* in the sheltered lee of Sok-To. Tied alongside as they were, it was natural that four of *Sioux*'s officers should cross the gangway for a chat and a cup of tea (the RAN was dry). The visitors seemingly ignored the treasured picture adorning the wardroom's forward bulkhead.

Had the Aussies been alert, they might have noticed the order in which their guests had seated themselves. They had taken chairs in a direct line from the door to a point below the picture. The Australians seemed not to notice the seating arrangements. Beneath the picture, seemingly half asleep sat Lieutenant "Pop" Fotheringham. Next to him sat Lt. Howard Clark. Two chairs away was Lt. Cdr. Patrick Benson, *Sioux*'s first officer, and beside the door was Lt. Neil Norton, the ship's navigator. Clark seemed engrossed in small talk. Fotheringham, far from being asleep, was actually watching Clark. Attention was most important for the quartet had come, not for tea, but for abduction. Their plan, arranged in minute detail, depended on timing—and total surprise.

Benson, an interesting spinner of yarns at any time, soon had his hosts engrossed in a "salty dip." All their attention was on him as they waited for the punch line. Knowing the time had come, Clark reached up and lifted the picture from its hook. At the same instant Fotheringham leapt to his feet, took the picture from Clark and raced for the door. The second Fotheringham made his move both Benson and Norton swung away from the table, blocking intervention by the startled Aussies. The swiftness of the move caught them totally by surprise, and by the time they could react Fotheringham was already at the door. He ducked through it and ran for the ladder to the upper deck, Clark right on his heels. At that point Fotheringham passed the picture to Clark who rushed across the gangway to *Sioux*. Meanwhile, Benson and Norton had blocked the hatch from the wardroom flats, keeping the pursuers confined below for a few minutes.

Esther remained in *Sioux* until the ship sailed for Canada at the end of her first tour when, a few days before departure, she was returned to *Bataan* with pomp and ceremony. The ceremony was held in *Sioux*'s wardroom so that the participants could properly toast the erstwhile captive, not with tea but with the more potent Horse's Neck, a favourite drink in Canadian ships.[5]

Sioux had returned to the disappointing news that Esther had gone home. *Bataan* would return to Korea shortly, but without Lieutenant Brand. He and Esther had been drafted ashore.

* * *

Sioux was given no time to mourn Esther. The ship was sent into action almost at once as part of Task Element 95.12 to work the patrol area between Inchon and Chinnampo. TE 95.12's job was to persuade the Chinese to maintain defenses against attack from offshore, keeping large numbers of infantry in constant readiness along the west coast. It was necessary for the UN to ensure that those troops remained where they were instead of being more gainfully employed along the wavering lines inland.

TE 95.12 therefore staged raids here and there, as though preliminary to an amphibious landing. There were several points along the coast where such a landing could be made, and the Chinese were determined to keep the coast as secure as possible from such an attack.

Sioux took part in several of these small raids, but on 18 May was involved in a rather large attack against the Chinese garrison at Go-Chin-Riki Point. Then, on 20 May, she joined six other ships and proceeded to the city of P'ungch'on where she bombarded the area prior to a landing by Royal Marines from HMS *Ceylon*.[6]

Sioux remained with TE 95.12 until 2 June when she was transferred to the east coast for a stint with TE 95.28 in the Tail-light patrol area.[7]

* * *

Nootka had spent the spring of 1951 productively, most of the time at sea on various patrols, including the aptly named Dick Tracy Run on which the assigned ship raced here and there, recovering bodies and rescuing the occasional downed pilot.

For the most part, however, *Nootka* was a solitary night prowler. She spent her days on the established routes, but as dusk fell would slip quietly away from the others in the group to steam at full speed into northern waters. The Australian naval historian, Norman Bartlett, mentions *Nootka* in his book *With the Australians in Korea* when he recalls that "the departing Canadian destroyer glided quietly into the fog, a huge Jolly Roger fluttering from her mast."

Nootka, like all the RCN ships, was particularly effective in night operations as she had the great advantage of HDWS Sperry Radar.[8] HDWS was capable of detecting even very small objects on the surface of the water, such as rubber rafts and low-riding boats. It gave the Canadians a distinct edge over the other UN ships. An added feature of HDWS was its ability to remain undetectable, unlike conventional radar. Because of this, the HDWS units could stay operational on a constant basis, and because the RCN had installed HDWS when the system was first brought out, the ships' operators were highly skilled in using it.

Cayuga demonstrated the accuracy and effectiveness of the HDWS as a gunnery guidance system during the night of 21 and 22 December 1951, when at 5,000 yards and without benefit of starshell illumination, she dropped two 4-inch HEDA shells directly onto a small craft making at top speed into a restricted zone.[9]

* * *

The night of 13 May 1951 was one of dense fog. The water was calm as there was no breeze. *Nootka*, cruising at 10 knots, was on course for the Yalu River. Lookouts posted at the "eyes" of the ship peered intently into the darkness, alert for mines.

Midway through the Evening Watch word was passed from radar to the bridge that a cluster of nine objects had appeared on the screen off the port side at 8500 yards. A second report quickly followed, confirming the objects as fairly large, stationary ships. All main armament was brought to bear as boarding parties made themselves ready. At a distance of 500 yards *Nootka* was stopped. Like a silent ghost she lay still in the water among the swirls of fog.

Fraser-Harris, desiring a better look at the quarry, dispatched a boat with a heavily-armed party to check out the as-yet unidentified vessels. There was no way of knowing if they were armed, friendly or not, if they were warships or fishing boats. All he knew for certain was that they were in restricted waters and had not responded to IFF signals.[10] The ship's cutter, guided by radio and

HDWS bearings, approached the targets and took a long, careful look before withdrawing back into the enveloping fog. Returning to the ship, the party leader reported having counted five medium-sized sampans and four large junks. Visible markings indicated the boats were Chinese fishing vessels, riding at anchor with nets and line out.

The boats were fair game, and Fraser-Harris was at first inclined to sink them where they lay, but thought better of it. If appearances were correct, they were merely fishing boats and their crews not likely to be combatants. As well, the capture of an entire fishing fleet would have better propaganda value than a terse report of its sinking, and the armed-party leader felt it could be easily done. They would, the party leader suggested, cut out one boat and tow it back to *Nootka*. If that worked, they would go back for another. The operation offered little risk, and should an alarm sound, the destroyer's gunners could finish the job.

The cutter was once again steered away from the ship to head for the target. It was silently paddled to the nearest boat—a sampan—and a tow line attached. Then the nets and lines were cut away, and the captive sampan was silently towed away from the main fleet. When the sampan eventually bumped against *Nootka* its crew was rudely awakened, ordered to remain silent and hustled up the scramble net to *Nootka*'s deck. The frightened fishermen were herded into the Squid Bomb Room and informed of their new status as prisoners of war.

Seven times that night the cutter made the short trip, returning each time with a boat in tow. Soon the Squid Bomb Room was filled with frightened, bewildered fishermen. None of them fully understood what had happened. Two boats were left bobbing silently on the still water. Some of the cutter's party wanted to board one of them and leave a cryptic note, but that idea was vetoed. It had an appealing sense of the bizzare, but the risk was not worth it. Besides, the mysterious disappearance of seven boats might induce the Chinese to keep out of restricted areas.

The total haul included five sampans, two large junks and twenty-eight fishermen. The boats were devoid of weapons. None of the Chinese were armed. The fishermen were turned over to UN authorities and presumably spent the remainder of the war in prison camps.

Nootka remained in the area until 20 May, when she was transferred to the east coast, joining TE 95.22 on the Northern Patrol Line. She remained on the NP Line for some time, shelling bridges.

To many the shelling of bridges seemed a waste of time and ammunition. No activity was ever detected along the rail lines and

133

no trains were seen. It seemed doubtful that the Reds were even using the lines, but a closer look was ordered.

The assignment was given to *Nootka*, and on 26 May a sizeable party went ashore for a firsthand look, carrying demolition charges to be placed at the base of a nearby bridge.

The landing point was an open beach directly under the bridge. The site had been carefully chosen to offer the party a good defensive position in case of attack. The boat made the beach without trouble, but as it touched ground a squad of Chinese riflemen appeared and opened fire. The Canadians returned the fire and the Chinese fell back. The boat was quickly backed off the beach into the safety of the fog.

Returning to the ship, the party leader reported the presence of well-concealed artillery and infantry bunkers. The small squad of Chinese which fired on the boat was obviously part of a much larger group. The presence of the guns indicated that Chinese were indeed using the rail line and considered it important enough to defend. It seemed likely that the trains were being run at night and hidden during the day in nearby tunnels.

Shortly after 1630 the fog lifted,[11] giving the gunners their first clear look at the landscape. *Nootka's* 4-inch guns were turned against the emplaced artillery with good results. The bridge, however, proved too sturdy to be affected by 4-inch shells. *Nootka* called upon the heavy cruiser, USS *Manchester*, whose 11-inch guns did the job in three broadsides.

* * *

Nootka had trouble with bridges. Her gunners could close tunnels, tear up tracks and destroy gun batteries and bunkers with ease. They could not, however, claim great success against bridges. One in particular, located two miles south of Sonjin, became known as the Rubber Bridge because, despite constant shelling, it remained standing throughout the entire war. *Nootka's* gunners came to view it as a personal affront. The Chinese seemed to make the bridge a symbol of defiance, for regardless of how much damage it received they would often effect repairs overnight.

If the bridge was to be brought down, the ship would have to sail within a mile of the site in order to put sufficient numbers of shells directly into its base. The Chinese, however, had laid mines which made such an approach impossible. The large cruisers were unable to get close enough due to the shallow water along that stretch of the coast. Only the destroyers could do the job.

With this in mind Fraser-Harris submitted a detailed plan to the task element's commander. Cdr. J. B. Gay, USN, approved the plan and Operation Squeegee was underway.[12] The operation called for two cutters to sweep a wide channel to a distance of 1300 feet from the shoreline. *Nootka* launched the cutters early in the morning and, using a paravane strung between them, they swept back and forth within a closely defined area. The paravane cut loose the mines, which were destroyed as they bobbed to the surface.

The boats encountered little interference, except for one shore battery which opened fire on them as they began their initial sweep. It was put out of action at once. *Nootka* kept up steady shelling of the enemy positions throughout the operation, and the cutters remained unmolested during the two hours it took to complete the sweep.

Once the channel was cleared, *Nootka*, followed by USS *Stickle*, moved into position. From a range of 1300 feet both ships opened fire. A hitherto unnoticed marshalling yard was spotted, as were many wooden sheds and other buildings. Once the freight yards, the buildings and the assembled cars had been destroyed, the gunners turned their full attention to the bridge. Shell after shell was hurled into the structure. Girders split and parted as braces shattered. The bridge, the director crew happily announced, would collapse within minutes. The guns were called to check while their crews stood back to observe their handiwork. But the expected collapse did not happen. The Rubber Bridge never did fall, but it was so badly damaged as to be no longer usable.

The Chinese were forced to reroute all their trains from that time forward. The entire line remained out of service until long after the armistice, though the Chinese work crews laboured for months filling in the entire ravine so that new tracks could be laid.

Chapter Thirteen _____

HAPPY DAYS

I do not know as yet if this can be considered a happy ship.
Report of Proceedings, Cayuga, August 1951

I f one can take at face value the official records now in the National Archives, there had been few happy days for those who served in the Canadian ships from July 1950 to mid-1951. *Cayuga's* crew is shown as a dark and moody lot, given to fighting among themselves. *Athabaskan* and *Sioux* fared only slightly better. Morale had reached a low ebb from September to November, had risen in December following the Chinnampo affair, only to fall once more in January. The new year had offered little hope. Until well into April, few considered the possibility of better days being near at hand.

In July, however, there came a change. The fortunes of the UN forces had steadily improved to the point where they were in total control of the war's conduct. The Chinese were being beaten on all fronts. South Korea was secure. As a result of land victories, action at sea diminished. Shorter patrols and more harbour time became the rule rather than the exception. The food, which had always been good, became even better as fresh vegetables were more easily obtained. Mail began to arrive on schedule and Ottawa announced a pay raise of 6 percent for all ranks. An able seaman could now look forward to $108 each month. Morale soared.

The ships, because of longer periods in harbour, were kept in better trim. Fresh paint replaced the ugly patches of red lead which had been slapped on like badges of honour denoting the long, arduous days of patrol duty. Boats, rope work and brass fittings took on a new lustre. All in all, the ships and their crews took on a sharper appearance.

The sailors were now able to enjoy time away from their ships. Not mere hours, but several days at a stretch, when they headed to posh resorts far inland for Rest and Recreation leave.[1] Ironically, many who went on the R&R junkets returned to their ships thoroughly debauched, more worn out than when they had left, and more often than not with the military police close behind, warrants in hand.

At sea the patrols became more relaxed. The ships no longer spent most nights closed up at action stations. While the shelling of port cities continued unabated, the action was rarely so intense that the entire crew was needed. More often than not at least half were allowed an "all night in," though sleep was not easy owing to the pounding of the guns.

Daylight hours saw a relaxing of routine. The PA systems were tuned to the Armed Forces Radio Service, allowing music to reach parts of the ship normally silent. AFRS had programs for nearly every taste. Few who sailed the Korean Patrol Lines will not recall "The Kyushu Cowboy" or "Honshu Hayride," both aimed at the country and western fan. "Great Fights of the Century" simulated famed boxing matches of days long past, including many fought before the days of radio. Factual round-by-round descriptions, complete with crowd noise and reactions, brought vividly to life great fights of which most sailors had only read. "Pete Kelly's Blues" brought Kansas City jazz into the ships. "The Damon Runyon Theatre" treated the sailors to the antics of Sorrowful Jones, Apple Annie and the other denizens of Runyon's Broadway stories. American and National League baseball games, delayed twenty-four hours, were broadcast via transcription.

These better days, however, had their drawbacks. The rate of detected crime rose to new heights, and the lines at Captain's Defaulters grew longer by the week. More warrants, the official documents read out to announce the punishment meted for more serious offenses, were read during this time than would be normal in six years at home.

It was during this period that medical officers lamented the increasing incidence of venereal disease—the Great Green Bubble, as lower deck parlance put it. Known also as Cupid's Measles, Aphrodite's Revenge and Sasebo Flu, its toll grew as the months passed. Those afflicted were immediately struck off the spirits list, denied leave for a minimum of thirty days and ordered to report to sick bay daily for treatment. Further, they were restricted to a certain section of the heads, where two or three cubicles were roped

137

off for those who had fallen victim to the carnal fever. These sections were known by various names, two of the more popular being Chancre Alley and the Rose Room.

Despite shorter patrols, the freshwater shortage remained severe. Water rationing, imposed in 1950, remained in full effect until mid-1953 when cessation of fighting allowed a return to normal routine. The destroyers were capable of producing fresh water through the process of desalination. Under normal circumstances a ship could supply its own needs in abundance, but the rigors of the patrols, plus problems caused by the Yellow Sea itself, taxed the system to the limits.[2]

Rationing saw the beginning of a workable, though less than satisfactory, method of showering known as the bird bath. A daily shower had over the years become a tradition that few failed to enjoy. The bird bath could tax the patience of a saint, not to mention his sense of humour. The rules were strict. First, he who would shower filled a wash basin with hot water. Then, naked as a newly hatched bird, he soaped himself as well as he could, finally entering the shower stall to rinse as quickly as he could. The system worked well enough, but the ordeal of standing in shivering nakedness in full view of passersby proved difficult for the very modest. At first the old hands took to teasing the younger ones with embarrassing remarks, but eventually that passed. The bird bath became a way of life until its eventual discontinuance.

Shipboard crime became a major problem during this period. The term should not be compared to civilian crime, as the two have little in common. Theft among shipmates during the 1950s was perhaps non-existent, since no mention of such is recorded in any of the ships' reports. To the RCN shipboard crime was any act considered prejudicial to naval discipline. Well defined in King's Regulations, Canadian Navy, it covered everything from mutiny to leaving a wrinkle in a bedcover. KRCN was unique in that every offence, regardless of severity, was punishable by death unless another punishment was substituted. The official terminology following each paragraph in which the crime was described stated that anyone found guilty of any act "prejudicial to good order and naval discipline . . . would upon conviction . . . suffer death or such lesser punishment as is hereinafter mentioned." Fortunately for all, the latter was the only punishment ever meted out. So far as is known, no sailor in the history of the RCN was ever executed.[3]

Detection of shipboard crime meant that the accused, if found guilty, faced punishment ranging from two hours' extra duty to ninety days in a detention barracks under the watchful eyes of the military police. Shipboard crime, therefore, had become a sort of game played on a win-or-lose basis for fun or profit. In Korea the term "undetected crime" became a part of naval slang quite different from the same term used in World War II.

Over the five years of Canadian involvement in Korea and Japan, there appears to have been a large number of sailors engaged in any number of private scams, ranging from dealings in the black market—mainly in cigarettes—to shares in brothels. American cigarettes were much coveted by the Japanese, who would gladly pay 3600 yen for a carton of ten packs. As the ships' canteens sold American cigarettes unrationed for ten cents a pack, the profit margin was too great to resist. Contact was made easily in the night clubs and cafes, whose managers were ready to buy any amount. While the business was illegal, it was so safe that many sailors ventured into the trade. None were ever caught.[4]

A few of the more enterprising bought into the lucrative brothel trade. While legal under Japanese law, ownership of such shares was not legal under RCN laws. There is no record of charges being brought against any of the Canadian sailors, so either a blind eye was turned or suspicions were not carried beyond a preliminary investigation stage.

Most of the detected crime was associated with leave and intoxication infractions. Insubordination was a somewhat distant third in the number of charges laid. Most resulted in loss of pay and privileges. Detentions ranged from fifteen to ninety days, but the rigors of the detention barracks were such that few risked a return. There were, however, enough first offenders to ensure a steady flow to the camp.

At one point the situation became such that a roster was put into effect. The birds, as they were called, had become so numerous that to send them all away at the same time would have adversely affected the manning of the ships. At one point no less than fifteen birds were on the roster for *Cayuga* with the other ships only one or two less. The roster system worked fairly well. No more than three birds were away from any ship at any time. If, as occasionally happened, a ship returned home while her birds were still in detention, the unfortunate sailors would find themselves drafted to one of the other ships. This of course made return to Canada dependent on the schedule of the new ship, and an unhappy sailor might find himself in line for another full tour of duty. It could also effect his future over the long run, as the new ship could well be from the opposite command. This could mean an involuntary change of coasts upon the sailor's eventual return to Canada.

From time to time civilians were involved with sailors in a fling with crime. One such case occurred when two of *Cayuga*'s sailors, already under open arrest aboard ship on military charges, stole one of the motorboats as the ship lay moored in Sasebo's harbour. Once ashore they sold the boat for 36,000 yen (CDN $100) and fled inland. *Cayuga*, minus two sailors and one motor boat, sailed for Korea the following morning. When she returned three weeks later the culprits, having been captured by the MPs, were returned to the ship. Charges were laid and a quick hearing was held. The following morning the two were sent off to serve their ninety days in close detention.

The boat, however, remained missing. It had been almost forgotten when, months later, it reappeared. Filthy beyond imagination, reeking of swill and garbage, its once gleaming paint and beautifully woven rope-work now blackened and rotting, it chugged slowly up to the ship. The boat's motor, once tuned to perfection, wheezed and gasped as its driver, an unconcerned garbage collector, steered it under the stern "gash chute." The operator and the boat were immediately arrested.

The civilian, it turned out, had purchased the boat for cash, and he produced a tattered receipt in proof. He objected to his arrest. The boat, he stated, had made him the finest garbage collector in the harbour. Its speed had enabled him to make many calls each day. His business had improved considerably since his most opportune purchase. The man was eventually persuaded to give up his boat, but he made a tidy profit in the settlement. The boat was taken inboard, scrubbed over and over, and had its engine overhauled. But it never regained its former lustre. Despite all the work it was never quite the same. On warmer days the pungent odour of garbage swirled about it as it hung from the davit.

Naval crime held different meanings for different people. What might be deemed just a skylark on one ship could be a misdemeanour on another. A remark made in jest could be termed insubordination or ignored, depending on the mood of the moment. What might bring on laughter one day could end in charges the next. For the most part common sense prevailed.

One instance when it did not, concerned a padre who sought to lay a morals charge against a sailor for his conduct ashore, which the padre deemed sinful. Fortunately the ship's commander felt there were no grounds for the padre's complaint and refused to consider it. The padre, a misfit in a rowdy crowd, was from a rural area of Quebec where he had served as parish priest prior to entering the navy. He had found the transition extremely difficult and, in fact, never did manage to adjust from the role of shepherd to a more or less obedient flock of villagers and farmers to spiritual advisor to a carefree group who knew the delights of foreign ports.

The priest had been sent to Korea as replacement for the worldly Father Ward, but he possessed neither the understanding nor the charisma of his predecessor. The unfortunate man spent most of his time tracking down those sailors who appeared on his records listed as RC; and, when he found them, would lecture them on the errors in their life-style and issue grave warnings against incurring the wrath of a vengeful God. He devoted his Sunday services (not well attended) to ranting against the evil Suntory whisky, Asahi beer and the Butterfly Girls who were doing the Devil's work. So great was his disappointment in his flock that he was moved one day to complain loudly that the ship he was then aboard was "a ship of Hell. This crew is akin to the beasts of the fields." Fairly strong words, but apparently heartfelt.

Naval crime, detected and otherwise, continued in varying degrees of severity until the final days of the RCN presence in Korea. For the most part little harm was done. In his *Report of Proceedings* for February 1952, Commander Plomer justifiably lamented that his ship had "too many habitual offenders." The problem, as he saw it, "has compounded itself from the start [of the second tour of duty] as the ship departed Esquimalt with twelve bad-hats and inherited a thirteenth from *Nootka* on arrival in Sasebo." Plomer went on to recommend that the "twelve originals be returned to Canada via the RCAF [which could then fly in] their replacements."

On 12 March, Rear Adm. Wallace Creery made reference to Plomer's suggestion in a memo to the navy secretary. Creery expressed sympathy for his beleaguered officer, but rejected the idea out of hand. In paragraph five he commented, "the cost of transporting 24 personnel across the Pacific is not justified from the taxpayer's [sic] viewpoint." He made the suggestion that such offenders "be refused the honour of re-enlisting when their contracts expired."

Surprisingly, perhaps, several of the so-called bad-hats in Plomer's report did remain in the navy to serve to retirement. More than one rose to fairly high rank, and at least one ended his career as an officer. For all its idiosyncrasies the RCN did not hold grudges.

Differences in punishment also varied from ship to ship. In 1952, the commanding officer of *Nootka*, Cdr. Richard Steele, RCN, who had replaced Fraser-Harris for the ship's second tour, sentenced a communicator and his buddy to ninety days' detention for their parts in a fracas ashore in which no one was hurt and no damage was done. Yet only a few weeks before, a group of sailors from *Cayuga* wrecked the Queen's Beer Hall in Kure while fighting with a group of British merchant seamen. The Royal Marine Military Police, who broke up the fight, laid charges against three of the

141

sailors. A few days later Plomer dismissed the charges without comment.

On the same day he sentenced to thirty days' detention an able seaman who, during an argument with a petty officer, had expressed the opinion that petty meant small and insignificant. This slur on a NCO was considered a crime, whereas the wreckage of the beer hall and the battering of the British seamen were the result of youthful exuberance. The entire incident lies dismissed in one curt sentence in the *Report of Proceedings* for April 1952. The insult to the PO was deemed very serious. It rated an entire paragraph.

Punishment was, therefore, a matter of individual interpretation by individual commanders. Each drew on his own experience, personal standards and prejudices. While the judgements handed down were, by and large, fair and equal, some were patently ridiculous. The many and varying differences gave rise to the labelling of Captain's Defaulters as June brides. "The June bride," the saying went, "knows what she is going to get; she just doesn't know how much."

* * *

During the period of the happy days, changes in dress regulations were introduced. The white uniforms which had been the pride and joy of Jeffry Brock disappeared from the scene for all ranks. They were replaced by a lightweight khaki for officers, chief petty officers and petty officers (first class). The regular blue uniforms remained standard dress for all other ranks on shore leave, but without jackets. The demise of the white uniforms went unlamented by lower deck ratings, who agreed they were the least practical and most uncomfortable uniforms ever devised. While officers' whites were of lightweight material, those of the sailors were heavy, almost canvaslike. They were hot and almost impossible to keep clean.

The introduction of different uniforms for officers and NCOs had actually taken place prior to the 1950 departure for Korea, but for reasons of his own, Brock had managed to scuttle the conversion for the ships going to Korea. In his book *The Dark Broad Seas*, he describes at length his efforts to veto the change for the Korean flotilla. He attempts to justify the move by claiming his men and officers preferred the old uniforms, but the truth was quite the opposite with few exceptions.

Brock was opposed to any change in uniform for the NCOs and officers because they would look too much like those of the USN. Brock had little respect for that navy, and was scornful of its gunnery, seamanship and anti-submarine expertise. One suspects that this arose mainly from the prejudice inherent in the RCN at that time for the USN. Whatever his reasons, Brock carried his dislike of things American to the point of denying his own men a uniform distinctly better than the one they had.

When Commander Plomer took on the responsibilities of CAN-COMDESFE in 1951, the first thing he did was to retire the whites for all ranks. At the same time NHQ ordered the end of black caps in favour of white ones. The RCN uniforms were beginning to take on a more Canadian look.

Plomer also made changes that affected the lives and morale of his sailors. Unlike Brock and Fraser-Harris, Plomer held no illusions that his sailors wished to be copies of Royal Navy seamen. He encouraged the adoption of Canadian ways on his ships. He issued baseball caps for use at sea, allowed overnight leave on request in certain harbours (Sasebo excepted) and cared little about formality. Plomer was Brock's direct opposite, and was just what the tiny fleet needed. He was certainly the remedy for his own ship. *Cayuga*, on her second tour, had a crew open and happy. The pessimistic paragraph in his July *Report of Proceedings* proved unfounded as time went on. The new-found morale in *Cayuga* soon appeared in the other ships.

Possibly the happiest ship was *Iroquois* under the command of Cdr. William Landymore, O.B.E., CD, RCN. During her three tours of duty the *Reports of Proceedings* for that ship mention fewer problems than do all others. Her numbers of warrants served were less than any other ship, her crime lists and punishment records shorter and all in all, her crews seem to have enjoyed a standard of morale uncommon to other RCN ships of the time.

This, according to former members of *Iroquois*, was a direct result of the rapport enjoyed between the sailors and the man they referred to as "Billy." Landymore took intense interest in the welfare of his men. He worked at keeping morale as high as possible under trying circumstances, and encouraged them to seek their personal goals. He urged the lower ranks to upgrade their educational standards by introducing correspondence courses for those who wanted them.[5] Landymore insisted his men put forth their best efforts, and in return extended to them his best efforts.

When the Flag Officer Atlantic Coast forwarded to the Secretary of the Navy in Ottawa his usual memo on the *Report of Proceedings, Iroquois,* December 1952, his remarks were generally routine except for Item 2:

> Attention is invited to Paragraph 5 of this report. *Iro-quois* has been doing an excellent job in furthering the training of her men, particularly in passing B.E.T. A

143

further and more detailed report is being called for as to how and how much has been accomplished [sic]. This will be forwarded to all ships in this Command as a challenge to them.

Original signed by
R. E. S. Bidwell.

Commander Landymore ran a taut ship, his command fair and equitable. He earned the respect and admiration of his men by respecting them. His concern for his men was never more in evidence than when, on 2 October 1952, he disengaged *Iroquois* from action so he might reach a hospital ship, in an effort to save the life of a gunner who had been wounded. Though his efforts were in vain, his concern for the mortally wounded seaman solidly cemented the already strong bond that existed between him and his crew (see Chapter 16).

Of the twenty-one officers who captained the destroyers through the five years of the Korean campaign, Landymore appears to have enjoyed the closest rapport with his crew. Plomer would seem a very close second, with Welland and Taylor following. The others remain distant in varying degrees. Certainly, none did as much for the betterment of the lower deck than did "Billy" Landymore.

* * *

No account of the happy days can be complete without the mention of the pedi-cab, a ricksha with a bicycle as its motive power. This hybrid vehicle was made by taking a conventional ricksha and welding to it the front half of a bicycle. The bicycle's drive chain was then extended to a sprocket on the rear axle. By this conversion the runner could become a driver. The finished contraption was several pounds heavier than a ricksha, but faster.

The pedi-cab, describable as a cumbersome racing sulky with one-wheel bike and rider in place of the horse, became the favoured mode of transportation among the Canadians. They were comfortable and inexpensive, unlike taxis which smelled because they used charcoal instead of gasoline as their fuel.

It was not long before the sailors discovered that the pedi-cab could be used for recreation. With longer periods ashore the problem of entertainment became acute, so any diversion was welcome. There were, after all, only so many hours of any leave period which could be devoted to beer-guzzling in the dubious atmosphere of servicemen's clubs. In their relentless pursuit of entertainment, the Canadians revived the ancient Roman sport of chariot-racing, the arena being the streets of Sasebo. The chariots were the pedi-cabs and the horses were the protesting but yen-hungry drivers who went along with the idea because the money was good. It became a common sight for two, three or sometimes four of the odd-looking conveyances to be seen careering along the narrow, twisting streets of Sasebo, the drivers sweating profusely while being exhorted to greater speeds by a passenger intent on winning the race even at the expense of seeing his driver collapse with a heart attack.

These races, always impromptu, went on for many weeks until they were called off by mutual agreement following the ultimate race, which took place one chilly night in April 1952. According to several sources a match race between *Cayuga* and HMAS *Bataan* had been arranged during an afternoon of celebration in the Anchor Club. The course, the ground rules and the two jockeys were quickly decided. The losers would, as usual buy the beer for the remainder of the evening.

Having set the course—approximately two miles in length— the search began for two pedi-cabs. This proved difficult, as all the drivers knew from past experience what was expected. They also complained that the course was too long. Finally two drivers were located, but neither was willing to drive the two-mile course. They would, however, rent their cabs for a suitable sum payable in advance. The arrangements were made and the two champions mounted their vehicles, ready for the race. At a signal the two started for the harbour, travelling neck and neck most of the way in their headlong flight through the narrow streets, scattering pedestrians as they went. After a few blocks *Bataan*'s driver managed to gain the lead by a length or two. With the jetty fast approaching, the Canadian increased his speed in a final effort to overtake his opponent.

The jetty was crowded with sailors of all nationalities. Most were waiting for the boats which would take them back to their respective ships. As the two pedi-cabs careered onto the jetty, the throng parted, leaving a clear path straight down the middle.

The pedi-cabs, now at breakneck speed, ran the length of the jetty as the drivers tried frantically to stop. This, as was so often the case with pedi-cabs, proved difficult for they all had inferior braking systems. The Australian managed to stop by locking the brakes and slewing sideways into a piling. The Canadian, however, could not stop. Worse, he lost control of the steering. He crashed his front wheel into the low barrier at the end of the jetty. The pedi-cab arced out into the air, then splashed into the murky water and sank like a heavy rock. A white cap floated lazily in the centre of the ripples, mute testimony to the mishap. On the jetty, shocked sailors, chattering in the excited babble of many tongues, milled about in confusion uncertain of what to do. Suddenly, in a burst of bubbles and frenzied splashing, the sea expelled the human intruder. The hapless sailor broke the surface and began treading water. At that moment a cutter from a USN ship drew near. Its astonished crew dragged the swimmer aboard and returned him to the jetty. He was quickly hustled aboard a boat from his own ship, which had been tied alongside awaiting the return of libertymen. Once safely aboard, the chilled fellow was handed a coat by some good Samaritan as a relief against the chill evening air.

Some ten minutes later, when the boat scraped against the ship, the sailor, dripping and hatless, clambered up the gangway and fled at full speed to his messdeck. Both the quartermaster and the officer of the day stared after the man, perhaps too astonished to speak. The quartermaster quietly retrieved the sailor's station card from the ashore rack. He would give it to him later. The OOD decided to check the wardroom. This was one of those times when it was prudent to be somewhere else.

There was no winner declared that night. One pedi-cab was gone forever, the other damaged beyond repair. There were no charges laid, nor was there even an official enquiry. *Bataan* and *Cayuga*, perhaps providentially, sailed for Korea the following morning. When they returned, weeks later, the issue had either been covered up or written off by the authorities as a misadventure.

* * *

The Japanese, regardless of their involvement with the sailors from the Canadian ships, never fully understood their visitors. They simply looked upon them as a source of income or trouble—or both. Shopkeepers, accustomed to the Oriental habit of haggling over all purchases, never got used to the Canadians' "take-it-or-leave-it" first offer. Taxi and pedi-cab drivers soon learned it was unwise to overcharge. Mama-sans would have preferred to have nothing to do with the Canadians, but the money they spent overcame their reluctance. The Japanese, who bow on meeting with others, did not like the handshake proffered by their Canadian guests. They were also critical of the amount of meat Canadians ate. They claimed meat caused a strange odour which permeated the skins of white men.

For all the differences, troubles ashore were remarkably few. Only two or three incidents of a serious nature were recorded as involving the civilian authorities. *Athabaskan*'s *Report of Proceedings* for May 1952 makes reference to a problem involving personnel from *Nootka*. While sketchy in detail, the report indicates the incident had its beginnings in a skivvy parlor. Skivvy parlours were strip-tease cabarets also known as Butterfly Bars. Japanese police entered the picture because the Allied Occupational Authorities had just returned control of civil law to the Japanese who, intent on asserting their newly restored powers over foreigners, decided to make the incident a test case.

The adventure in the skivvy parlor was viewed very seriously by the Japanese police. The RCN, on the other hand, was inclined to look on the caper as a misunderstanding and wanted to handle the matter as a court-martial offence only. The navy saw the incident as warranting a sentence of perhaps ninety days' detention; the Japanese were thinking in terms of years in prison.

According to the initial report written by Commander King, it became a matter of necessity to keep the sailors involved out of the clutches of the Japanese police at all costs. Thus ensued a remarkable game of hide-and-seek. Cdr. Dudley King, RCN, had just assumed the position of CANCOMDESFE from Commander Plomer. King knew only the bare outline of the story, and probably had wished Plomer could have stayed on a few more weeks in order to deal with the case. Nonetheless, King tackled the messy situation in good spirits.

Nootka's captain, Cdr. Richard M. Steele, had already decided the best way to deal with the issue was to convene a court-martial as soon as possible, but had been thwarted by Japanese insistence that they held jurisdiction. The matter was then forced into the diplomatic arena, with the final decision depending on the outcome of talks between Tokyo and Ottawa. Under no circumstances, however, was Steele about to turn his sailors over to the Japanese until Ottawa so ordered. King agreed with him, as had Plomer. There was always the possibility the Japanese police would grab them, and getting them back might be difficult. It was decided the men must be kept well away from Japan.

The two captains played a stalling game for weeks while awaiting word from Ottawa. Ottawa, apparently in no hurry as the delicate negotiations went on, agreed that the men should be kept at sea until such time as a decision was reached. For weeks the men were kept at sea in Korean waters, shuttling back and forth between various ships. At last the word came through. Ottawa had convinced Tokyo that authority over the four men rested in the hands of the military. Japan waived all claims on condition the men be punished to the full extent of the Canadian naval law.

Though final victory in the matter had gone to the navy, there had been some tense moments. The four sailors, aware of the close call they had, were only too willing to plead guilty to the charges as read. They accepted the punishment, served their time and returned to Canada. There were no discharges, however.

Commander King, in his final report on the matter dated 26 May 1952, reflected at length on the case:

> Paragraph 21—It is unfortunate that just before my assumption to [the position of CANCOMDESFE] four courts-martial were about to be convened to deal with [the accused], all from *Nootka*. . . . The subsequent activities and actions in connection with the covering of these and later counts were strangely reminiscent of Gilbert and Sullivan. [The navy's efforts] to prevent the accused from falling into the clutches of the Japanese civil police . . . would be humorous were it not for the gravity of the charges.[6]

The Gilbert and Sullivan case notwithstanding, goodwill and mutual tolerance for each others' behaviour patterns and customs kept the Canadians and the Japanese on generally friendly terms. What the average Japanese citizen thought of the visitors will never be known. Though always polite and gracious, there was never much doubt some misgivings were felt. The Canadians, for their part, seem to have genuinely liked both Japan and its people, but neither host nor visitor ever fully understood each other. The differences were too great, and their time together too short.

LEOPARDS, SALAMANDERS AND DONKEYS

You Canadians should stop fighting your own private war.
Senior RN Officer

Since the early days of 1951 the Chinese had held control of the mainland north of the 38th parallel, but had been unable to capture more than a few small islands. The few islands off the east coast, securely in the hands of the UN, were never in any real danger of invasion, but those on the west coast were a different matter.

The security of those islands was the direct responsibility of the fleet. In general, this responsibility was carried out successfully, but the islands of the Chorusan group and two unimportant islets near Chinnampo were lost to the Reds in December. The Chorusans were part of a peninsula just south of the Yalu River and, considering their proximity to mainland China, it was remarkable that the navy could maintain their security for the entire year. The fight to do so became known as the Island Campaign. While it was not the exclusive patent of the Canadian Navy, no other contingent took it more seriously.

The Island Campaign began with modest activity in January 1951 when it became obvious the Chinese intended to occupy all of Korea, including its myriad islands. The navy was determined to hold them as long as possible, a sizeable undertaking considering that there were more than 2500 of them.

As the defence of all the islands was out of the question, priorities were assigned to the various areas. Cho-Do and Sok-To were to be held at all costs, as was Pengyong-Do, a large island just south of the 38th parallel. The Chorusans were to be held as long as possible, in particular the largest of the group, Taewha-Do. With this in mind the garrison of irregular fighters who called the island home was increased. Nearly all these brave men, South Koreans and North Korean dissidents, were lost when the Chinese eventually took the island.

The four large islands to the south, having been made priority zones, saw their defences increased, although the increase was pitiably small. Cho-Do and Sok-To became sheltered bases for the destroyer fleet, so their defences were more than adequate. Pengyong-Do's main defence was its distance from the mainland. An invasion by Red troops would have had to start with a crossing of several miles of open water, and there would have been plenty of time to rush ships there from Cho-Do.

The importance of these islands lay not in their strategic positions, but in their capacities as bases for the numerous guerrilla units which played a great part in the Korean fighting. Mainly ill-disciplined gangs, these irregulars ranged in number from a couple of dozen to several hundred. They were composed exclusively of South Koreans and North Korean defectors, and were supported in varying degrees by either the ROK or the United States. Some, not recognized by anyone, lived off the land (which meant they stole everything in sight), lived by their wits and had little concern for loyalties. They knew only the roughest form of discipline, usually geared to the philosophy that only the strongest could be the leader. It was commonplace for these gangs to change leaders every few days, often through personal combat. Their members were often more brutal than their foes.

The larger, organized groups with official patronage were usually well equipped and worked under a stricter code. Those with American support had officers and NCOs from the U.S. army to advise them. The groups under ROK auspices were actually agencies of Syngman Rhee's political machine and little was—or is—known of them.

The Canadians worked throughout the Island Campaign mainly with two groups: the Leopards (U.S.) and the Salamanders (ROK). Later in the campaign there would also be dealings with a large but little-known outfit call the Wolf Pack. The Wolf Pack had only a loose affiliation with the Americans, but did not seem to be sponsored by the ROK. They disbanded at the end of the war and were heard from no more.[1]

The Leopards, controlled from the island of Pengyong-Do, were assigned to various islands in varying strength. They had a large force on Taewha-Do and kept substantial numbers on both Cho-Do and Sok-To. The Leopard chief was always a career officer or NCO of the U.S. army. Leopard, as he was known, would be changed every few months, as were his assistants. (There were, from time to time, civilians who served in that capacity, and these were thought to be CIA agents).

The Koreans called the NCOs *tognagi* which meant *agent*. Canadians had trouble properly pronouncing the unusual word so they simply pronounced it as donkey, which eventually became the universal word, even among the agents themselves.

The donkeys worked under the most trying conditions as they did their best to control the guerrillas who were, in theory at least, under their command.

Without doubt the best of them all (from a Canadian point of view) was a career soldier, Master Sgt. Hubert Frost, U.S. army. As the donkey on Sok-To during most of 1951, Frost became a familiar figure to those who served during that year. Frost personified the popular image of the career soldier. Tall, muscular and slim, he kept his uniform always crisp and fresh despite the rigors of life on Sok-To.

Frost preferred to deliver his information in person, partly because he did not trust his Korean communicators and partly because he could always get a cup of strong coffee and a decent meal aboard ship. The information Frost supplied was always top quality. He had an ability for separating reliable reports from worthless ones. It was he who made the discovery that Chinese troops at Amgak were spending their nights in the woods to avoid the nightly bombardments. The only purpose of the shelling had been to keep them awake, so the routine was changed to daylight shelling. Night shelling continued, but was more or less restricted to a starshell once every twenty minutes. The shelling proved effective in that it kept the Chinese from their sleep. Small things played great roles in the unusual war being fought in Korea.

Until July the campaign remained low-key. Patrols were routine, with most of the ships' time spent in random shelling of fixed positions. Because of the relative quiet the RCN ships were sent to the east coast. During this period the contingent was reduced to two ships, since *Sioux* had gone to Hong Kong for boiler repairs.

Not until September did the action swing back to the west coast, as the Chinese began expeditionary moves against some of the smaller islands in the Chorusans. *Cayuga* and *Athabaskan* were immediately recalled, and *Sioux* returned from Hong Kong. The Canadians were overjoyed at being freed from the mundane duties of carrier screening and blockade patrol. They threw themselves into the new task with a zeal that annoyed the British task group and task element commanders.

The British, never greatly enthused about the naval aspect of the Korean War, had loudly lamented the lack of an enemy fleet to engage in battle. They were even less ecstatic about having to prowl about among a group of islands in the dead of night. To the Royal Navy the Korean War was a most un-English war. However, it was the only war available to them at the time.

The Canadians regretted their attachment to the Royal Navy during those days. Because the commanders of the various elements and groups were all RN, their permission was needed to carry out whatever action was felt necessary to conduct the campaign. While permission was rarely denied, it was usually given with obvious reluctance. On more than a few occasions the covering signals of approval suggested that the type of warfare espoused by the Canadians was hardly in the best interests of naval prestige. One senior RN officer was particularly outspoken in his criticism when he told Commander Plomer the Canadians would be well advised to stop fighting their own private war. Plomer, who in later years recalled the incident without identifying the officer, deeply resented the advice.[2]

Comments of that sort did nothing to improve the usually touchy relations between the two navies. Contrary to popular belief, the Canadians did not get along at all well with the Royal Navy. A number of *Reports of Proceedings* refer with sarcasm to the direction of the patrols under RN command. Brock certainly had his share of disagreements with his RN colleagues, as did Plomer and Landymore.

The snide remarks from the British finally ceased when Rear Adm. Wallace Creery visited the Korean theatre in September 1951. He set the matter straight in talks with RN officials, and there were no further opinions expressed aloud about private wars. Creery had never liked the cavalier attitude which the RN held toward its Commonwealth partners, and showed his displeasure during his meetings with the RN on his Korean visit.

The Canadians noticed the definite change in attitude. Suddenly they were being given a freer hand in their dealings with the island guerrillas. Until the end of hostilities the RCN destroyers remained busy among the islands.

Those who lived on the islands, whether guerrillas or peasants, impressed the sailors with their stoic acceptance of the situation into which they had been thrust. These people had seen their homes, their rice paddies and their gardens shelled by both sides. Their chief livelihood had been denied them when the fishing areas were declared off limits by the UN fleet. When, in 1951, the prohibition was lifted they resumed fishing on a limited basis.

Through the entire tragedy of the war the islanders held together as few others could have. The young men had, of course, all been pressed into the ROK army, but the very young and the very old remained in the villages with the women. Life went on as it had for centuries, with the children being taught by the grandparents. It was not an uncommon sight for landing parties to see a very old man with children gathered about him telling stories and giving lessons. The Canadians were always amazed at the rapt attention these elders commanded from the children. There was never any sideplay or wandering off. There was never any sign of boredom and there was never any backtalk. The sailors refrained from approaching these groups, and the Koreans seldom acknowledged their presence.

When the necessity of talking to villagers arose, one of the elders would act as spokesman. All others would stand silently by as if indifferent. This was their defence, the same defence Korean peasants had used so successfully for centuries against a succession of invaders. It had kept their society intact and isolated from outside influence. It was this philosophy which had been the cornerstone of the Hermit Kingdom, and it remained unchanged on the islands.

The Canadians, having no wish to disturb the villagers, came and went as their patrols dictated. The sailors would often leave small, and therefore acceptable, amounts of food and other supplies. Medical attendants were sometimes taken ashore to treat burns and abrasions. These attentions were never refused. When children were treated, the medical kits were often found to contain candy bars. Canadian sailors were tough, but they were also very soft-hearted where children were concerned.

Each ship provided as much as possible in an effort to alleviate the sufferings of the villagers. There were few sailors who would not have given more, but a strict protocol had to be observed. The villagers would never accept what could be considered charity. Such acceptance would have caused them to lose face. Only small amounts could be offered, and these would be graciously accepted. The islanders would have been mortified to appear as beggars, a total reversal of the situation on the mainland, where civilians stole

153

anything that was removable, while shamelessly bartering or selling their children—especially their daughters—into virtual slavery for a pittance of food or material.

* * *

In October the action intensified. The Chinese increased their probes along the Chorusan Islands. By November the situation in the area had become tense. On 5 November, *Athabaskan* relieved *Cayuga* near Sok-To, not far from Amgak, where the Chinese had installed several batteries of 75mm guns. Proceeding with extreme caution, Commander King positioned his ship just out of the batteries' range, recalling that *Cayuga*, on 30 October, had barely escaped with her life.

Cayuga had become the fifth UN ship to draw fire from the Amgak guns and the second RCN ship to come under the same guns. She had been the first, however, to encounter fire from competent gunners. The Chinese were, for the most part, very poor artillerymen. But on 30 October the Red gunners, having found the range quickly managed to straddle the ship with several shells before the Canadians could even react. *Cayuga* had gone into the zone with little concern many times over a period of days. The area was considered safe, and this day seemed unlikely to be any different. The donkey on Sok-To[3] had signalled a request that a pesky gun be put out of action, as it was interfering with his junks on their routine runs. Plomer took *Cayuga* into the zone and dropped anchor.[4] There being no hurry, the ship remained silent for two hours before firing two shells at the targeted gun.

Suddenly, shells splashed into the sea some fifty feet astern. Ensuing waterspouts drenched the quarterdeck, soaking its sole occupant, A/B Don Cathcart. He and everyone else rushed to action stations. Because no action had been foreseen, the ship was on green alert with near-normal routine in effect. The stern spar had even been extended with two of the ship's boats tethered to it. Within seconds of the first waterspouts another appeared some fifty feet off the port bow. This was followed immediately by two spouts twenty-five feet off the starboard side. The Chinese had found the range and held the ship firmly in their sights.

At the first fall of shot the action bell had sounded, the bridge had come to life and the order to raise anchor and put the engines full astern had been given. When the port-side salvo landed, the hook had not yet cleared the water. The shipwright, knowing the danger the ship was in, sledgehammered a coupling and freed the anchor from the ship. At the same time the ship's engines churned into life, moving the ship sluggishly astern. The two boats tied astern were crushed. Fortunately, no one was in them at the time.[5]

Cayuga had not moved twenty feet before another shell hit the water, dousing the forecastle and the bridge. Had the ship's departure been delayed by five seconds, a direct hit would have been received. With shells landing all about her on both sides and ahead, *Cayuga* hustled out of range, firing as she went. In full reverse, the remains of her boats dangling from her stern, she backed around the southern tip of Sok-To to safety.[6]

Cayuga's hasty, and embarrassing, retreat delayed the action against the Amgak guns. Some reconnaissance was needed. So it was that *Athabaskan* drew the assignment when she relieved *Cayuga* some days later. King moved his ship in with great caution, but did not anchor. Unlike *Cayuga*, *Athabaskan* had not gone in alone. HMS *Belfast* was just out of sight, ready to bring her 8-inch guns into action and a flight of Sea Furies from HMAS *Sydney* hovered overhead.

Athabaskan opened fire on the village of Mumbonch'on, known to house a large garrison of Chinese soldiers. A few shells scored hits on the larger buildings, but the Reds made no reply. The guns were then swung over to known gun emplacements, but again failed to draw answering fire. The gunners then turned their attention to a large junk moored near a rocky beach. If anything was to draw fire, it was felt, it would be the shelling of the junk, for the Reds were known to protect their boats with diligence. The junk was totally destroyed, but still the Amgak guns remained mute.

Commander King signalled *Belfast* and *Sydney* that he was calling off the combined attack and the two ships departed the area. *Athabaskan* stayed a couple more hours before leaving. The Chinese never did bother to answer the attack. It was a characteristic of the Chinese that if they chose not to fight for whatever reason nothing could induce them to change their minds.

Athabaskan left The Slot and returned to Cho-Do. There, while she refuelled and took on ammunition, a signal was received which informed King that he should steam at full speed to Taewha-Do. The Reds had attacked the island in some force, and the destroyer's guns were needed. As the ship drew close to the island, fires and columns of smoke were plainly visible. A few minutes later the island's donkey arrived in a small sampan to relate the sequence of events to Commander King.

Chinese bombers had attacked the island in force and had scored direct hits on villages and supply dumps. The bombers, eleven in all, had struck accurately, and jets had later strafed the island. The donkey said the reports of a sea attack had been erroneous, although one was still expected. He stated that the guerrillas under his command had been withdrawn to more strategic positions inland, and that the villages had been evacuated.

King, feeling his best plan was a delaying tactic, took his ship to the nearby island of Ka-Do, which was held by the Chinese. As it was but a few miles north, it posed a direct threat to Taewha-Do, for it was the likeliest point of embarkation for any Chinese attack.

Once in a favourable position and using maps supplied by Leopard agents, *Athabaskan's* gunners spent the night shelling the island. The following morning reconnaissance aircraft reported extensive damage. It was also reported the photos showed many casualties, but casualty reports were always suspect during the Korean War. The Americans, for instance, using aerial photos, would count the visible bodies within a confined area, then multiply that number by the total area of the battlefield.

At 0400 *Athabaskan* departed Ka-Do for Taewha-Do where once again the Leopard agent came aboard. The ship at once set course for Pengyong-Do so the agent could attend a conference with the chief Leopard.

While the meeting ashore was taking place, King took advantage of the time to visit with the CTE aboard *Belfast.* King wanted to return to the larger island in order to evacuate the islanders wounded in the Chinese air raids. He knew there was little chance for any of them to survive the cold nights in the hills, and even less chance of surviving a further raid. It was during this type of action that the Canadians regretted the need to seek permission from others. The CTE, however, not only gave immediate authority for King to embark on the venture, but told *Cayuga* to tag along in support. The Leopard agent once again aboard, *Athabaskan* raced north at 28 knots, covering the distance in less than seven hours. Midpoint she was joined by *Cayuga*, and the two arrived at the island at 2130.

Cayuga then proceeded to a point midway between the island's northeast coast and the mainland where she could keep watch with a good view. King took his ship around to the west side, where many precious minutes were wasted attempting to persuade the guerrillas to venture out in a sampan to collect their boss. Those otherwise doughty warriors were none too fond of the sea at any time, and they felt the water was too rough for safety.

Eventually, a couple of sampans were coaxed out and the agent took his leave. He promised to send the wounded out at once. The hapless donkey, however, had underestimated his warriors' dislike of the sea. Once back on shore they refused to go out again until the water had calmed down. Try as he might, he could not persuade them to relaunch the boats into the light to moderate waves.

King, meanwhile, knew he could not stay long. He was getting edgy, as the area was a poor place to be during the daylight. The Chinese air bases were much too close for comfort, and King had no intention of allowing his ship to be caught in shallow water by a venturesome plane. Fortunately, the waters calmed shortly after midnight and the sampans began arriving with the sick and wounded. By 0350, 7 November, a total of forty-seven wounded in the care of one ROK nurse had come aboard. King took a southern course for Cho-Do.

Cayuga, who had remained idle all night, also left for a prearranged rendezvous with *Bataan*, and the two spent the remainder of the day shelling Chinese positions farther north.

It was the following day that the situation in the Chorusans took a bad turn. During the night of 8 November, Paegun-do and Sowha-do fell to the Reds. The loss of these smaller islands left only Taewha-Do in UN hands. Commander Plomer, now in full charge, took immediate action and moved *Cayuga* to a position midway between Tan-Do and Ka-Do. There he was to remain for several hours, during which 268 rounds of HEDA shells were hurled into the targets the islands offered.[7]

Meanwhile, some miles to the south, Commander King had gone to *Belfast* for a conference with the CTE. Both were now convinced the situation on Taewha-Do would soon become untenable. They discussed, but were reluctant to recommend, immediate withdrawal of the guerrillas. HQ Tokyo replied to their signal in vague terms and suggested nothing concrete. The CTE, however, could not act on his own initiative beyond certain limits, and he was unwilling to risk his ships in daylight patrols so close to the Chinese mainland. His only possible action could be delaying tactics. King suggested that the destroyers proceed by night to the vicinity of Ka-Do, to spend as much time as possible in heavy bombardment of that island. This type of harassment, he felt, might keep the Chinese on edge enough to discourage any immediate plans they might have for an attack on Taewha-Do.

These, then, were the tactics employed for the next two weeks. By night the destroyers shelled the Chinese-held islands, and by day they hit targets further to the south. *Athabaskan* was probably the busiest ship in the fleet as she ran various errands, which included ferrying guerrillas to Taewha-Do and carrying supplies to more outlying islets along the coast.

The tactics obviously worked, since there was no Chinese movement during that time. Taewha-Do remained in the hands of the

Leopards, and it seemed the Chinese had abandoned plans for an immediate invasion. November had been the most ideal month for an invasion, and as the month drew to a close, it appeared the danger had been forestalled at least one more month. It was hoped the delay might extend into January 1952.

* * *

The immediate threat to Taewha-Do over, the Canadian ships were sent back to the Cho-Do area. On 27 November, intelligence reports from a Salamander agent indicated the probability of invasion against Sok-To and, perhaps, Cho-Do. King, now commanding the destroyer group, moved quickly to forestall that possibility. King assigned USS *Edmonds* the task of covering the southeast zone and *Athabaskan* the northeast. As the ships moved out shortly after 2030, the wind began to increase. As they ploughed into the heavy seas, it was obvious no invasion could be made, and King radioed *Edmonds* to return to Cho-Do.

Athabaskan was back at Cho-Do only a few minutes when word was sent to the bridge that a crew member was missing. A thorough search of the ship failed to locate him. A/B Robin Jensen Skavberg disappeared from *Athabaskan* during the Last Dog Watch (1800-2000), 27 November. A Board of Enquiry, convened to look into the disappearance, determined that he had last been seen at 1827 while helping raise the starboard motor launch. Following the pipe for the White Watch to close up to cruising stations, he proceeded in the direction of "B" gun deck, but never got there.

The Board heard varying testimony from several crew members. Skavberg's divisional officer testified the man had gone through a period of mild depression because an expected transfer to the Physical Training Branch had failed to come through. The ship's medical officer, Lt. C. A. West, confirmed this, but pointed out that it had been in August and coincided with an injury Skavberg suffered in a boxing match with a very good middleweight from the Royal Navy. An eardrum had been punctured by a solid blow but had healed nicely. The MO further stated that Skavberg had long since regained his usual cheerful nature, and neither officer felt there was any probability that the sailor might have jumped.

His messmates testified that Skavberg had returned to normal, but some felt that physical fitness had become almost an obsession with him. Some felt Skavberg was out of his element in the navy, and that the army might have provided him with better avenues for his particular interest in boxing, running and general P.T.

Further testimony showed that a wire guardrail had been disconnected from the stanchion on the port side of the forecastle, just opposite the ladder leading to "B" gun deck. It was thought Skavberg had accidentally gone over the side at that point.

The Board of Enquiry concurred and returned a verdict of "accidental death."[8]

* * *

On 30 November, during late evening, HMS *Cockade*, a destroyer, was on routine patrol near Taewha-Do. Suddenly a radio report from the island broke the silence in her radio room. The island, the radio crackled, was under a full-scale attack by hundreds of Chinese infantrymen. They had stormed ashore from boats and sampans and established a beachhead. *Cockade* immediately dispatched a flash signal to all units as she steamed toward the island.

King, upon receipt of the signal, turned *Athabaskan* about and steamed northward at full speed. The irony of the situation was not lost on those in the Canadian ship. Taewha-Do had been left unwatched by Canadian ships only two days during the past three months, and it was during the second of those two days that the Chinese had struck. *Cockade* had relieved *Cayuga* less than thirty hours previously; *Sioux* had been sent around to the east coast only days before, and *Athabaskan* had gone to Cho-Do on a routine mission less than forty-eight hours before. During those few hours there had been no HDWS radar covering the island's approaches.

Cockade, with no HDWS, had been unable to detect the boats that had ferried the invaders across the narrow strait. She had, in fact, been unaware that anything was amiss until the message was picked up. By that time the first wave of Chinese were already wading ashore. Once aware of the situation, she had taken immediate action. Her guns sank one large junk and damaged several others, but her efforts came too late. Then, to add to her troubles, batteries from the mainland found the range, scoring direct hits on the ship that killed one sailor.

By the time *Athabaskan* arrived the time for warships had long ended. Only the possibility of rescuing survivors remained and this became the priority. King, unable to use his guns against the island for fear of hitting the defenders, steamed instead to the sheltered lee of Tefa-to, a tiny islet not far from Taewha-Do. There he could see the large island. What he saw was not encouraging. Taewha-Do was ablaze with scattered fires, but sounds of rifle and machine-gun fire indicated resistance had not stopped. Chinese troops were visible everywhere. A large group appeared on the beach and opened fire on the ship with medium artillery. Both "A" and "B" guns answered and destroyed the gun in one salvo. A large junk then appeared from behind an outcropping and several shots were fired by those aboard. It was also destroyed by the destroyer's heavier armament. King, concerned with the fate of the defenders, sent a signal to the CTE, stating his intention to dispatch an armed party to search for Leopard survivors, but was ordered to return to Paengyong-Do.

Athabaskan's *Patrol Report*, dated 18 December, tells of the mission:

> Item 84. I proceeded to Paengyong-Do to anchor in the vicinity of Ceylon off the EAST BLUFF at 1500 1st December. I proposed to CTE 95.12 that I should return to TEFA-TO under cover of darkness to see if by any chance any other survivors from TEFA-TO had by that time managed to escape to Taejomgjok-to or adjacent islets. This was approved and on completion of fuelling I slipped and proceeded toward TEFA-TO. [sic][9]

> Item 85. As it was not known whether or not the enemy might by this time have set guns on these islets eastward to TEFA-TO, I decided to anchor in a position $210°$ one mile from Sojongjok-To sending in the motor cutter to reconnoitre their beaches. I came to anchor in this position at 0011 2nd December and dispatched the well-armed motor cutter in charge of Lt. Comm. CA Hamer, RCN(Reserve) 0-3-264. The crew was composed of:

> Communicator—P1CV A. HEYS 3384-E
> Coxswain—ABRC J. Bryan 7545-E
> Stoker—P2ER F. Meridith R-2275
> Bren Gun—AB(NQ) E. Howard 7630-E
> Lanchester—ABQR D. Turnbull 8166E

> During the passage from TEFA-TO I had briefed them fully on all aspects of the operation.

The motor cutter left the ship at 0015. It prowled about in the bays and inlets for two hours but no one was found. At 0215 the boat was called back and the *Athabaskan* departed the area at 0230.

* * *

The fall of Taewha-Do brought shocked reaction from HQ Tokyo, although HQ had been warned many times by those who worked the patrols that Chinese invasion plans included the islands. All the Leopard commanders as well as the Salamander chief had sent numerous reports to their respective HQs. The Canadian commanders plus the RN and USN CTEs had also reported many times on the matter, but nothing was done to bolster the defences. Interest came only after the loss of Taewha-Do, too late to save the Chorusan Islands or the Leopards who had done their best to hold their positions.

It would be wrong to imply that the mere presence of the RCN ships would have denied the Chinese their victory at Taewha-Do, or for that matter, that the Chinese would not have invaded despite such a presence. HDWS radar would, however, have spotted the invasion fleet the instant it put to sea, given the islanders early warning and prompted CTE to move ships into the area sooner.

Had either of the Tribal Class ships been in the immediate area, their heavier armament and multiple Bofors would have supplied the fire power needed to wreak havoc among the junks and sampans en route to the island. *Cockade*, with only 293 radar and two single-barrelled 4.7-inch guns, was at a distinct disadvantage under the circumstances. She cannot, however, be faulted for her efforts that night.

With Taewha-Do lost, the remainder of the northern islands fell in rapid succession. The Chinese, using the big island as their base, had little trouble in securing the myriad smaller islets in the area.

Full coverage of the entire coast now became impossible and the CTE was forced to change his tactics once again. Priority now shifted to the exclusive defence of Cho-Do, Sok-To and Pengyong-Do. These islands, it was decided, would be defended at all costs. The loss of even one would have dealt the UN war effort a major blow.

Haste in reinforcing the three islands became a matter of grave concern. There was no longer any doubt the Chinese would attempt the capture of at least one. Commander Plomer, in his capacity as CANCOMDESFE, wrote a top-secret report entitled "Defence of Sok-To" in which he detailed the minimum requirements for the area's defences. He noted there were only 240 ROK Marines on the island, that they possessed 29 Browning automatic rifles, of which only 24 were serviceable, and for which there were only 3500 rounds of ammunition—enough for a few seconds of firing. The guerrillas had rifles and pistols, but lacked sufficient ammunition for a prolonged fight. There were no artillery pieces at all.[10]

Plomer's report bluntly stated that a Chinese attack could not be repulsed, that defence would be a matter of hours at best, and that HQ should immediately either increase the defensive capabilities of the islands or evacuate them. Anything less than a complete commitment to the immediate needs, he stated in very blunt words, would be a flagrant waste of lives.

Plomer's report, even if acted on quickly, would take some time, so the CTE concentrated his ships near Cho-Do. His immediate task was to convince the Chinese that the islands were heavily defended. Also, along the way, the CTE had learned a valuable lesson. The fall of Taewha-Do had shown him the advantages of having HDWS radar at his disposal, and in order to fully utilize this invaluable tool, he released the Canadian ships from routine patrols. Henceforth, the three would form a special patrol group between the mainland and the three islands.

Plomer's report hit a nerve in HQ. Within days Cho-Do and Sok-To saw their defences bolstered. The U.S. 5th Air Force sent heavy bombers in a series of devastating raids against Chinese mainland positions and supply depots. ROK Marines arrived in six LCVs, and Oerlikon and Bofors guns were installed along the shoreline in strategic places. Mortars and machine guns were also brought in in large numbers. Within a week the islands had increased their defensive capabilities to where the heaviest attack could be repulsed.

On 11 December, *Sioux* was brought around from the east coast as the third prong of the defensive patrol. For a total of five days she moved between Amgak and Walsi-ri in a series of heavy bombardment operations.[11]

At 0345, 16 December, a cold Sunday, a signal was received in *Sioux*, informing Commander Taylor that an attack was imminent against the tiny islet of Ung-do. Taylor, knowing the islet, had good reason to suspect such an attack would be a ploy to draw attention away from Chongyong-do, a more likely target. *Sioux* was therefore positioned midway between the two islands so that both could be watched.

Suddenly, the radar operator reported a series of tiny blips moving toward Ung-do. The blips proved to be infantrymen slogging across the mud flats. The ROK Marines on Ung-do were notified at once as *Sioux* moved closer. A pattern of star shells was fired above the flats, illuminating the invaders. The Chinese, fully exposed and hindered in their movements by the sticky mud, became easy targets for both shipboard and island gunners.

Taylor's first thoughts had been correct however, for while Ung-do was being attacked another force of Chinese had moved against the larger island. This sector, by chance, was beyond the range of the radar and the attack went undetected. The island fell at 0800, but remained in Chinese hands only until 1830, when ROK Marines drove them off. *Sioux* had aided the retaking of the island by keeping the guns at Walsi-ri out of action while the marines made their successful attack. She knocked out a heavy mortar battery and three heavy guns. It had been a good evening's work.[12]

The attacks against the two small islands indicated that the larger islands were on the minds of the Chinese generals. When a few hours later the news that Chongyong-do had once again fallen came through, there remained no doubt about what was on the generals' minds. HQ Tokyo ordered that the two islands be retaken at once.

CTE 95.12 called an immediate council of the ground force leaders and his senior naval commanders. The result of that meeting was a proposal to launch a two-pronged attack. Coded Operation Cheerful in keeping with the Christmas season, the plan, on paper, showed merit. In reality it proved to be less than cheerful.

Aimed at retaking the two islands in simultaneous attacks backed by full naval bombardment, the plan called for a combined force of Leopard and Salamander units. This was the first error. The groups had never worked together, took their orders from separate commands and were not sufficiently disciplined to understand the need for co-operation in a venture of that sort. Error number two was the planners' failure to remember the lessons of the previous year. They forgot that the Korean soldiers had often shown the greatest reluctance to stand and fight when outnumbered. Error number three was the planners' assumption that the Salamanders were basically the same as the Leopards. They were not. The Salamanders were expert at sabotage, given to sneaking about in darkness, blowing up a bridge, then melting away into the night. They could live off the land for days while avoiding contact with anyone. The Salamanders were rarely involved in full-fledged fire fights. They were not suited for full frontal attacks, and it was this trait which spelled out the disastrous ending to the operation.

Plomer was named overall commander of the operation. He would direct the landings from *Cayuga*. Supervision of the actual landings was to be the responsibility of one Lieutenant Pack, a most able officer in command of the ROKN minesweeper JML.302. Pack was to see the guerrillas to the beaches and, should the need for retreat arise, to get them off safely.

At 1800, the operation got underway. *Cayuga* moved into The Slot to commence shelling Pongyong-do, while *Belfast*, from a distance of ten miles, began shelling Ung-do.[13] As this was going on, the Korean minesweeper went to Cho-Do, where four junks filled with guerrillas waited. The junks were taken in tow and the little convoy headed toward The Slot. Only a few hundred yards had been covered, however, when one of the junks began to ship water in large volume. It seemed some of the guerrillas had a change of mind about the upcoming adventure and had scuttled their boat. Pack was forced to stop, cut loose the sinking junk and transfer the occupants to the other boats. The loss of the junk meant that the landing at Ung-do would have to be modified. Lieutenant Pack, however, decided to go with one boat, and that was error number four.

At 1939, the two Chongyong-do boats slipped their lines to head for the beach. The minesweeper and the remaining boat continued to Ung-do. The boats landed at Chongyong-do and the guerrillas landed unopposed. For awhile it appeared the Chinese might have abandoned the island. That hope was dashed a few minutes later when heavy mortars opened fire, followed by rifles and machine-guns. One of the mortars scored a direct hit on one of the junks, ripping a gaping hole in its side. The five crewmen aboard were killed. The stricken junk sank quickly, while the other junk withdrew into safer water some five hundred yards offshore.

The sinking of the junk and the guerrillas' inability to advance spelled the end of the operation. Plomer, from his vantage point on *Cayuga*'s bridge, saw at once that the show was over, and ordered the evacuation of the fighters ashore. He signalled the minesweeper to return at once with its junk, as it had covered only half the distance to Ung-do. Plomer's first thought had been to use those in the Ung-do junk in a second landing to reinforce those already ashore. Obviously, those in the junk feared this was what was on the commanders's mind because, as soon as Lieutenant Pack cut them loose and pointed to the shore, those in the junk took it over and headed to sea. *Cayuga* was brought about to cut off the path of retreat, and the junk turned and headed back toward the island. Then, however, it swung away to port. Lieutenant Pack, meantime, had swung his minesweeper onto an intercept course, but the junk headed at full speed into very shallow water where the larger ship could not follow. When last seen, the junk was headed toward a rocky islet well away from the battle area.

Plomer considered using his 4-inch guns against the fleeing boat, but decided against it.[14] When asked years later why he had let the junk escape, he replied that he felt the boat would eventually find its way back to Cho-Do, where the Koreans themselves would handle the matter. This is what did, in fact, happen. The perpetrators of the desertion were quickly pointed out by those who had no say in the commandeering of the junk, and summarily executed.

With the desertion of the junk and its passengers, all hope of salvaging Cheerful was lost. The order went out to those on the beach to withdraw, which they did with great alacrity. Operation

Cheerful had failed, but from failure had come a small success. The landing had given the Chinese doubts. From that moment they seem to have abandoned any plans they might have had for Cho-Do or Sok-To. They obviously overestimated the strength of the ROK forces on the islands; and they knew they could not match the firepower of the combined fleet. Cho-Do and Sok-To were never invaded, and when they were handed back in 1953 to North Korea, it was a part of the agreement negotiated under the terms of the general armistice.

* * *

For those who sailed the Canadian ships, 1951 came to its close with no further incident. The few days between the bungled Cheerful and the end of the year were spent routinely.

On New Year's Eve *Cayuga* steamed quietly into The Slot, dropped her hook in the sheltered lee of a small island and, at the stroke of midnight, thumped sixteen broadsides into the Chinese garrisons on Ung-do. The gesture was a break in the RCN tradition of sounding the ship's bell to ring in the new year (the only time the "silent hours" were ever disrupted) with eight bells for the old year and eight for the new. The break seemed appropriate: eight broadsides for each year, a total of ninety-six 4-inch HEDA shells from the six barrels of three guns.[15]

With echoes of the explosions still reverberating through the stark hills, *Cayuga* turned from The Slot to set course for Taewha-Do, scene of victories and defeats during the past year. She arrived just in time to rouse the Chinese from their slumber with a savage hammering which left buildings ablaze. With the fire of the burning buildings lighting the skies, the ship turned southward for Japan. The early morning mist through which she sailed covered her departure that first morning of 1952. The patrol had been long, and the crew happily took their salt-encrusted ship into Kure for a well-deserved rest, some R&R leave and a few repairs to the ship.[16]

Despite the frustrations and disappointments of 1951, the losses at Ung-do, Chongyong-do and Taewha-Do, and the impossibility of alleviating the sufferings of the islands' villagers, spirits remained high enough going into 1952. Probably the most important was the sense of humour the sailors had managed to keep through their trials. This never wavered. The following bit of bad poetry, while hardly of epic stature, sums up the attitude of those who sailed the ships during those wearying and hectic days. The doggerel was composed in reply to a signal (CTE95.12 30/0800) from *Belfast*, reminding all ships in the element that a severe shortage of star

165

shells had become a problem. It admonished the ships' gunnery officers to limit their use of the star shells to no more than five per night.

Entitled "New Year's Eve, Korean Style," it was penned by an unknown watchkeeper during the Middle Watch (0001-0400) just after *Cayuga* had delivered her sixteen-salvo salute to the Chinese:

'Twas New Year's Eve when in The Slot,
A mere stone's throw from the Commie lot,
With sixteen salvos over and under
We hoped to catch the cads aslumber.
Eight for the old; eight for the new,
Conserve your 'Stars' where five will do.
My crystal ball tells our fortune true
But we must have licht the nicht the noo.[17]

There exists no record of the CTE's reaction, and it appears he declined to send a reply. This omission could be construed as meaning he had not been amused. No matter. Master Sergeant Frost, Lieutenant Beaudette, Captain Patterson and the other donkeys would have seen the humour in it.

Chapter Fifteen_____

ALL THE WORLD'S A STAGE

All the world's a stage, . . .
And one man in his time plays many parts.
Shakespeare, *As You Like It*

_____

The recruiting officer at HMCS Brunswicker in Saint John, New Brunswick, had reported for work on the morning of 13 March 1951 anticipating another routine day. There would be the usual enquiries from prospective recruits, mostly lads of seventeen and eighteen and perhaps one or two older men who wished to re-enlist. He and his small staff would probably process final papers for a couple of new entries, swear them in and arrange for their transportation to HMCS Cornwallis just a ferry ride across the Bay of Fundy. He was delighted, therefore, when his secretary asked him if he would like to talk to a Dr. Joseph Cyr about the possibility of enlisting in the navy.

The applicant told the young officer of his wish to serve his country. He had, he mentioned almost casually, been approached by both the Canadian Army and the Royal Canadian Air Force, as they also were in need of doctors but he would really prefer the RCN. He went on to say that he had recently sold his practice but time was beginning to weigh on him and he would like to get back to work. He had brought his credentials with him in the hope the process might be expedited.

He could not have uttered more magical words than his reference to the other two services. There was no way the navy would willingly lose such a prospect to their rivals. The officer, barely able to contain his excitement, bade the good doctor make himself comfortable in a room adjoining his office while he made a phone call to set the wheels in motion. He saw in the doctor a true prize.

The RCN at the time was suffering an acute shortage of medical personnel, and had been actively recruiting with discouraging results. Many of the few enquiries from would-be naval surgeons came from men unsuited to the navy. To add to the problem, Canada was in the midst of postwar development. All types of professional people were needed throughout the land, not the least of which were those of the medical discipline. Having to compete with the other two services, the navy also had to cope with the civilian sector. The navy's great disadvantage was the time which would have to be spent away from home. Few doctors wanted to be away for months on end.

Confronted, therefore, with a fully qualified doctor professing eagerness for a life at sea, the navy took no chances on losing him. He was pounced on with the swiftness of an eighteenth-century press gang. By 16 March the RCN's newest surgeon had been flown to Ottawa, processed and sworn in, then flown to Halifax to take his place on staff at HMCS Stadacona. The induction process which usually took up to ten weeks took only three days.

The recruiter's catch was, however, not quite what he seemed. Born Ferdinand Demara at Lawrence, Massachusetts, in 1921, he had embarked at an early age on a series of professional jobs in teaching, psychology and zoology, among others, obtained by presenting forged or stolen documents, always bearing a name other than his own. This variegated career was punctuated, for some reason, by brief sojourns in monasteries, and one of these took place in 1950 at Grand Falls, New Brunswick. By the time he moved on the following spring, Demara, as "Brother John," had established a friendship with a local physician, Dr. Joseph Cyr, and had helped himself to some of the doctor's credentials. And so it was as Dr. Joseph Cyr that Demara presented himself at the recruiting office of HMCS Brunswicker. With his ill-gotten shingle hanging from the main mast of the Royal Canadian Navy, this would prove to be his greatest—and probably his last—adventure as an impostor. It would also become the navy's greatest embarrassment.

Even the brash Demara was surprised at the speed with which the navy had moved. He had not anticipated such haste, and had planned on spending a week or two in a library, cramming medical information into his head. Now he found himself a practising physician with real patients, suffering real ailments. He had no trouble with sore throats, rashes and other minor illnesses. These he treated with doses of well-known drugs. More complicated cases, he dealt with by referring them to others. Because of his superb memory, he became a master of referral. Stadacona had a large staff of doctors, so Demara was able to play his game long enough to enable him to learn enough to begin treating even serious cases.

He had been at Stadacona a few weeks when he received a draft to HMCS *Cayuga*, then in Esquimalt preparing for her second tour of duty in Korea. The fears he might have felt at the thought of being the sole doctor aboard a destroyer in a war zone did not deter him for a moment. He packed his kit, collected his travel warrant and journeyed to the west coast, reporting to *Cayuga* 16 June 1951.

Three days later the ship departed with a full complement of officers and men. Among them was 0-17669 Surgeon Lieutenant Cyr, Joseph, C., RCN.[1] If Demara harboured any fears, they were brushed aside. He found that very little illness befalls those in a ship. For the most part his work was limited to steam burns, cuts and rashes and other minor complaints. Further, he was fortunate in having as his medical assistant a very competent petty officer, Robert Hotchin, who, naturally, had more medical knowledge than Demara. Knowing this, Demara was smart enough to let Hotchin do most of the work. Hotchin, it was learned later, had harboured some very real doubts about his boss's abilities, but his reluctance to mention them can be readily understood by anyone who served in the navy of that era. One simply did not raise questions about an officer.

Demara soon became a familiar figure to the entire crew. Because the ship's doctor was also morale officer, he was in a position to roam about the ship talking freely to one and all. He made friends easily and no one ever felt reluctant to talk to him. He was considered a bit eccentric because he carried a .45 calibre automatic on his belt most of the time—unusual apparel for a medical officer. Although he was a large man—about six feet and weighing in the neighbourhood of two hundred pounds—his personality was such that most looked upon him as a friendly giant. His sparkling eyes and hearty laugh put people at ease, and because he was interested in everyone's problems, he gained the confidence of most of those on the lower deck. Only one man besides Hotchin had doubts about the ship's doctor. Petty Officer J. Vale, who was familiar with New Brunswick, wondered why anyone named Cyr from Quebec and New Brunswick could not speak even a little French. His suspicions had been aroused first by the doctor's accent, definitely American, and then by his refusal to converse in French with one of the cooks, a lad from Quebec. However, like Hotchin, he knew better than to voice his doubts too loudly.

Once *Cayuga* reached Japan to resume her place in the UN fleet, the patrols and routine duties allowed Demara to fade into the background. He carried out his daily business, filed his morale reports with the captain and spent his spare time cleaning his .45 automatic.

In mid-August the ship became heavily involved in the Island Campaign. Her main activity was in support of the island guerrillas, whose wounded were often treated aboard the ship. It was then that Demara came into his own. The ship's records show Demara to have performed several operations during a two-month period, ranging from the amputation of a gangrenous foot to the removal of bullets from arms and elsewhere. He operated quickly and efficiently, and gave no one any reason to question his talents as a surgeon. His performance is all the more amazing when one realizes that, until be began practising medicine in the RCN, his only exposure to the medical field had been as an orderly in a Boston clinic before he embarked on his life of deception.

Demara had learned quickly that a ship's doctor had to be a jack-of-all-trades, of which one was dentistry. The shock of that sudden discovery had come to him one afternoon while *Cayuga* was mid-ocean between Hawaii and Guam. It had come with a summons to the captain's cabin. Demara had thought the call to be of a social nature, but to his dismay, it turned out to be a demand from the captain that Demara alleviate a massive toothache.

Commander Plomer was suffering and he expected, quite rightly, that his ship's doctor could do something about it. Demara had no idea of what to do, but he peered inside the open mouth and asked a few cautious questions. He gained the information that the tooth had been scheduled for extraction prior to the ship's departure, but that Plomer had kept putting it off. Demara, stalling for time, took the opportunity to chide Plomer about his neglect, but realized he would actually have to pull the tooth. He also knew he had no idea whatever of how to proceed. He was now well and truly trapped. The ship was four days from the next port so there was no way of making a referral. No miracle drug was available. He had met his moment of truth.

Demara gave his patient some pain tablets, told him he could not do an extraction until the following morning, and fled to his cabin. He knew nothing of dentistry, had never given it a thought. He had never even so much as read on the subject. He had no idea whatever of how to pull a tooth, how to give novocaine or even where to inject it. It had never occurred to him that a ship's doctor might be called on to perform dental services.

In desperation he searched the tiny medical library, and there found a small book on dentistry. It was only a thin booklet and extractions were dwelt on very briefly, but it gave him the information he needed. During the night he made his final decision and early the next morning selected the instruments the book described as necessary, took a deep breath and began what would be the longest walk of his life to that date—the thirty-six steps to the sick bay.

Plomer, having been alerted by Hotchin at Demara's request, had seated himself as comfortably as possible on a wooden chair. Demara carefully laid out the instruments on a side table, filled a syringe with novocaine (he said later it was probably far too much) breathed a silent prayer and jabbed the needle into the gum adjacent to the sore tooth. While he waited for the freezing to take effect, he ran his memory once more through the procedure he had read in the book. Then he went to work.

Motioning Plomer to open wide, Demara applied the pliers to the tooth, closed his eyes and, with sweat beading his forehead, twisted first one way, then the other, and pulled. Out came the tooth leaving no bone chips or gum damage. Plomer suffered no complications, Demara's dentistry having proved as miraculously good as his practice of medicine.[2]

Until well into October, life for Demara passed without incident. The crew remained healthy, and except for a suspected appendicitis attack, nothing occurred to cause him uneasy moments. Even had removal of the appendix become necessary, he would have faced the problem. The ship at the time was sailing with a task group that included two heavy cruisers and an aircraft carrier, with sick bays equipped for such surgery. The operation would have been performed on the carrier. He might have been asked, out of courtesy, to assist, but would have been expected to decline. It is more than likely, however, that he would have accepted.

Demara might have carried off his masquerade for years, had it not been for his skills, a guerrilla raid and a dearth of news for home consumption. These three circumstances, combined with Demara's penchant for bragging, led to his unmasking.

On 7 September, a message was received which ordered *Cayuga* to Cho-Do where Plomer was to use his guns in support of a group of Salamanders engaged in a raid on a Chinese garrison near the Nanch'on River. The raiders had slipped ashore during the night and would proceed into battle at first light. The ship took up station and at 0745, after the fighting had been raging some three hours, the first call for the heavy guns came in. For the next five hours a steady bombardment was kept up and the Salamanders gained a major victory. By 1425, the objective had been secured, the last building destroyed and the last of the raiders returned to their boats. There had been many casualties, of which three were serious. Plomer's offer of medical assistance, however, was declined. *Cayuga* departed for points north.

On 10 September, she returned to Cho-Do on a routine call. Plomer was then informed that the three seriously wounded Salamanders had not responded to treatment received on the island. All were close to death. Plomer then ordered them brought to the ship and at 1440 they arrived.

Demara took one look and made a snap decision. He ordered the startled Hotchin to bring his surgical equipment to the upper deck at once. He quickly explained that he felt at least one would die while awaiting his turn in the sick bay. By treating all three at once, he might be able to pull them through. Demara did an admirable job. The worst of the three would surely have died had treatment not been swift and expert. By the time he had finished he had collapsed the lung and removed a bullet from the man with the chest wound while successfully treating the other two as well.[3] Demara had indeed saved the three men, but the greatest feat was the work he did on the chest wound. While the collapse of a lung might have been accomplished by any qualified medical assistant, Demara had known exactly what to do and how to do it.

Such heroics made great stories in those days. The war, so far as naval operations were concerned, had lost its newsworthiness. Things were too routine. The great stories of 1950 were no longer forthcoming. Stories of value were being suppressed by the censors. Canadian newspapers, as a result, were not giving much print to Korea.

The saving of human life with a steel deck as an operating table, however, was a godsend to the Public Relations Branch. A public relations officer, Lt. (SB) R. A. Jenkins, was elated. He approached Demara about a press release and a statement. Demara turned Jenkins down on the grounds that what he had done was not of sufficient importance to warrant a press release. Jenkins, though greatly disappointed, did not press the issue. But a couple of days later, for reasons known only to himself, Demara had a change of mind. He told Jenkins to proceed with the story. It was duly written and dispatched for release through Canadian Press. The account of the skilful surgeon's actions in the shadow of the torpedo tubes was read by Canadians across Canada with great interest.

One of the most interested was the legitimate Joseph Cyr. At first he dismissed the story as a case of mistaken identity. Surely there were other doctors of the same name in New Brunswick. Then he began to think of the missing documents and made a phone call to the local RCMP office. A constable called at his surgery, asked a few questions, then left. Two days later he was back. Cyr was shown a photo from a RCN identification card and asked if the likeness was familiar. Indeed, replied Cyr, the photo was that of Brother John Payne, late of the local seminary. At that moment the entire picture became clear for both the doctor and the RCMP constable.

On 24 October a signal from NHQ Ottawa was decoded in *Cayuga*'s signal centre. It advised Commander Plomer that his ship's doctor might not be the man he claimed to be. Plomer sent at once for the duty messenger and told him to escort Dr. Cyr to his cabin. Plomer had no doubt about the doctor's skills, no reason to doubt his credentials. He decided to show the signal to the man and ask him to verify or deny its implication. Plomer's reasoning was pragmatic. The ship needed a doctor and the man, whomever he might be, was good at his work. The ship was going into action that very night and might well require those skills.

When Demara entered the cabin Plomer silently handed him the signal which Demara read without comment. Plomer said years later that the colour seemed to drain from Demara's face and he muttered something to the effect that he should not have entered the navy, but outside of that he had said nothing definite. Plomer then asked if the doctor could verify his identity as Joseph Cyr. Demara replied in the affirmative. Plomer then ordered him to return to duty and prepare the sick bay for expected casualties from a guerrilla raid planned for that night. Demara left the sea cabin without comment.

The following day a second signal arrived stating in no uncertain terms that the ship's doctor was indeed an impostor. The RCN, however, still had no idea of his real identity. The signal ordered Plomer to place him under close arrest, pending transfer to HMS *Ceylon* which would take him to Tokyo for return to Canada. Demara was immediately placed under guard in his cabin. Plomer was to recall in an interview with the *Kingston Whig-Standard* in 1982 that Demara had been dressing a steam burn on a stoker's arm when Plomer and two seamen took him into custody. Plomer recalled that Demara's entire body seemed to sag and "a look of total defeat and a terrible sadness entered his eyes."[4]

Transfer to *Ceylon* was to have been made 25 October, but had to be postponed until the following day. The delay had near-disastrous results. On a routine check of the prisoner during the early hours of 26 October, a guard discovered Demara unconscious on the cabin deck. The distraught man had taken an overdose of drugs, probably tranquilizers. Officially there were denials that his intention had been suicide, but those who had sailed with him were inclined to lean toward that probability. In any case, quick action by Petty Officer Hotchin pulled him through the crisis.

Cayuga overtook *Ceylon* quickly and a medical officer from the cruiser came aboard, made a rapid examination, then ordered immediate transfer to the larger ship. Although satisfied that Demara, still unconscious, was in no immediate danger, he deemed the situation to be critical.

Cayuga's log states simply, without detail or emphasis, the final word of Demara's career in that ship: 1400—Surgeon Lt. J. C. Cyr left the ship to join *Ceylon*. The October *Report of Proceedings, Cayuga*, gives the details:

> Surgeon Lt. J. Cyr, RCN, 0-17669 had taken an overdose of drugs and numerous attempts were made to bring him back to consciousness. Whether this was taken to commit suicide or as a sedative on the receipt of the news that he is an imposter [sic] is not known."

> He was examined by the MO from *Ceylon*, but Cyr had not recovered appreciably and was still not conscious(sic). He was however transferred, not without difficulty, to HMS *Ceylon* and placed under medical custody [sic].

> Lt. (S) W. E. Davis and Lt. (TAS) D. R. Saxon were detailed to search Cyr's cabin and personal effects. Their long hours of investigation did much to throw light on this interesting case.

The detailed search of the vacant cabin did indeed throw light on the case. From letters and notes found strewn about, the two officers pieced together much of the now identified Ferdinand Waldo Demara's strange history.

The RCN, thoroughly embarrassed by the entire affair, declined to prosecute Demara. The whole episode, Ottawa decided, was best forgotten as quickly as possible. On his return to Canada Demara was very quietly, and honourably, released from the service, issued re-hab and back pay plus active service credits in the amount of just under one thousand dollars. He was then driven to the border and turned over to the United States Immigration Office at Blaine, Washington. The Americans had nothing against him in the way of outstanding warrants so, after a few routine questions, they let him go on his way. The RCN, meanwhile, did everything in its power to obliterate the memory of its great embarrassment. The official history of the navy has allowed him one terse footnote.[5]

Demara's adventures in the Canadian navy had, however, received a good deal of attention in the States and there is no doubt he could have made a fortune had he capitalized on it. He chose not to. Fred Demara would not be heard from for ten years, until 1961 when Universal Studios in Hollywood, producing mainly Grade "B" movies, made a film called *The Great Impostor*. Based on the book of the same name by Robert Crichton, it purported to tell the true story of Demara's escapades. Its release (some say it escaped) brought Demara into the open just long enough to denounce the movie as a parody filled with errors. He also criticized the book on which it was based.

The movie, insofar as it portrayed his time in the RCN, was plainly flawed. Commander Plomer had accepted an invitation to attend the filming, presumably as an adviser for the RCN segment. The film's producer, however, paid little attention to his suggestions. The two actors who played the parts of Plomer and Demara—Edmond O'Brien and Tony Curtis respectively—were miscast. Curtis, in particular, in no way resembled the stout Demara either in manner or appearance.

Demara was discovered once again, quite by chance in 1970, when a Canadian reporter, vacationing with his family in the Gulf Islands of Washington State, recognized the pastor of the tiny Baptist church at Friday Harbour on the island of San Juan as Fred Demara. The reporter asked for, and was granted, an interview. He was warmly greeted and was pleased to find Demara in a talkative mood. The reporter's article appeared later in the week in the *Victoria Colonist*, as a human interest feature. Fred Demara was at last legitimate, the story said. During the nineteen years which had elapsed since his RCN adventure he had returned to a religious vocation, having been ordained a minister of the Baptist faith. Following his ordination, he had served in numerous small parishes, until he was called to the little church on San Juan Island. In 1974 Demara accepted an appointment as resident chaplain at Good Samaritan Hospital, Anaheim, California, where he remained until his death.

In 1979, during the Labour Day weekend, Demara returned to Victoria for a three-day visit. Although in poor health he could not bring himself to pass up the opportunity of attending a reunion of those who had served in *Cayuga*. Canadian Immigration officials, at the request of the Reunion Committee and a personal letter from Plomer, then a retired Commodore, granted a special pass which allowed Demara entry to Canada. It was issued on the conditions that he stay no more than four days and refrain from speaking with the press.

Demara arrived in Victoria, where a small welcoming party met him. He was quickly whisked away. It is unlikely the press knew of his visit, although a column devoted to him appeared in the 5 September edition of the *Victoria Colonist*. When Demara arrived at HMCS Naden for the reunion, he was greeted with warmth by those who had known him as a friend and shipmate twenty-eight years before. The welcome made it obvious that Demara had made no enemies aboard *Cayuga*. By all accounts he enjoyed the party.

Demara's exploits had at various times led to arrests, charges of fraud, forgery, embezzlement, theft and vagrancy. Yet he was never sentenced to a single day in jail. The Reverend Fred W. Demara, Doctor of Divinity, died of a heart attack at Anaheim, California, on 7 June 1982. He was sixty years of age. As a hospital chaplain he had at last found his true role in life.

There is one final, ironic footnote to Demara's story. Dr. Joseph C. Cyr—the legitimate one—eventually left Grand Falls to practice medicine in the United States, and settled in Anaheim. One of the hospitals to which he was accredited was the Good Samaritan Hospital. During his first week there he saw, and recognized immediately, the man he had known as Brother John. Fearing the man was still posing as someone else, Dr. Cyr made a few discreet enquiries. He was told of Demara's status and attempted to make conversation with him. Demara pretended not to know his old friend but, as time went by, talked to him about hospital matters. Demara never did, however, acknowledge their previous relationship.

The outbreak of the Korean War in the summer of 1950 found *Huron* (right) at Halifax, awaiting refit, along with *Micmac* — the only RCN Tribal not to see service in Korean waters. *Ken Macpherson*

HMCS *Athabaskan* refueling at sea from a British cruiser, circa 1950. *Author*

Huron awaiting repairs in dry dock at Sasebo, Japan, following her grounding on the island of Yang-Do. Note the missing anchor; it was jettisoned on the island to facilitate her rescue. Bill Mushing

HMCS *Huron* during a practice torpedo run off the coast of Korea, circa 1951. *Bill Mushing*

Nootka during full power trials, 1950.   *F.C. Polischuk,* NAC/DND PA133592

HMCS *Haida* on Korean patrol, 1 April 1953. *Norman Keziere* NAC/DND PA151995

HMCS *Iroquois* off Halifax 26 January 1952.   *D.F. Quirt* NAC/DND PA136243

HMCS *Cayuga,* 3 December 1950, a few hours before entering the Daido-Ko to Chinnampo. *NAC/DND PA167313*

HMCS *Sioux*   *Ken Macpherson*

HMCS *Athabaskan*   *Ken Macpherson*

Chapter Sixteen _____

SHOOT-OUT
AT PACKAGE ONE

Relentless In Chase
Motto of HMCS *Iroquois*

HMCS *Iroquois*, the fifth of the six Tribal Class destroyers from the RCN to serve in Korea, arrived for her first tour of duty on 12 June 1952 to relieve *Cayuga*. The ship and her restless crew then were forced to languish ten long days in the filthy water of Sasebo's harbour.

On 23 June orders were received which sent the ship to the Cho-Do patrol zone as part of Task Group 95.11. The ship had left Sasebo with a crew eagerly awaiting and anticipating action and high adventure, only to spend seven tiresome days "chasing the wind" astern of the carrier USS *Bataan*.

There had been one break in the tedium. On 28 July, HMNZS *Taupo*, a New Zealand frigate, spotted a large fleet of junks heading at top speed toward the strategic island of Pengyong-Do. *Taupo* called for help and waded into the fray. *Iroquois* responded. The destroyer, however, had several miles to steam, and by the time she arrived, *Taupo* had already sunk seven of the junks, damaged several others and scattered the remainder. *Iroquois* spent several hours searching the area without success, then returned to her task of screening the carriers.[1]

August was little better. The reasons for the lack of activity were simple enough: there were too many ships and the enemy was being

177

less than combative. Even the Leopards and Salamanders rarely called for assistance during that slack time. They were also having trouble finding the enemy. The war had come to a virtual standstill so far as the fleet was concerned. In their efforts to draw out the enemy, the ships had taken to venture dangerously close to the shoreline along the Chorusan Islands. Still they had little success. It was a dictum of the Korean experience that the Reds, once they decided not to fight, would remain unshaken in their resolve. Because there was little to do, the UN fleet carried out exercises in which the RCN ships, their crews always eager to escape the ho-hum drudgery of carrier patrol, took part wholeheartedly.

But idleness is truly the Devil's workshop. This old idiom proved itself during those times as ships' companies began taking special delight in badgering each other. The more annoyance a crew could heap upon their counterparts the better. Plots led to counterplots as each mischievous deed spawned reprisals in kind. A plot to unfurl a huge Russian battle flag from *Nootka*'s mainmast was thwarted when the perpetrators from *Iroquois* were caught in the act. But the idea of such a gag so appealed to the men of *Nootka* they joined forces with those from *Iroquois*, and the combined force played the trick, successfully, on HMS *Cossack*. The captain of that ship was less than pleased when dawn broke to reveal the flag snapping briskly from the halyards.

Annoyance was not confined to skylarks and trickery. Verbal abuse became prominent. In this the sailors from *Nootka* excelled, especially when the target was *Iroquois*. *Nootka* had seen a great deal of action during the days of heavy fighting, while the newly arrived *Iroquois* had seen none at all. To make matters worse, it was beginning to appear that the war might end before she saw any. This possibility was not lost on *Nootka*'s crew, and they increased their taunts accordingly. Their favourite theme was that *Nootka* was a seasoned veteran into her second tour, had seen fierce battles, had shelled trains on the east coast while her sister had done little more than screen carriers and patrol the Dick Tracy Run.[2] Those of *Iroquois* grew tired of *Nootka*'s exploits, but the Nootkans remained relentless in their reminders that *Iroquois* had been less than productive and that had made *Nootka* cock of the walk in Korean waters.[3]

Iroquois' crew had taken all they were willing to endure when, on a quiet afternoon as the two ships steamed slowly abreast with less than twenty feet between them, a group of seamen aboard *Nootka*, being less than gainfully employed, began shouting insults across the water. Among the catcalls was the suggestion that

Iroquois might best serve the war effort by remaining in Sasebo for use as spare parts for the more warlike *Nootka.*

In the navy of those years what a sailor might call his own ship was one thing; what others might say of her was quite a different matter. The *Iroquois'* crew members would not tolerate such an insult. Suddenly, one of the deck petty officers shouted, "The spud locker. To the spud locker!" and those on deck saw at once the solution to their immediate problem.

Spud lockers were large, wire-screened bins which held a great quantity of potatoes when full, generally enough for a month at sea. Most ships had two, one on each side. On that particular day the locker of the starboard side was still half full of potatoes. In minutes it was empty, its entire contents having been tossed, grenadelike, at *Nootka.* Her deck was littered with the remains of shattered potatoes. The boats, funnels, torpedo tubes and the ship's side bore the splash marks of hundreds of potatoes. The pulp made the deck slippery. *Iroquois* had clearly won the round. Before the astonished victims could regroup and retaliate, the ships drew apart, widening the gap out of potato range.

The rivalry between the two ships continued unabated. The pranks were tolerable to *Iroquois'* company because they could be avenged. The long stories were not. Finally, the CPOs and POs decided to do something about it. Their opportunity came the first day the two ships were tied alongside in Sasebo.

At 1300, just after lunch, a large group from *Iroquois*, led by CPO George Perigo, the gunner's mate, marched in solemn procession across the gangway to *Nootka.* The group had come, Perigo informed the startled Officer of the Day, to sit at the feet of the masters and hear once again the thrilling saga of *Nootka's* heroism. For the occasion, he continued, they had dressed in appropriate garb, the better to enjoy and appreciate the great war stories as told by *Nootka's* great warriors. All were indeed dressed appropriately, in full battle-dress, anti-flash outerwear, steel helmets, gas masks and life jackets.[4]

* * *

September brought better days for *Iroquois.* During that month she spent time on both coasts, becoming the first RCN ship to see east coast action since the previous June.

The first part of September was spent on the west coast, the scene of previous disappointments, but this time things were different. There had been a resurgence of activity by the Chinese in the vicinity of the important island of Mu-Do. A medium island close to the mainland, it was the base for a large group of guerrillas known as the Wolf Pack. The group had no direct affiliation with either the ROK government or the U.S., but worked with both. The Wolf Pack did good work and had good leadership at all times. Their main force was stationed on Yongmae-Do, a large island farther south, but the brunt of the fighting was borne by those on Mu-Do.

The Chinese, tired of the constant raids from Mu-Do, had brought up heavy artillery and commenced a constant shelling of the island. This led to speculation that the Reds were planning to invade the island, and a decision was made to launch a full-scale raid against the Chinese mainland. There were two sound reasons for this. First, was the desire to silence the Chinese guns. The second was a matter of morale. In August the guerrillas had launched a raid against the Chinese, only to be beaten off with losses which included the capture of several of their key people. The defeat had left the guerrillas with a severe morale problem, worsened by the inactivity that followed. When *Iroquois* entered the picture the guerrillas were a morose, discouraged group.

Those who advocated the raid felt the timing was at its best. The Chinese, knowing they had inflicted a sound defeat upon the raiders, were not likely to expect another raid so soon. *Iroquois'* ship's company had their own reasons for wanting the action. In the failed raid *Nootka* had been one of the covering ships. To succeed where she had failed would be a point scored in their ongoing rivalry.

Operation Siciro took its code name from a combination of the first three letters from USS *Sicily*, the aircraft carrier which would provide the air cover, and from *Iroquois*, who would provide the surface fire. The plan of attack was to land at 0400, 10 September, fan out and take cover until first light. Following an intense bombardment by *Iroquois* and an air strike by planes from *Sicily*, the guerrillas would strike their selected targets. They were to regain their sampans and clear the area by 0800. They were under strict (and unwelcome) orders to take prisoners.

The raid went well. The bombardment by *Iroquois* (assisted by HMS *Belfast*) began at 0230. The raiders hit the beaches on schedule, undetected, and right at dawn the fighters from *Sicily* took to the air. The planes directed their bombs and rockets at points away from the zones being attacked and thus there was no chance of hitting the raiders. The planes scattered the Chinese, and before they could regroup the raiders struck.

Three of the previously captured Wolf Pack agents were rescued, a reasonable number of prisoners taken, and the big guns put out of commission. The raid was considered an overwhelming success.

The Chinese prisoners were quickly taken out to the *Sicily* along with the wounded Wolf Pack agents.

The *Iroquois* sailors left the area feeling pleased. It had been their first good night and they felt things might get better. They were right. The ship would enjoy some great days within the next few weeks.

* * *

It was on 27 September that *Iroquois* sailed for the east coast and her date with destiny. She reported the following day to Task Unit 95.22, a mobile group of five U.S. destroyers and two ROKN torpedo boats. *Iroquois* became unit commander. The next five days were spent by Commander Landymore in getting to know his unit and assigning them their duties.

The five days were spent patrolling the area in company with the five U.S. destroyers. The area was a dangerous one, so the lookouts were told to pay sharp attention and the guns' crews remained closed up at all times. The ship had been shelled on her first day, but luckily the shells fell short. Only the quarterdeck had been sprayed, but it had brought home to the newcomers the fact that east coast gunners were better than those on the west coast.

Naval patrols are not unlike the adventures which await boys who move into a new neighbourhood. *Iroquois* was the new kid on the block, so it was natural for the established residents to watch and wait. There may have been some resentment at the new kid having taken command, but if so it was soon put to rest.

On the second day of patrol, while in company with USS *Walker*, *Naifeh* (strictly speaking, a destroyer-escort), *Thompson* and *Carmick*, *Iroquois* steamed slowly in the lead along the rugged coastline. A lookout in one of the trailing ships spotted a gun emplacement at the mouth of a cave halfway up a hill which overlooked the strait through which the convoy had to pass. The gun, of large calibre, commanded the entire strait.

Landymore directed the four destroyers to use their main armament against the target. Each took several shots but missed.

Landymore moved his ships closer and called for one more salvo. Again all shots were misses. Telling the others to check their fire, he took *Iroquois* as close in as he dared. Then he told his gunnery officer, Lt. (G) D. F. Tutte, DSC, RCN, to display to the Americans the fine art of naval gunnery. Tutte, seeing the opportunity to enhance the ship's already solid reputation, took extra care in the laying and training of the guns. Finally satisfied, he gave the order to fire. The 4-inch guns spoke and from the mouth of the cave there

181

erupted a single explosion as the gun, its crew and its store of ammunition all went up at once.

Landymore, his entire countenance one large grin, swung his ship about in a wide, lazy arc. The others fell into line and sailed through the narrow strait without incident. Several more bombardments were carried out that day, but none was as satisfying to the *Iroquois* sailors as had been the one-salvo lesson they had given the USN.

The Korean War, from a sailor's point of view, was a gunner's war. To this end each ship's company, from gunnery officers to magazine loaders, did their utmost to keep the Canadian gunnery reputation at a high level. Their hard work paid off. No ship of any navy proved superior to the RCN. Indeed, few were equal and most never came close to the excellence shown by the gunners of the Canadian contingent. This excellence rushed to the fore and enabled *Iroquois* to take her vengeance against the Chinese for the losses she was to suffer at Package One on 2 October.

* * *

HMS *Charity*, a British destroyer, had demolished a train and ripped up a section of track at a site code-named Package One on 28 September. No one could foresee it at the time, but her action would have a dramatic effect on HMCS *Iroquois* and her crew. *Charity* had set the scene for the Canadian ship's worst and finest hours of the war; and it would also change the entire attitude of the Canadian sailors toward their allies.

A few hours after *Charity* had done her work at Package One, she gave over command of her task group to *Iroquois* and set her course for Japan. *Iroquois*, with nothing to do for the moment, dropped her hook a few thousand yards offshore.

Package One was the first in a series of five tunnels along the rail line from Songjin to Sinpo, some eighty miles to the south. Each of the tunnels had been given a number for easy identification and each intervening stretch of track was known as a package. Thus, the open stretch between tunnels one and two became Package One, the stretch between tunnels two and three became Package Two, and so on. Package One was the most northerly point in the line.

The Chinese, hard pressed on all fronts, worked desperately to keep their trains running, and were quick to rush repair crews to the scene of any damage. It was with this in mind that *Iroquois* was kept at the scene of *Charity*'s earlier work.

As expected, the repair crews appeared at the package as if on a schedule. The ship's gunners allowed them to begin their work, then dropped a 4-inch HEDA shell into their midst. They scattered and sought refuge inside the tunnel, where they were kept by the simple expedient of firing a shell into the tunnel's opening every few minutes. *Iroquois* stayed a few hours before turning the job over to another ship. She then went out on a routine patrol.

Thursday, 2 October began routinely. The skies were clear, the sea calm with only a gentle breeze. Reports indicated the fine weather would remain at least two more days.[5] Landymore decided to spend the entire day on patrol in the company of three U.S. destroyers. The four got underway at 0700, leaving USS *Marsh* the task of keeping the Chinese repair crew in their tunnel prison.

Marsh kept up a steady barrage all morning but, and perhaps this should have been considered an omen, she was forced to move several times because fire from shore batteries had begun to fall too close for comfort. Eventually, *Marsh* signalled for assistance, and *Iroquois* responded.

The lunch hour had just ended as *Iroquois* sailed into the zone, her crew at action stations on full alert. Landymore signalled *Marsh* to take up position as back-up support. Then he took his ship in close to shore. The shore batteries remained silent. For two hours and thirty minutes, *Iroquois* fired round after round into the mouth of the tunnel. She also found time to shell two of the still-silent shore batteries. At 1600 the order to check was given, and the ship began a slow turn seaward.

As she turned she was for the moment fully broadside to the shore, and at that moment the shore batteries opened fire. One shell landed twenty feet short of the port side, but a second whistled directly over "B" gun. A third shell hit the ship directly below the bridge just aft of "B" gun. The impact of the explosion was taken mainly by the gun's crew. In the split second of the explosion every member of "B" gun's crew was knocked down by the concussion. Engulfed in acrid, choking smoke, many lay on the deck, some unconscious, all in some shock. One sailor, semi-conscious, dragged himself to the portside ladder, intending to escape to the deck below. Unable to properly grip the ladder's handrails, he fell to the steel deck below, a distance of some nine feet. He was saved from further injury by his padded anti-flak suit and his steel helmet.

Inside the gun housing (destroyers did not have enclosed turrets as did larger ships) the blast had slammed the gun's trainer A/B Jerry Stokke against the gun-shield. Stunned and choked by smoke, he managed to regain his station, readjust his headset and resume listening to the director's pointers. He discovered his gun could still bear an additional ten degrees shoreward and managed, despite the increasing pain in his right arm, to swing the gun to the proper line.

183

The smoke had not yet cleared when several things began to happen all at once. While Stokke was realigning the gun, L/S Gerald Jamieson, the gun captain, reassembled his crew. By sheer exhortation he got them back into action, and the crew managed to load the left barrel. Meanwhile, A/B John "Scotty" Moxham, alone and unaided, loaded and made ready the right barrel. "B" gun was back in action. The moment the ship was hit, the crew on "A" gun (on the deck immediately below) swung their gun shoreward. They kept up a full barrage on the shore batteries and continued firing non-stop until bearing was no longer possible. On the bridge, Commander Landymore ordered the engine room to lay on heavy smoke. The shore batteries continued to fire into the smoke screen, but none of their shells hit the ship.

While "A" and "B" guns were replying and the engine room was making smoke, a medical party headed by PO Emile Fortin arrived on "B" gun deck. They were shaken by the scene that lay before them. The explosion had opened a gaping hole in the ship just aft of the gun housing. Beside it lay A/B W. M. "Wally" Burden, mortally wounded. Not far away lay the bodies of A/B Elburne A. Baikie and Lt. Cdr. John L. Quinn. Both had taken the full blast of the explosion. Nearby, A/Bs J. A. Gaudet and E. M. Jodoin, both seriously injured, groped about trying to get back to the gun. They were immediately taken to the sick bay. PO Fortin then turned his attentions to Burden. As he worked a shell, exploding close to the ship, hurled a jagged piece of shrapnel into his arm. He continued his work, refusing treatment, until the ship was well out to sea.

With *Iroquois* now clear of immediate danger, Commander Landymore called for damage control reports. He was pleased to learn that outside of the damage to the upper deck area the ship was unharmed. His first concern was for his casualties, in particular Burden, and he decided to make a run for the Danish hospital ship, *Hope*, which he knew was lying at anchor a few miles to the south.

USS *Marsh*, meanwhile, had fled. Her officers had watched the duel between *Iroquois* and the shore batteries, but made no effort to intervene. *Marsh*, whose duty had been to provide cover, had fired not a single shot. She had instead been taken quickly out of range. A photographer on her bridge[6] had taken pictures of the action, but his were the only shots from *Marsh*.

Once *Iroquois* had made open water, the damage was assessed and repairs begun at once. The wounded, now all in or near the sick bay, were given more thorough treatment, while the ship continued her race against time in search of the *Hope*.

Landymore, knowing his crew was concerned for the wounded, addressed them over the ship's P.A. system to appraise them of the situation. He cautioned them against being too optimistic for the stricken Burden and assured them the shore batteries would be dealt with in due course.

Two hours later he spoke to them again. His voice at times broke as he informed them that Burden had died. There was, he told them, no further need to proceed to the *Hope* as the remaining wounded were in no danger. He had made arrangements to transfer the dead and wounded to USS *Chemung*, a tanker bound for Sasebo. Landymore spoke at some length, telling his crew of the pride he felt for them. He spoke of the *Iroquois*, of her battle honours, of her reputation in the world of naval affairs. He reminded them that her motto—Relentless In Chase—had originated with the Indian tribe for whom the ship had been named. He told them how Iroquois warriors, once they had defeated their enemy, would run them to ground so that none would escape. That, he told them, was how the ship would treat the batteries at Package One.

Early the following morning *Iroquois* transferred her fallen warriors to *Chemung*. Of the injured, only two were sent over as the others had elected to remain in the ship. With transfers completed, the crew held a short memorial service for their dead comrades, then they returned to their stations to make ready for their special mission. Two hours later *Iroquois* steamed into the waters below Package One, this time alone.

With a single spotter plane circling high above to report the fall of shot, *Iroquois* raced in with all guns firing in salvos. As she approached, the Chinese guns opened up, but as a moving target the ship had the advantage. Her gunners made short work of the main batteries. Then, working from the aircraft's reports, they began systematically to obliterate the smaller batteries. Shell after shell was hammered into the objects of their wrath and there was no cease-fire called until the spotter plane's pilot gave a report that he could see no further targets. The pilot added, in almost awed tones, that in his service career he had never seen as fine a display of pinpoint shooting. This was high praise indeed from a flier who had spent many years in spotting duties.

The incident at Package One taught the Canadians two valuable lessons. One, sadly belated, was that shore batteries should be treated with greater caution. The second was that allies are not always to be depended upon. For the remainder of the fighting those lessons were never forgotten. The RCN ships, from that moment on, rarely made requests for support; and those requests, whenever possible, excluded the ships of the USN. USS *Marsh* to this day has not been forgiven by the crew members of *Iroquois* for her failure to provide support that day at Package One.

The final tally from the action at Package One was three dead, two critically injured and nine seriously wounded plus many injuries. There were also six medals awarded, including a Distinguished Service Medal to L/S G. E. Jamieson for his courage in rallying his gun crew. He was later promoted to petty officer 2/c.

* * *

On 8 October, under the clear sky of a warm autumn Wednesday, A/B Wallis M. Burden, A/B Elburne Baikie and Lt. Cdr. John Quinn were borne by sailors from *Crusader* to their final resting places in the Commonwealth Cemetery near Yokohama, Japan. Chaplain (P) John Wilson conducted the service. The three volleys were fired over the flag-draped coffins, the plaintive notes of the "Last Post" were played, and then the coffins were lowered into the ground. There were in attendance representatives of the U.N., various armed forces, and a small group from the Canadian Embassy in Tokyo.[7]

Meanwhile, *Iroquois* was ranging along the east coast. She returned to Sasebo on 15 October and remained there for thirteen days before sailing to Hong Kong for a short visit. The departure from normal routine had been considered a good chance for the crew to wind down from the experience at Package One.

Iroquois returned to the war on 15 November. She spent the final days of her first tour of duty on the west coast. A week later she greeted *Athabaskan*, who was about to begin her third tour, and the following day departed for Halifax via Hawaii. *Iroquois* would return to Korea the following year. She would be there, on patrol, when the final cease-fire ended three years of fighting.

Chapter Seventeen _____

THE TRAINBUSTERS CLUB

Acknowledge receipt of your final dues to the Trainbusters Club.
Lifetime membership now recorded. Well done.
CTF 95 in signal to HMCS *Haida*

Of the various clubs formed by the naval forces in Korea, the most prestigious was that of an elite group that devoted much time to chasing the trains which ran the deadly gauntlet among the rugged peaks of Korea's Taeback Mountain range. The Trainbusters Club had its beginnings in July 1952 when the American destroyer *Orleck* destroyed two trains within a fourteen-day period. The commander of Task Force 95, recognizing a morale booster when he saw one, declared *Orleck* the trainbusting champion, and issued a challenge to the entire task group to best her record.

From its concept the TBC was considered a USN project, but to make things fair, membership was extended to any qualifying ship in TF 95. As TF 95 only rarely included ships outside the USN, and then only for a few days at a time, the odds were heavily stacked in favour of the Americans. In the spirit of competition, however, the other navies were invited to try for membership whenever the opportunity presented itself.

From the beginning of the war to *Orleck's* hour of glory, dozens of trains had been destroyed or damaged. It is rather unfortunate the club was formed at such a late date, for had the idea been conceived earlier a great many ships would have qualified for

187

membership, and the "kills" would have greatly exceeded the official count of twenty-eight trains.[1]

The first rule for admittance required that the train's engine be destroyed. The engine was the fee for membership, but after that had been recorded all subsequently destroyed trains were counted as kills, regardless of the engine's fate. The rules were so strictly enforced that all kills recorded were legitimate. Membership, however, was not an easy matter because of the engine clause.

Once the club was formed, the crews who ran the trains learned the true meaning of hell on earth. Those brave men often found themselves running just a few feet ahead of the explosions which dogged their daily existence. They took their trains across damaged tracks and over quickly repaired trestles that were usually swaying precariously. They hid during the daylight hours in tunnels, hoping their tormentors would leave before managing to seal both ends. Hiding in the tunnels was probably less safe than running. The gunners became adroit at blocking those openings, and once they were closed a lingering death awaited those trapped within.

A grudging respect was extended to the prey by the hunters. The trainmen, hounded as they were, kept the trains moving, although schedules became a thing of the past. They earned the respect to an even higher degree because, even under heavy shelling, they would do their utmost to save their trains by attempting repairs.

In July 1952, the RCN was represented by *Athabaskan*, *Haida* and *Crusader*. All had gunners eager to try their skills against the elusive trains, but the handicap they faced was all too obvious. Because the Canadians worked almost exclusively within the Commonwealth fleet, their time was spent mainly on the west coast. When they did draw an east coast assignment, the chances of going to TF 95 were slim indeed. They knew that any chance they might have at winning the championship—or even gaining membership in the TBC, for that matter—was slim. To add to the problem, even should they be assigned to TF 95, they could not expect to spend much time on the train patrol as TF 95 was a multi-purpose force and train-hunting was only a small part of the duty.

By placing their priorities in proper order, the destroyermen managed, despite the little time they were allotted, to amass a creditable number of kills. Of the twenty-eight kills tallied officially by the TBC, the RCN accounted for eight. That gave the RCN the proportional record, a significant feat in itself. The main achievement, however, was the winning of the championship by *Crusader*, who bagged four trains, three of them in a single twenty-four-hour period. *Crusader* was about to kill two more during that time, but was forced to leave in order to refuel. While she was taking on oil orders sending her on another assignment were received.

The business of trainbusting was based on extreme patience, a degree of luck, and superb gunnery. The gunnery skills were important, not only because of the craggy hills and the undulating tracks of the railway system, but because of the vagaries of the Korean weather. Fog often kept the ships well out to sea. Thus the guns were operating at maximum range much of the time, and had to hit a speeding target from ranges of 8,000 to 12,000 yards. If the clouds hung low over the jagged peaks or the fog was heavy, hits were difficult to verify.

For the RCN trainbusting began in earnest on 26 October 1952, as *Crusader* lay at anchor some 10,000 yards off the coast, one mile south of Sonjin. She had been there for some time seeing and doing very little, and was due to weigh anchor at 0600. Shortly after 0120, Lt. F. Copas, RCN, the gunnery officer, spotted a train as it emerged from a tunnel. He was elated and immediately alerted the gun crews, gave pointer directions and told them to commence firing.

The 4.7-inch guns roared into action. Two direct hits were verified as the last two cars were seen to topple off the track into the ravine below. A spotter aircraft confirmed the hits the following morning.[2] While not sufficient to gain membership into the club, this caused some excitement within the ship. They were particularly pleased with their shooting at such extreme range.

The following night *Crusader* was once again on that station. The night was clear, brightened by a full moon. The sea was dead calm. The ship's captain, Cdr. John H. Bovey, DSC, RCN, took the ship to within approximately 3,000 yards of the coast and dropped anchor. The crew went to action stations to wait. At 2020, a long train was sighted steaming in a southerly direction. Southbound trains were considered true prizes, usually being laden with supplies, ammunition or troops. Northbound trains were usually empty. *Crusader*'s first broadside toppled several cars and the train came to a dead stop. The second and third salvos hit near the front of the train, obscuring the engine in smoke and dust. When the smoke cleared, the engine was gone. Obviously the trainmen had managed to uncouple it and hightail it into the tunnel. Once again *Crusader*'s bid for membership had been thwarted. More in disappointment than in anger, the gunners spent several hours placing carefully aimed shots into the remaining cars and coaches. By midnight none remained.

At first light a spotter plane was dispatched from a nearby carrier to assess the damage. The pilot prefaced his remarks with the news that the engine was lying on its side on the far side of the track. Far from having escaped, it had been knocked over the edge into the ravine below. *Crusader* had joined the club.

With their spirits high but fuel tanks low, the happy sailors took their ship in search of an oiler. The hope was to refuel quickly, then return to Sonjin before the morning was gone and be free to search for trains for the remainder of the day. It was not to be. While at the refuelling station orders were received which sent the ship back to the west coast. She would not return until the following April.

No RCN ship saw the east coast until December, when *Haida* was sent over. Her crew then began to think about trains and a place in the TBC. Of all the ships that have served in the RCN, *Haida* was the one which garnered the most glory, served in the most theatres of war and saw the most action. During her career, *Haida* did everything a small warship could be expected to do, and seemed destined for honours in excess of her share. Yet she earned them all, her various crews working her as well as any crews ever worked any ship.

Her crew in 1952 were well aware of their ship's history, and they were determined to make Korea a prominent page of that book. *Haida* had arrived late in the war, however, on 6 November 1952 when the sea action was already waning. It was therefore imperative that *Haida* join the Trainbusters Club, if only to add one item more to her list of accomplishments.

The opportunity came at 0300 19 December[3] near Sonjin, but was lost when the engine escaped. Her gunners contented themselves with pounding the remainder of the train, but their hearts were not fully in it. They left most of the cars standing as a gift to USS *The Sullivans*[4] when that ship came on the scene at 0516. *Haida's* crew felt their chances of joining the TBC had slipped away with the escaped engine. The ship was due to head for Sasebo within a few hours, and was then to proceed to the west coast for a lengthy patrol.[5]

With *Haida's* departure the east coast was devoid of RCN ships, and would remain so until the following February, when *Athabaskan* joined TG 77. That task force was not involved in trainbusting, so *Athabaskan* had no opportunity to exercise her gunners' skills in that way. *Haida*, however, returned in late March, slated for a two-week patrol. During that time only a single engine was seen and fired on. But the range was too long and once again the ship went away empty-handed.

Crusader, the sole RCN member of the TBC to date, was reassigned to TF 95 and put on the coveted train-watch near Tanch'on. Ordered to remain on station until relieved, she arrived at 1400 and anchored not far offshore.

At 0400 the following morning, 15 April, a train of fifteen cars was spotted as it proceeded slowly along a twisting track, running without lights. All guns were brought to bear and the first salvo stopped the train on a high trestle. Scurrying frantically, the train's crewmen managed to unhook the engine and escape with it into a nearby tunnel. *Crusader*, no longer obsessed with engines, stayed until 0700, systematically picking the train apart car by car. Then she made a quick run to a nearby oiler to refuel. Returning, she dropped her hook and settled down to await another train.

At 1630 another train chugged into sight, but it was far beyond the guns' range. Commander Bovey, after consulting with Lieutenant Copas, felt an attempt should be made. He moved the ship as close to shore as safety would allow, but even then the train was estimated to be at 13,000 yards, a great distance for the destroyer's guns. Distance and elevation were carefully checked. Satisfied that a shot could be effectively made, Lieutenant Copas ordered the firing of one salvo. The shot went high, so new settings were made. The next two shots were direct hits. The train ground to a halt, its engine derailed and several cars blown off the track.

As that train was not about to go anywhere, the guns were brought to bear on a second train which had been spotted. One shot was fired. The shell slammed into the engine, a direct hit. Engulfed in steam and smoke the engine toppled over on its side.

For two hours *Crusader*'s guns alternated between the two victims. One of the trains had been carrying ammunition or other explosives for several cars erupted in great balls of flame. The fire quickly spread to the other cars, most which were constructed of wood. Both trains destroyed, *Crusader* returned to the scene of her early-morning kill. The crew hoped they might get a chance at another train so the lookouts kept very sharp watch as they moved southward. But the hunting had gone cold and no more trains were seen that day. *Crusader* ended the patrol on routine gunnery assignments along the Northern Patrol.

Crusader now had four trains to her credit and was declared undisputed champion of the Trainbusters Club. It was a title she was never to relinquish, though several ships would eventually tie for second place. *Crusader* was to have two more chances to better her record, but on both occasions her targets managed to escape, and after that she never saw another train. On 27 April, the ship was recalled to Sasebo, and in early May she sailed for the east coast where she made one final patrol. In June she departed for Esquimalt.

After 362 days under the UN flag, *Crusader* sailed for home on 18 June 1953, the championship firmly in her grasp and her crew rightly proud of their trophy. She had won the prize, working on a part-time basis, against other ships whose full-time employment had been that of train hunting. She had bested the others because her gunners were at their very best while working at long range.

Crusader's superb gunnery was recognized by others, a fact attested by signals the ship received from such highly ranked officers as Vice Adm. R. Briscoe, USN, Commander in Chief of Naval Forces Far East. His dispatches hail *Crusader* for "displaying the finest gunnery seen in Korea on either coast."[6]

The first signal received in *Crusader* following confirmation of her fourth kill was one from the Commander Task Force 96. His signal authorized a change of code name. *Crusader* had been designated Leadmine, but henceforth, the signal read, she was to be called Casey Jones.

* * *

The news that *Crusader* had bagged four trains took little time going around the fleet. *Haida's* crew, when they heard the news, were determined to best her record, though they knew the going would be all uphill. The odds had been made even longer by a decrease in the number of trains being seen; and there had been an increase in the number of hunters. It seemed as though every ship in the USN had been sent to the east coast in a determined bid to wrest the coveted trophy from the upstart Canadians.

Haida's sailors were not concerned by the Americans, but they did give a troubled glance at *Athabaskan*, who was also due for an east coast assignment. If she got a head start she could open a gap which might prove insurmountable. They brooded about the situation as they prowled among the rocks and islets of the west coast. Then, on 25 May, *Haida* was ordered to the east coast.

On 26 May at 2215 *Haida* anchored near Tanch'on. The night was bright under clear skies. The sea was calm. Both "A" and "B" guns were closed up to action stations. The waiting began.

At 2320 a train was spotted. Mindful that the engine must be knocked completely out of action, one of the guns was trained with the accuracy of a sniping rifle directly on it. Carefully, the gun was swung to lead the engine as a seasoned duck hunter leads the bird. The gun captain pressed the red firing button, the gun roared forth, the seconds were counted and the shells found their mark.[7] The engine, hit dead centre, exploded and toppled onto its side. The trailing cars spilled along the track. *Haida* had joined the club. For the next three hours *Haida's* guns picked clean the bones of their victim. Then the happy crew took their ship into the Northern Patrol zone.

Three days later the ship was back, this time several kilometres south of Sonjin. At 2200 a train was sighted, heading north.[8] Sightings taken, all guns opened fire. A star shell revealed the train standing scant yards short of the safety afforded by a tunnel. The guns spoke once more, but the lull had given the trainmen the seconds they needed to uncouple the engine and move it into the tunnel. But *Haida* had made her two kills in one patrol, a feat few others could claim. *Haida* always managed to add a touch of class to everything she ever attempted.

Haida departed Korea for Halifax on 14 June. She made the trip via Hong Kong and the Suez Canal, thus becoming the second ship of the RCN to circumnavigate the globe.[9] She would return to Korea in 1954 as part of the Armistice Patrol.

During her single tour of duty, Canada's most celebrated warship ran up a total of six east coast and three west coast patrols. She had spent more than half of her 217 days in Korea on active patrol, had been fired on twice by shore batteries and both times destroyed her assailants. Two of her ship's company had earned honours for their service: The DSC went to her CO, Cdr. Dunn Lantier, RCN, while PO Ralph Smith earned a Mention-in-Dispatches for some superb gun-laying while downing a bridge.

* * *

With *Haida* gone and *Crusader* preparing for departure, those in *Athabaskan* began to look at the TBC. They had thought their chances of an east coast patrol slight, but on 20 June she was assigned to the Tanch'on area in command of CTU 95.2.2, arriving on 22 June. She spent two days on routine patrol and saw little action.

Throughout the patrol, however, the lookouts kept a sharp watch for trains. Because their task unit was part of TF 95, a train kill would gain them membership in the TBC. On 24 June fortune smiled on the ship. The First Watch (2000-2359) had barely begun when a train was seen. "A" gun fired two salvos. The second stopped the train in its tracks.

Visibility was poor that evening. The famed Korean fog had settled in, but the train could still be seen well enough to determine that the engine had been derailed. A signal was duly sent claiming membership in the club for *Athabaskan*. Because the train was clearly unable to proceed, the ship was moved a few miles north to undertake another mission.

When she returned at 0330 she pumped a couple more shots into the engine, which blew apart. Then a few shells were hurled into the cars. *Athabaskan* then proceeded south on a short patrol, returning at dawn to finish off the remaining rolling stock. While the gunners were finishing that task the signal welcoming them to the Trainbusters Club was received in the radio room.

On 30 June *Athabaskan* scored direct hits on a train, but it escaped into a tunnel and therefore could not be counted. The following day was Canada's birthday, at the time still designated Dominion Day. The crew celebrated by bagging their second train—this time a kill, as no tunnel was available for refuge. Now that they had two trains the possibility of a third seemed within reach; and if they could get three, *Crusader*'s four could at least be tied.

Late that afternoon a most welcome signal was received, relieving *Athabaskan* of patrol duties. Henceforth the ship was to hunt trains. The ship's company was elated, for they had sighted many trains on the downleg of the last patrol. Cdr. J. C. Reed turned his ship on a course for Tanch'on. *Crusader*, it appears, had friends among the gods. No sooner had *Athabaskan* arrived at Tanch'on than a thick fog began to settle. As the ship lay at anchor the sailors could hear trains rumbling between the tunnels, their plaintive wails frustrating the hunters as they sat at their idle guns.

Athabaskan reluctantly returned to the task force, but before she made her departure she fired a salvo blindly into the fog at a train heard but not seen. The train was heard to stop for a few minutes, then rumble on southward out of further danger. That train was the last one to come under *Athabaskan*'s guns. Later that day she was relieved by *Huron* and, after a few days in Sasebo, returned to the west coast. *Athabaskan*'s hopes for the championship had been thwarted, but she had scored two official kills, both on the same patrol, and had brought the RCN total to eight.

Athabaskan had been cheated by the fog, but the fog was not finished with its mischief. The fog was about to combine with carelessness and neglect of operational procedures to rob *Huron* of much more than a mere championship.

_____

Chapter Eighteen

ADELINE
WAS NOT
SO SWEET

We find HMCS Huron took the ground at 0038 13 July 1953.
Board of Enquiry, July 1953

O n 6 July 1953 HMCS *Huron* sailed out of Sasebo on a course for the east coast of Korea. She had already completed one patrol which had been dull and unproductive. This would be the second patrol of her second tour of duty. The ship's company was looking forward to some action that might break the monotony of what was becoming a winding-down process as the end of the war was now in sight.

Huron had arrived from Canada on 18 June but, as the first patrol would indicate, there was little left to do. The signal ordering the ship to the east coast to join Task Force 95 near Tanch'on was welcome news. The entire crew, from her skipper, Cdr. R. C. Chenoweth, MBE,CD, RCN, to the most junior seaman, was chafing under the prolonged inactivity and eager to do something. The upcoming patrol was seen as a chance to get into the Trainbusters Club, take out a bridge or two and perhaps support a commando raid.

Huron's first tour had been less than spectacular. She had arrived after the initial excitement of the war had waned and the sea war had settled into long patrols and monotonous stretches of carrier screening. She managed one patrol on the east coast and three on the west side of the peninsula. While on the east coast she had destroyed one gun battery, one train and one bridge. For the latter, CPO Reg Winter had received a Mention-in-Dispatches for gunnery.[1] While on the west coast *Huron* had captured a large junk that had been laying mines, and towed it into Inchon. There had been some routine assignments, but none had been spectacular.

Although *Huron*'s first tour had been put down as a case of rotten luck—the ship always seemed to be on the coast opposite to the one seeing the action—the crew now manning the ship was hopeful that this tour would be better. *Huron* was considered a happy ship. The crew members got along with each other and interbranch co-operation seems to have been good. The commanding officer was liked by his men. There appears to have been little friction between lower deck personnel and the officers. The lone exception was the gunnery officer, whose abrasive manners had earned him the sobriquet "Little Iodine" after an obnoxious cartoon character in *Stars and Stripes*.[2] His subsequent woes, the direct result of his own errors, produced no sympathy from his peers.

But there were no thoughts of trouble ahead as *Huron* plowed her way through the choppy waters of the Korea Strait. Only one note of sadness touched the ship that day. Her mascot, a small terrier of uncertain lineage, had disappeared while the ship was tied alongside a jetty in Sasebo. The little dog, named Bubbly after the daily tot of rum and coke, may have been unique in that he was a Canadian dog and had boarded the ship in Halifax prior to the first tour. In light of future events his disappearance may well have been an omen.[3]

On 7 July, not a minute off schedule, *Huron* appeared out of the fog near Tanch'on for her rendezvous with *Athabaskan*. The usual exchanges were made and the ships parted company. *Huron* turned on an easterly course in search of the task force.

The heavy fog remained until 11 July, when it lifted sufficiently to allow a resumption of coastal patrols. *Huron* was assigned an area coded Cadillac Two. This was a stretch which ran north and south, and was part of both the Northern Patrol and the Tail-light Patrol. Cadillac Two then was further divided into several shorter runs. One of these was Sweet Adeline, a protective patrol designed to cover the defence of Yang-Do, an island of some political value but no strategic worth.

Yang-Do was high priority. A rugged, uninhabited island with high peaks and a boulder-strewn shoreline, it had become a pawn in the ongoing peace talks being held in Panmunjom. In their belief that Yang-Do was of importance to the Chinese, the UN commanders ordered the fleet to protect the island at all times. The Chinese had sent two expeditionary forces toward the island on earlier occasions, but both groups had been chased off by the patrolling ships. These raids had convinced the UN of the island's worth, so Sweet Adeline was made into a full patrol line. One ship each day was assigned to the patrol.

Sweet Adeline, a stretch of forty miles, covered the narrow strait between the island and the mainland. It was a dangerous area. *Iroquois* had been hit near there the year previously, and along the entire stretch were Chinese guns in great numbers.

Huron, having drawn the patrol for 12 July, spent the entire day steaming back and forth along the route. Because the day was a Sunday, the ship's routine was slightly relaxed. The weather had remained reasonably tolerable with fog just thick enough to thwart the shore batteries, yet not too heavy to make sailing dangerous. All that day and into the night *Huron* plied the circuitous route—WSW on a heading of 230 degrees to the south end of the patrol line then a sharp turnabout to the reciprocal heading of ENE 50 degrees. In the dying minutes of 12 July, the First Watch gave way to the Middle Watch. *Huron's* log duly notes the changes of watchkeepers and mentions the weather as deteriorating, with increasing fog and wave action. Not recorded is either the ship's speed or its course, an oversight which would prove costly to the 1st OOW, Lieutenant Commander Thomas, RCN.

Because the fog had thickened, Thomas, upon taking over the watch, ordered speed reduced to twelve knots. He then sent S/Lt. E. P. Webb, the 3d OOW, below to the operations room to check on several items. On his return to the bridge, Webb reported to Thomas that the radar readings supported the compass readings. The course was then logged, tardily, as 230 degrees and the time of log entry marked as 0015.

At 0018, Lt. G. H. Emerson, the ship's gunnery officer, called the bridge from his duty station in the operations room. As 2nd OOW he was responsible for setting the ship's course from the radar readings. Emerson informed Thomas that the end of the patrol line had been reached and the ship should be turned to a heading of 050 degrees. This was done at once, but again the time of change of course was not entered in the log. As the ship was making its turn, Thomas left the bridge, made his way down to the operations room and spoke briefly with his 2nd OOW. He then returned topside.

Thomas was no sooner on the bridge when Emerson called up, requesting an immediate change of course to 030 degrees. A twenty-degree change in course made no sense to Thomas, who asked Emerson for his reasons for wanting to change course. Thomas, from experience, knew 050 degrees was the correct heading, that a change to 30 degrees would put the ship on line with the island which, though he could not see it through the thick fog, he knew had to be close. Visibility at that moment was no better than one cable, about 608 feet. Emerson, however, insisted the course-change was necessary. The ship, he stated, was running inside the track. Thomas ordered the change and the helm was turned to 030 degrees. The change was noted in the log, as was the time.

Meanwhile, in the operations room, the HDWS radar operator noted with alarm that the ship was turning. He immediately reported to Emerson that land was bearing dead ahead at a distance of less than a kilometre. By his reckoning *Huron* was within 2500 feet of Yang-Do and closing at twelve knots. The distance would be covered in less than three minutes. Emerson ignored the radar operator's warning, but did look at the screen. He then ordered the operator to range on a point of land about three-quarters of a mile distant, returned to his chart table, picked up a comic book and leaned back to read. The course of 030 degrees was maintained.

While the radar operator was trying to convince Emerson that *Huron* was in danger, the ASDIC operator suddenly detected the presence of solid ground directly in the path of the ship. At the same time two lookouts and two officers on the bridge saw the island looming out of the fog, dead ahead. The rocky shore was already under the bows. The high cliffs towered above the ship. None of the horrified men had a chance to shout a warning. At 0038, 13 July 1953 *Huron* took the ground on the rocky shore of Yang-Do at a speed of twelve knots. For her the war had ended.

* * *

At the moment of grounding only six men aboard the warship knew what had happened—the radar operator, the ASDIC operator, the two lookouts and the two officers on the bridge. Within seconds the hapless Lieutenant Emerson also realized his ship had gone aground. He rose unsteadily to his feet, turned to stare at the radar screen and realized his world was about to change dramatically.

The remainder of the ship's company, most of whom had been sleeping, had no way of knowing what had happened. The absence of explosions told them the ship had not hit a mine or taken hits from the shore batteries. They tumbled from their hammocks to find out what had happened. Those in the lower compartments scrambled up the ladders, trampling on feet and fingers in their haste. These minor mishaps caused sharp exchanges in the semi-darkness. A signalman, whose habit it was to sleep in the nude, got all the way up the ladder before he realized he had not had the presence of mind to don some appropriate clothing. His efforts to descend the ladder against the upward flow of traffic brought him much verbal abuse.

Within a few minutes the ship's precarious position became obvious. Being hard aground was serious enough, but should the fog lift with the dawn the ship would be a stationary target for the shore batteries. There were eight known gun emplacements within the range of the ship and *Huron*, being unable to move, would be blown apart by the artillery ashore.

The shore guns were only part of *Huron*'s problems. The hull of a Tribal Class destroyer was not thick, and the successful refloating of the ship hinged on the condition of her hull, in particular the forward plates. The ship's forward section was high and dry, making inspection a simple matter. A party of damage control specialists was lowered over the side to the beach below. What they saw was not encouraging. Approximately ninety feet of the lower hull had been holed or fractured. Several plates along the lower compartments had buckled and loosened. Fearing the lower compartments would flood, these were emptied at once and the hatches dogged tightly.

In order to lighten the forward section of the ship all ammunition was removed from "A" and "B" magazines. The Bofors magazines were also emptied, as were the contents of the forward freezers and storage lockers. This weight was shifted to the stern. The two anchors and their cables were slipped, and may well remain to this day conversation pieces for visiting fishermen. The task of moving the ammunition and stores was not easy, and took the better part of ten hours. Fortunately the fog remained as thick as it had ever been concealing from the Chinese what was taking place beneath the muzzles of their guns.

At 1005 a tug appeared in answer to *Huron*'s signal for assistance, and the combined power of both ships finally pulled *Huron* into the water and uncertain safety. No one was certain that the ship would remain afloat. It was a nervous crew that turned her bows into the choppy waters. Within seconds the sailors knew their ship would be unable to proceed in a normal fashion. The forward motion of the ship was causing the weakened plates to strain alarmingly. Several began to flap in the waves' action. Her only remaining option was to proceed by the stern. Mile after desperate mile, the wounded ship made her way toward Japan at an agonizing pace of three knots. Steaming in reverse was not only slow, it caused other problems. Those on the bridge and forecastle were engulfed by smoke from the funnels.

199

During the second day a floating dry dock appeared, but it proved to be of no use. The ASDIC arm had been extended when the ship struck the ground and had bent on impact. It could not be retracted and the ship, therefore, could not enter the dry dock. All efforts to cut away the arm were unsuccessful. Despite the best efforts of skilled technicians from the three ships, nothing could be done to help the crippled ship into the safe confines of the dry dock. After many hours of frustration a halt was called. The unusual armada continued the voyage southward at three knots.[4]

On 20 July, seven days after taking the ground, *Huron* arrived at Sasebo. She immediately went into dry dock for complete evaluation of her damages. Damage proved to be more extensive than originally thought. The ship was to remain in dry dock until 25 October. During that time the armistice which brought an uneasy peace to Korea was signed, the islands north of the 38th parallel were turned over to the North Koreans after their population was evacuated and *Huron*'s captain and two of his officers became the principal players in an enquiry into the grounding. (See Appendix J for excerpts from the enquiry.)

The enquiry found that *Huron* had gone aground owing to errors in pilotage, in circumstances that could not be re-established because no record had been kept. It also appeared that a number of normal bridge and operations room procedures had been ignored, especially as respected navigational aids. After two days deliberation, the Board recommended that disciplinary action be taken against all three officers, in particular the 2d OOW. The three were returned to Halifax within days.

On 21 September Cdr. T. C. Pullen arrived from Canada to assume command of *Huron*, which remained with the UN fleet until 5 February 1954. On that date she sailed for Halifax via Hong Kong and the Suez Canal. The misfortune which had plagued the ship in Korea played one last trick on *Huron* on the way home. As she was negotiating a difficult turn in the Suez Canal, a sudden gust of wind caught the ship, and before anyone could react, her bows grounded on the sandy bank. She was freed without trouble, but her crew had a fleeting moment of deja vu.

Huron returned to Halifax on 17 March to a quiet reception by a small group of friends and relatives. The boisterous crowds of earlier days, when the ships' returns were treated as gala events, were now part of the past. The war in Korea had ended and was already being forgotten.

Chapter Nineteen

CEASE-FIRE!
CHECK ALL GUNS

The word of peace is rendered. Hark, how they shout.
Shakespeare, *King Henry IV, Part II*

Throughout 1952, while the situation at sea remained steady, the land forces saw the various fronts change several times. The truce talks (the site was changed to Panmunjom in 1952) dragged on with neither side willing to compromise. For that matter the negotiators had wasted weeks arguing about such ridiculous items as the height of the flagpoles, and whether the negotiation tables should be round, square or oval. The Chinese, masters at the game of patience, toyed with the frustrated westerners, who time and time again walked into the little traps set by the highly amused Chinese. This pleased the Chinese and provided them with the confidence they had lacked at the first round of talks.

Among numerous stumbling blocks, the thorniest was the disposition of prisoners of war. The UN held thousands of North Korean and Chinese soldiers in the camps on Koje-Do and elsewhere. Many of the POWs had no desire to return home. The Reds, naturally, wanted all of them returned. That issue burned on and on.

Syngman Rhee, having had his share of Korea returned to his control, became belligerent both toward the Chinese and his UN allies. In an unwise speech Rhee announced that South Korea would fight on, alone if necessary. Fighting alone was the one thing South Korea was in no condition even to consider, but the statement set the talks back several days. Rhee's ridiculous speech was no sooner smoothed over when, in an action which outraged both the Chinese and the UN, he released some ten thousand POWs from camps under ROK control. This came close to scuttling the talks completely, but the negotiators were told to struggle on and work something out.[1]

From a UN point of view, a binding armistice was imperative. Time was beginning to run out on the alliance of nations which had troops in Korea. International interest in the war had begun to wane; contributing nations wanted to withdraw their soldiers and sailors. China also wanted out, for Peking could see their troops were getting the worst of it. As the fighting had come to a stalemate, everyone knew it was time to call a halt. Those with a sense of history saw Korea as likely to become another Flanders, with thousands of troops bogged down in the grinding siege of trench warfare. Only the feisty Rhee, who was beginning to see himself as the saviour of Asia, continued to place obstacles in the path of progress.

Finally an agreement acceptable to both sides was hammered out. It would not bring the war to an unconditional conclusion (to this day the Korean War is not officially ended), but it was enough to ensure peace if both sides would abide by the terms. The document provided enough security for South Korea that UN troops would be able to leave within a reasonable time, without the likelihood of having to return. This was most important, since there was little chance that contributing nations would resume a war already over.

Hostilities, the document stated, would cease on 27 July 1953 at 1000. The troops along the fronts would then withdraw, leaving a strip of vacant land across the width of the country. Two and one-half miles wide, it was marked on all maps as the Demilitarized Zone (DMZ). This zone was then divided into two equal strips marked on all maps by a line called the Military Demarcation Line (MDL). A time limit of three days, later extended, was set for the dismantling of gun emplacements and bunkers and the removal of personnel and equipment.

As a condition of the armistice, North Korea was to regain possession of the offshore islands north of the 38th parallel on both coasts. Those who lived on the islands, however, were to be allowed the opportunity to go to South Korea if they desired. A period of ten days was agreed as being sufficient for the evacuation of these islands.

Iroquois was assigned to the task group responsible for clearing the west coast islands. She was responsible for Cho-Do, Sok-To and several of the Chorusan Island group. She was the only RCN ship so assigned, as *Huron* was still in dry dock and *Athabaskan* was helping to monitor the withdrawal of Chinese troops from the ports and islands ceded to South Korea.

In the pre-dawn hours of 1 August, *Iroquois* landed a team of explosives experts on Cho-Do. The team placed heavy explosive charges among the bunkers and gun sites. The few islanders who had not been evacuated earlier were gathered up and placed in waiting vessels. As dawn broke the charges were exploded, and all military installations went up in smoke. With the glow of the fires astern, *Iroquois* left the waters off Cho-Do and Sok-To, the scene of memories good and bad, for the last time. Cho-Do, while not the final assignment of the patrol, was probably the most memorable.[2]

As *Iroquois* was moving among the islands, *Athabaskan* was scouting the coastal inlets keeping a wary eye on the Chinese as they trudged steadily northward. Five days after the armistice had been signed, she sailed for Sasebo, the only RCN ship to divide a patrol between war and peace.

Athabaskan claimed the honour of firing the final shell from a RCN warship in the Korean War. On 20 July, a week before hostilities came to an end, she bombarded Chinese positions on the mainland. Lying at anchor in the lee of Mu-Do (still in the hands of the redoubtable Wolf Pack) she spent the entire night placing shots into gun emplacements and troop encampments.[3] Returning to Sasebo on 14 August, she became the first RCN ship to serve a postwar patrol.

* * *

The armistice was at best shaky. There were well-founded fears that it might be broken, intentionally or otherwise, at any time by either side. With this in mind the UN allies agreed that no troops would be withdrawn until peace had taken a reasonably firm grip.

Some of the smaller nations began to recall their troops, but those with large numbers kept theirs at full strength. Canada had agreed to keep troops in the area for as long as required, but had tentatively decided to decrease her commitment to one battalion in Korea and either a destroyer or a frigate in Japan. It was, therefore, somewhat of a surprise when *Athabaskan* and *Iroquois* were each in turn relieved by the two veterans *Crusader* and *Cayuga*, the latter newly recommissioned and boasting a complete remodelling. Gone was her top-heavy afterstructure and she sported new, radar-controlled guns. On 18 November *Athabaskan* sailed eastward for Esquimalt, and on New Year's Day 1954, *Iroquois* headed for Halifax via Hong Kong and the Indian Ocean.

203

With no war to fight, the crews now found time to look at Korea in a different light. The patrols, confined now to the waters below the 38th parallel, became tame and routine, though the vigilance for mines remained. The ships were now free to roam farther afield, and trips to Manila as well as the ever-popular Hong Kong were allowed more frequently. Training exercises with other warships were resumed. The RCN began once more to work with USN and RN submarines in order to regain much neglected anti-submarine skills.

When in Japan the ships shunned Sasebo, whose harbour had become a sewer, and smaller, cleaner ports were visited. In his *Report of Proceedings* for August 1953, Captain Landymore summed up the sailors' feelings toward Sasebo:

> The days in Sasebo from 15 to 20 August were swelter-
> ing. The living spaces throughout the ship were never
> below 90° and were generally over 100°. The harbour,
> which is always a dirty one, surpassed its worst and was
> literally a sea of fuel oil and garbage.

During 1954 all the destroyers but *Nootka* served for varying times, but by December only *Sioux* remained. She would be the last Canadian ship to serve on the Korean patrols. On 17 August 1955, *Sioux* left Japan for home. Her departure closed the book on the Royal Canadian Navy's involvement in the Korean affair.

Chapter Twenty

THE
LAST SUNSET

Sunset, sir. Make it so.
RCN Sunset Ceremony

On 20 July 1953, HMCS *Athabaskan* became the last Canadian warship to fire a shell during the Korean war. It was also, though no one could have foreseen it at the time, the last shell to be fired in anger by any ship of the Royal Canadian Navy. Within fifteen years the fiercely proud, highly efficient and well respected naval force would be ended, not by enemy guns in battle, but by the stroke of a politician's pen.

When Bill C-243, the Canadian Forces Reorganization Act, was signed into law in 1967, the Royal Canadian Navy passed into history. Canada's navy, the act stated, would henceforth be known as Canadian Forces Maritime Command. Canada's sailors sullenly exchanged their traditional blue uniforms for green uniforms which bore no resemblance to anything seamanlike. At the same time, all ranks, titles and insignia were replaced by those of the army. Leading seamen became corporals, petty officers became sergeants and lieutenant commanders were suddenly majors. Parade drills, supply forms and trade classifications were changed to conform with those used in the army. All three services became one as unification became a fact.

Unification, to use the common term for the reorganization, struck at all three services. The Canadian army, hit less hard than the others, accepted the changes with little outcry, lamenting mainly the passing of several famed regiments. Hardest hit was the navy, nearly all of whose cherished and time-honoured traditions were scrapped.

The officers were particularly stricken, as unification meant a virtual end to their Wardroom Society, modelled lock, stock and English accent on that of the British Navy. Seemingly overnight the elitist officer corps of the RCN found itself a minority within a larger body. The smug security of the wardroom had gone, and many were unable to cope with the change. New officers coming into the navy no longer found it necessary, or even advisable, to cultivate the wardroom accent, intended to emulate the Oxford English of British gentlemen. For fifty years the affected accent had grated on the ears of lower deck personnel. Few RCN officers had ever mastered it anyway, and now there was no longer a need to use it in order to fit into a social order perpetuated by senior officers filled with reverence for such English heroes as Drake, Nelson and Beatty.

The demise of the Wardroom Society, however welcome it may have been to lower deck sailors, proved little compensation for the overall pain of unification felt by all ranks. The navy began to resemble the army, as shipboard routine changed to accommodate the new order. The daily rum issue was replaced with a more civilized privilege—the shipboard cocktail lounge. The White Ensign was hauled down one evening, to be replaced the following morning with a flag of new design.

Many sailors could not adjust to the changes. These men left the navy in protest, taking with them a store of much needed experience. The navy quickly fell into neglect. The ships grew old and were not replaced. Repairs were delayed—at times for weeks on end—owing to lack of spare parts. By 1975, the navy had been reduced to a collection of tired warships no longer able to keep up with their NATO counterparts.

Training cruises, which once saw Canadian warships ranging from Europe to Australia and Asia, became rare. Eventually, the once commonplace home waters operations became the highlight of a sailor's routine. Morale, which even in the best of times had never been high, fell to an unprecedented low as the navy deteriorated under a series of ineffective defence ministers.

* * *

Unification was the brainchild of Paul Theodore Hellyer who, as an enlisted man, served in two of Canada's services during World War II. During his short military career, Hellyer had seen enough duplication and inefficiency to inspire a desperate resolve to make some corrections should the opportunity ever present itself.

Hellyer had joined the RCAF during the war in the hopes of becoming a flier. He completed the rigors of basic training, but before he could be sent to flight school the end of the war was in sight. Those who were in the program were to be released into civilian life. They were, however, informed they would be welcome to apply for entry into the Canadian Army if they so desired.

Hellyer (and some 4,000 others) applied for transfer to the army, and at this point discovered how ludicrous the military system could be. Transfer was not possible between the services. The RCAF would first have to release the men to civilian status, from which they could apply for enlistment in the army. The army would then have to seek permission from the RCAF to sign them, because the men were still on the RCAF reserve list. The entire process could take weeks, perhaps months.

Hellyer, disgusted, took his RCAF discharge and applied for entry to the army. In due course the call came and he reported to the recruitment centre, where he was signed on and sworn in. Then, to his chagrin, he was told he would have to go through the army's basic training. The RCAF basic, he was told, held no status with the army as the drills were different. Then he was informed he was to be assigned to the artillery. He did not particularly wish to go to the artillery, but when he questioned the decision, he was told he had to be so assigned because his school records indicated a very high proficiency in mathematics. That automatically slated him for a career as a gunner. It mattered not what he might want; he was good at math and that meant he would be a gunner.

It is hardly surprising that, upon his final re-entry into civilian life at war's end, Lance Corporal Hellyer had endured his full limit of military stupidity. His sentiments were shared by thousands, but he was determined to do something about it. With just that in mind he entered the world of politics, and from the moment of his first victory at the polls, a collision course was charted which would make the navy the victim of this misguided concept of military reform.

* * *

The navy's eventual woes were nowhere in evidence in 1955, when *Sioux* left Korea for the last time. Indeed, the navy's future looked bright. Korea had alerted the Western world to Russia's aims in global affairs. In alarm many nations began to intensify their defence capabilities. The Canadian government announced its intention of increasing Canada's forces and moved quickly to that end.

In its publication of 14 June 1952, the *Financial Post* printed an article which forecast substantial increases in the size of the RCN.

From a force of 26 ships and 18,000 men, the paper noted, the navy would be expanded to 100 ships and a proportionate number of sailors. The navy rejoiced. When Ottawa made the speculation official the RCN moved at top speed to comply.

By 1953, the first of the new destroyers, the ultra-modern, Canadian-designed *St. Laurent* had been completed, romped through her sea trials with ease and took her place as the pride of the fleet. In rapid succession more ships of her class were built and commissioned. By the time *Sioux* came home six new ships were in service. The future looked bright.

Then, in 1957, the Liberal government was swept away in the landslide victory of John Diefenbaker's Conservatives. An immediate halt was called to all existing construction of warships. With a long way to go to its total of one hundred ships, the RCN hove to and prepared to ride out the doldrums. For the next six years, dreams of expansion remained a faint hope, but at least the six new ships were among the world's best.

In 1963, Lester B. Pearson led the Liberals back into power with a small majority. As the Liberals had traditionally been good to the navy, hopes for expansion arose once more. Then suddenly, like a spent candle, the flame of hope was snuffed out. Hellyer was named Minister of National Defence. The once-upon-a-time corporal, now the boss of all three forces, laid into his former employers with a vengeance. Within weeks the RCN's long-awaited expansion program was cancelled outright. The army was refused its request for new personnel carriers. The RCAF was told to forget about replacement planes. There began to seep down from high places rumours of a complete overhaul of the forces. The three forces were to become one: one chief of staff, one postal service, one supply branch. The forces recoiled in horror.

The day Hellyer had been sworn into office, unease had been felt by the generals and admirals. He was the first to hold that office who had not been a serving officer. Also, he was very young. The generals and the admirals, however, reasoned that because he had never gone higher in the ranks than that of lance corporal, he would probably retain the feeling of subservience he had known in the army. What the generals and admirals failed to consider was the age-old disdain most lower ranks have always felt for the Brass. Rarely have privates or ordinary seamen looked on their officers as being second only to God. The new DND minister soon made it perfectly clear he held no general or admiral in awe.

In March 1964, a new policy was formally announced to the House of Commons, and on 16 July a White Paper was introduced which spelled out in detail the plans to integrate the forces. The long, often bitter, journey to unification had begun officially.

Before the White Paper had been presented, changes had already been made which had effectively stopped most of the duplication and modified many of the regulations which Hellyer had so despised. Had he stopped at that point he would have achieved his primary goal as those changes had actually been welcomed. But he moved relentlessly into what would become known as Hellyer's Folly.

In 1966, when Hellyer made a speech in the House of Commons detailing the final plans for unification, the mood within the RCAF and the RCN turned ugly. His announcement meant, purely and simply, the end of the two services as separate entities. There were cries of outrage from many quarters both inside and outside the services. The officers who had already left voluntarily or, like Jeffry Brock, had been forced into early retirement, rallied much opposition. For a while they appeared to have considerable support.

As with all bills tabled in the House which receive second reading, C-243 went to committee (the Standing Committee on National Defence) for clause-by-clause study. There began a long scrutiny of the proposed legislation. Over many months the committee called on former and serving members of the Armed Forces for their views. Long, often bitter, debates raged, but in the end the committee returned Bill C-243 to the House for its third and final reading.

The committee, ironically, had been chaired for many of its early sessions by David Groos, the Liberal member for Victoria. Groos had retired from the RCN a few years previously with the rank of captain and had entered political life. Many felt his connections with the RCN would move him to support the views of his former colleagues. His conduct as chairman proved quite the opposite. Dedicated as he was to the party line, he could not quarrel with official policy. No doubt he suffered the angst of mixed emotions from time to time, but even after ill-health forced him to resign his seat and return to private life, he never said a word in support of his former friends or the navy which had been his life's career.

Hellyer, confident of success, spent the months of committee hearings weeding out those he deemed in opposition to unification and bestowing promotion on those who supported it. In July 1966, Hellyer retired Rear Admiral Landymore, who had risen to the position of Flag Officer Atlantic. He justified this unpopular move by citing Landymore's opposition to unification. It was the same justification he had used in retiring Brock two years earlier. In firing Landymore, Hellyer finalized the intention he had harboured since

1965 when Landymore told the committee the minister had censored a statement he wished to make.

Hellyer, in reply to reporters' questions at the time, called Landymore's statement "insubordinate." Several months later he once again referred to the insubordination of the admiral, but this time he unwisely termed it as "consistent disloyalty." He almost immediately retracted his ill-chosen words, but the slur on a gallant Canadian enraged a number of people, many of them prominent Liberals. Landymore, no longer able to remain stoically quiet, went public. In an article published in *Macleans* (September 1966), he warned of the dangers in Hellyer's concept of defence planning. The article was the admiral's parting broadside.

With Landymore out of his way, virtually no one was left within the RCN who could offer resistance. Those who remained were content to live with the situation, although many, once they had reached the safe harbour of retirement, spoke out in retrospect.

Opposition within the House of Commons did grow loud enough to force Pearson to come to the defence of Hellyer. Unification, he told the House, was government policy and not the singular wish of Paul Hellyer. He went on the say the bill would not be amended or negotiated further. He reminded the loyal opposition that they would have the opportunity to vote on it and, if they could, defeat it. The government, he said flatly, was willing to take the issue to the voters if necessary. Pearson's challenge went unanswered. None within the ranks of opposition wanted to risk an election on a military issue, and Hellyer rushed Bill C-243 to the House for final reading. It was passed without much comment.

Unification, after twenty-four years, has not been the resounding success Hellyer dreamed it would be. Time and world affairs may give a final—perhaps fatal—answer. Arguments still persist as to its effectiveness. The sorry state of Canada's navy presents the strongest case against Hellyer's Folly.

Those who were overlooked in all the emotion and outcry over the case of unification were the ordinary servicemen. While admirals, generals and air marshalls wrangled with politicians over the status of the nation's defences, those in the ranks were ignored. They were rarely asked for an opinion. They could have contributed to a worthwhile degree had they been consulted, even obliquely. They would have mentioned their desire for a distinctly Canadian identity and, had unification promised them that, they might well have favoured the idea.

In all her wars Canada has sent her sailors, airmen and soldiers into battle as part of British forces. Even in Korea the Canadians found themselves part of the Commonwealth Force—and it was dominated by the British. Canadian services were patterned after Britain's. The only distinguishing features were the shoulder-flashes on the uniforms and, in the RCN's case, a red Maple Leaf on the ships' funnels. At sea they were usually mistaken for RN ships because of the White Ensign they flew.

The loudest lament heard from Canadian sailors in Korea was no louder, or different, than those of other sailors in other wars. The question of identity had never been solved or even properly addressed. The RCN always pushed it aside until it could no longer be ignored. Then a few minor changes would be made, mainly to uniform design, and the laments would fall silent for awhile.

By 1953, so many sailors were leaving the navy that Ottawa was moved to initiate a survey to determine the reasons. The results of that survey fill several boxes in the archives. They show that the sailors simply felt the RCN was still too British. Young men from all across Canada had joined the RCN in the years following the Second World War, seeking to serve their country in a Canadian navy, only to discover early in basic training that Canada's navy was really only a poor imitation of the Royal Navy. The survey begun in 1953, however, moved the navy to contemplate some changes. But by the time it got around to giving serious thought to those changes it was too late. The RCN had ceased to exist.

Paul Hellyer perhaps had the idea of a national identity in mind when he conceived his monster. Unification did bring about a sort of identity. It was, however, neither suitable, acceptable nor workable. Sailors dressed in green are out of keeping with the sea upon which they sail. Airmen in green clash with the skies in which they fly. Soldiers in green do not blend well with the soil they defend.

Lately much has been done to offset many of the disadvantages which unification brought to Canada's armed forces. Not the least is a long-overdue return to the traditional colours for the individual services' uniforms. At long last, steps are being taken to update the navy's fleet of aged ships. Fortunately, nothing is being contemplated which would return the navy to the days and style of the RCN.

Any such move would be regrettable. A return to the old navy would unlikely be acceptable to those presently in the navy. The RCN of World War II and Korea is gone, along with the ships from that era. Few of the men who served in the RCN still go to sea. Only memories remain. As it is with most memories, the good times, the exciting times, the happy times are the ones recalled. The hard times, the dangerous times, the bad times are forgotten, and that is the way it should be.

Chapter Twenty-One

RETROSPECT

From July 1950 to July 1953, the period of actual fighting, 3,621 officers and ratings saw active service aboard eight destroyers. Since a good many of the men served more than one tour of duty, the total in equivalence would have numbered 4,269 men. The eight ships served a total of fifteen single tours. To August 1955, when the last ship went home, the ships had performed twenty-one single tours, and more than 6,000 sailors had served.

The RCN expended more than 130,000 rounds of ammunition, not including small arms and machine-guns. Sixty-two medals were bestowed on twenty-six ratings and twenty-four officers. Nine sailors died—three by enemy gunfire, three lost at sea, two as a result of a vehicle mishap, and one while undergoing surgery.

These are impressive figures when one realizes the RCN drew its men from a force which numbered less than 25,000 men at any given time. Of the eleven ships in the RCN destroyer fleet during those five years only *Micmac, Crescent* and *Algonquin* saw no Korean service.

With the passage of time, events in history tend to become clouded. Records are mislaid. Memories fade. Also the question of worth arises. After three decades, the subject of Canadian involvement in Korea raises that question. That the war wasted thousands of lives and affected many more is not in doubt. Some recent movies and television programs (in particular the popular series "M*A*S*H") attempt to portray the Korean conflict as a massive blunder by those who participated. Others seek to compare the Korean intervention by the UN with the American involvement in Viet Nam. Korea was never like Viet Nam. The war in Viet Nam was against outside forces who sought to dominate. The Korean War was perpetrated by Koreans against Koreans.

Because the Korean outcome was ultimately a stalemate with a return to the status quo of 24 June 1950, and because forty years later the situation is still not resolved, it is easy to be critical of the UN action. It is equally easy to find grounds for its defence. Had the UN ignored the call for aid to South Korea, it is unlikely the U.S. would have chosen to fight alone, and the South Koreans could never have withstood the North Korean onslaught. It is doubtful if the average Korean peasant would have cared about such a turn of events beyond the initial shock of coming under Communist rule. Politics was not high on his list of priorities. The average Korean would probably have preferred a loaf of bread on his table each day over a chance to vote for Syngman Rhee once every four years.

Those who served in Korea have, understandably, a different view of the campaign from those who were not there. Most of them feel the Korean action was worthwhile. They know it was a stopgap measure, a wall that delayed—at least temporarily—the resolute advance of Communist influence in Asia. Had the UN turned its back on South Korea, the Reds could well have used the peninsula as a stepping stone to Japan.

To the members of the Royal Canadian Navy who served in Korea the UN action was, in general, considered justifiable. None who saw the poor villagers on the west coast islands and witnessed their suffering could likely be convinced to the contrary.

For those who served, it became a sore point that Canada's leaders—the very ones who had sent them in the first place— never saw the war as being anything other than a police action. To those who served in *Iroquois* the shells that struck down their shipmates were instruments of war.

What chafed the sailors most was the lack of recognition of the Korea veterans during the annual Armistice Day ceremonies. That slight was not rectified for many years, despite pressure from such organizations as the Royal Canadian Legion, the Naval Veterans' Association and the Korea Veterans' Association. Finally, in 1982, twenty-nine years after the last shell was fired, proper recognition was bestowed upon those who had served there. That year the Silver Star Mother (selected from among Canadian women who have lost sons in battle) was one whose son had been killed in action in Korea. Recognition, however late, had come.

The ships of those days are gone, and the men who sailed in them no longer go to sea. Of all those proud destroyers only one, *Haida*, remains afloat. *Haida*, fittingly, is now a permanent naval museum filled with the artifacts and mementos of a proud navy. She lies alongside a jetty in Haida Basin as part of Toronto's Ontario Place. Each year thousands of visitors walk her decks, peer into compartments and rooms and admire her 4-inch guns, while children clamber about within the housings and line up patiently to await a turn at sitting in the gunner's chair. The Bofors point skyward as if still expecting hostile aircraft. Many of those who visit *Haida* are former members of the RCN. They all take a moment or two to pause in silent reflection upon those distant days.

Of the seven other ships, only memories remain. Three—*Huron, Iroquois* and *Athabaskan*—bequeathed their names and battle records to others which are still in service. It is hoped that future ships will bear the names of *Cayuga, Sioux, Nootka* and *Crusader*.

Certainly they deserve as much.

APPENDIX A

DIMENSIONS AND ARMAMENT OF THE DESTROYERS

	DIMENSIONS/TONNAGE							ARMAMENT
SHIP/NO.	WT.	L.	W	MAIN	#	SEC.	#	ANTI-SUBMARINE
NOOTKA 213	2745	377'	37'6"	4"	6	40mm	8	4-21" torpedo tubes 6 Squid Mortars Depth Charges
HAIDA 215	2745	377'	37'6"	4"	6	40mm	8	4-21" torpedo tubes 6 Squid Mortars Depth Charges
HURON 216	2745	377'	37'6"	4"	6	40mm	8	4-21" torpedo tubes 6 Squid Mortars Depth Charges
IROQUOIS 217	2745	377'	37'6"	4"	6	40mm	8	4-21" torpedo tubes 6 Squid Mortars Depth Charges
CAYUGA 218	2745	377'	37'6"	4"	6	40mm	8	4-21" torpedo tubes 6 Squid Mortars Depth Charges
ATHABASKAN 219	2745	377'	37'6"	4"	6	40mm	8	4-21" torpedo tubes 6 Squid Mortars Depth Charges
SIOUX 225	2530	362'	37'6"	4.7"	2	40mm 20mm	4 2	4-21" torpedo tubes 6 Squid Mortars Depth Charges
CRUSADER 228	2500	362'	37'6"	4.5"	4	40mm	6	4-21" torpedo tubes Hedgehog Depth Charges

APPENDIX B

FINAL DISPOSITION OF RCN SHIPS
THAT SERVED IN KOREA 1950 - 1955

NAME	NO.	BUILDER	FIRST COMMISSION	FINAL DECOMMISSION	FINAL DISPOSITION
ATHABASKAN	219	Halifax Shipyards Limited, Halifax	20-01-48 at Halifax	1-04-66 at Halifax	Broken up in 1970 at La Spezia, Italy
NOOTKA	213	Halifax Shipyards Halifax	20-08-46 at Halifax	06-02-64 at Halifax	Broken up in 1965 at Faslane, Scotland
HAIDA	215	Vickers-Armstrong, England	30-08-43 at Newcastle	11-10-63 at Sydney, Nova Scotia	Permanent Naval Museum, Toronto, Ontario
HURON	216	Vickers-Armstrong, England	19-07-43 at Newcastle	30-04-63 at Halifax	Broken up in 1965 at La Spezia
IROQUOIS	217	Vickers-Armstrong, England	30-11-42 at Newcastle	24-10-62 at Halifax	Broken up in 1966 at Bilbao, Spain
CAYUGA	218	Halifax Shipyards	19-10-47 at Halifax	27-02-64 at Halifax	Broken up in 1964 at Faslane
SIOUX	225	J. Samuel White Co., Isle of Wight	21-02-44 at Cowes.	13-10-63 at Esquimalt	Broken up in 1965 at La Spezia
CRUSADER	228	John Brown Limited Scotland	15-11-45 at Glasgow	15-01-60 at Esquimalt	Scrapped in 1963 at Victoria, B.C.

APPENDIX C

THE COMMAND ORGANIZATION, UN NAVAL FORCES, KOREA, 19 FEBRUARY TO 3 APRIL 1951

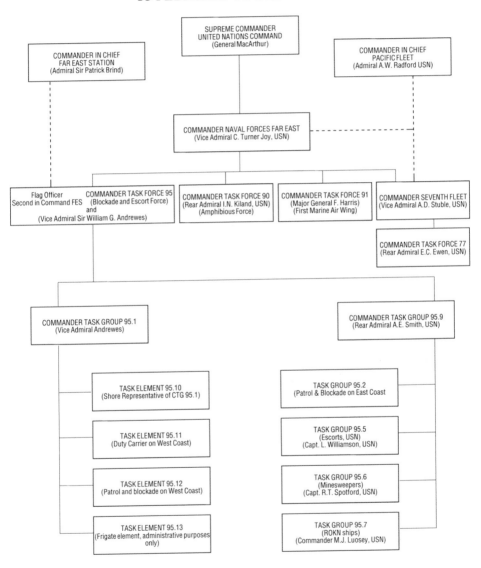

APPENDIX D

THE COMMAND ORGANIZATION, UN NAVAL FORCES, KOREA, 10 APRIL 1951

(Simplified Diagram)

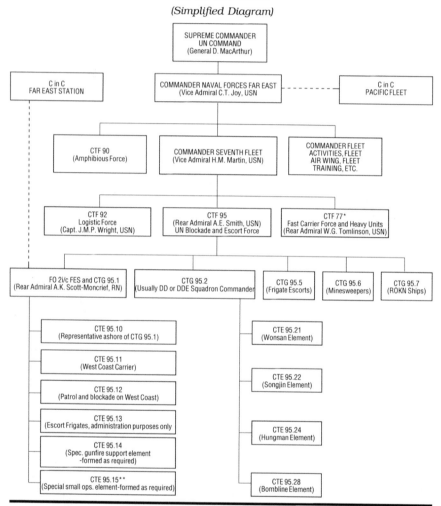

*TF77'S commander changed each time the senior officer's carrier was relieved. In the 37 months of the war there were 56 changes of command. This involved 13 rear admirals.

**TE95.16 was occasionally formed when extra minesweepers were sent to TG95.1. The ships usually kept the element number assigned by the commander of TG95.6.

APPENDIX E

MEDALS, HONOURS AND AWARDS PRESENTED TO
RCN PERSONNEL WHO SERVED IN KOREA FROM 1950 - 1955

Names are listed alphabetically, and the rank given is that held at the time of award being earned.

DISTINGUISHED SERVICE ORDER
Captain Jeffry V. Brock	Cayuga

ORDER OF THE BRITISH EMPIRE (MILITARY DIVISION)
Captain William M. Landymore	Iroquois
Commander James Plomer	Cayuga
Commander John C. Reed	Athabaskan

BAR TO THE DISTINGUISHED SERVICE CROSS
Commander Robert P. Welland	Athabaskan

DISTINGUISHED SERVICE CROSS
Lt. Commander John H. Bovey	Crusader
Lt. Andrew L. Collier	Cayuga
Captain Dudley G. King	Athabaskan
Commander Dunn Lantier	Haida
Commander Edward T.G. Madgwick	Huron
Lt. Commander Donald R. Saxon	Cayuga
Commander Richard M. Steele	Nootka
Commander Paul D. Taylor	Sioux
Lieutenant Douglas F. Tutte	Iroquois

DISTINGUISHED SERVICE MEDAL
CPO Albert L. Bonner	Nootka
Leading Seaman Gerald E. Jamieson	Iroquois

BRITISH EMPIRE MEDAL (MILITARY DIVISION)
CPO Douglas J. Pearson	Cayuga
PO Edward H. Randall	Nootka
PO Thomas Shields	Athabaskan
CPO George C. Vander-Haegen	Athabaskan

MENTIONED-IN-DISPATCHES
Lieutenant Nelson R. Banfield	Sioux
Captain Jeffry V. Brock	Cayuga
CPO Harry E. Brown	Cayuga
CPO Lennox Clark	Athabaskan
CPO Ralph E. Davies	Cayuga
CPO Edward V. Dear	Athabaskan
CPO Frederick C. Emmerson	Nootka
CPO Frederick Ewald	Crusader

PO Joseph E. Fortin	Iroquois
Commander Alexander B. F. Fraser-Harris	Nootka
Lieutenant Gerald J. Giroux	Athabaskan
CPO Alfred Gold	Crusader
Commissioned Gunner (TAS) David W. Hurl	Athabaskan
Captain William M. Landymore	Iroquois
CPO Joseph E. Leary	Nootka
CPO John L. Meads	Crusader
Lieutenant Paul L. McCulloch	Athabaskan
CPO Henry C. Morgan	Athabaskan
CPO William D. Moyes	Athabaskan
Lt. Commander John L. Quinn (posthumous)	Iroquois
Leading Seaman William J. Roberts	Cayuga
Lt. Commander Frank P.R. Saunders	Nootka
PO Samuel H. Shaw	Athabaskan
CPO John T. Shea	Athabaskan
Lt. Commander Harry Shorten	Athabaskan
PO Ralph Smith	Haida
Able Seaman James G. Stewart	Crusader
Commander Paul D. Taylor	Sioux
CPO George E. Vanthaaf	Sioux
Commander Robert P. Welland	Athabaskan
Surgeon Lieutenant Chris A. West	Athabaskan
CPO Richard Williams	Crusader
CPO Reginald Winter	Huron

AMERICAN AWARDS PRESENTED TO RCN PERSONNEL FOR KOREAN SERVICE

LEGION OF MERIT (DEGREE OF COMMANDER)

Commander Edward G. T. Madgwick	Huron

LEGION OF MERIT (DEGREE OF OFFICER)

Captain Jeffry V. Brock	Cayuga
Commander James Plomer	Cayuga
Commander Paul D. Taylor	Sioux
Commander Robert P. Welland	Athabaskan

LEGION OF MERIT (DEGREE OF LEGIONNAIRE)

Commander Alexander B.F. Fraser-Harris	Nootka
Commander Dudley G. King	Athabaskan

DISTINGUISHED FLYING CROSS

Lieutenant Joseph J. MacBrien	Task Group 77

BRONZE STAR MEDAL

Commander John H. G. Bovey	Crusader

APPENDIX F

COMMANDING OFFICERS OF RCN DESTROYERS IN KOREA
1950 - 1955

SHIP	COMMANDING OFFICER	TOUR
ATHABASKAN	Commander R. P. Welland, DSC and Bar, CD, RCN	1
	Commander D. G. King, DSC, CD, RCN	2
	Commander J. C. Reed, OBE, DSC, CD, RCN	3
CAYUGA	Captain J. V. Brock, DSO, DSC, CD, RCN	1
	Commander J. Plomer, OBE, DSC and Bar, CD, RCN	2
	Commander W. P. Hayes, CD, RCN	3
CRUSADER	Lt. Commander J. H. Bovey, DSC, CD, RCN	1
	Commander W. H. Willson, DSC, CD, RCN	2
SIOUX	Commander P. D. Taylor, DSC, RCN	1
	Commander P. D. Taylor, DSC, RCN	2
	Commander A. H. Rankin, OBE, CD, RCN	3
HAIDA	Commander Dunn Lantier, DSC, CD, RCN	1
	Captain J. A. Charles, CD, RCN	2
HURON	Commander E. T. G. Madgwick, DSC, CD, RCN	1
	Commander R. C. Chenoweth, MBE, CD, RCN	2
	Commander T. C. Pullen, CD, RCN	2
	(Pullen relieved Chenoweth 21-09-53)*	
	Commander J. C. Pratt, CD, RCN	3
IROQUOIS	Commander W. M. Landymore, OBE, CD, RCN	1
	Captain W. M. Landymore	2
	Lt. Commander S. G. Moore, CD, RCN**	2
	(Moore relieved Landymore 01-11-53)	
	Commander M. F. Oliver, CD, RCN	3
NOOTKA	Commander A. B. F. Fraser-Harris, DSC and Bar, CD, RCN	1
	Commander R. M. Steele, DSC, RCN	2

*In accordance with the recommendations of the Board of Enquiry into the grounding of HMCS *Huron*.

**Captain Landymore was returned to Canada to take up duties of higher responsibilities. He was eventually promoted to Flag Officer Pacific Command. Landymore, when he retired, was Flag Officer Atlantic Command.

APPENDIX G

SENIOR OFFICERS OF THE RCN DESTROYERS IN KOREA
1950-1955

Appointment	Name	Ship	From	To
CANCOMDESPAC	Capt. J. V. Brock	Cayuga	30-05-50	16-03-51
CANCOMDESFE	Commander A. B. F. Fraser-Harris	Nootka	16-03-51	20-07-51
	Commander J. Plomer	Cayuga	20-07-51	27-05-52
	Commander D. G. King	Athabaskan	27-05-52	20-06-52
	Commander (A/Captain) W. M. Landymore	Iroquois	20-06-52	26-11-52
	Commander J. C. Reed	Athabaskan	27-11-52	18-06-53
	Captain W. M. Landymore	Iroquois	18-06-53	06-11-53
	Commander (A/Captain) T. C. Pullen	Huron	06-11-53	05-02-54
	Captain J. A. Charles	Haida	05-02-54	12-09-54[*]
	Commander (A/Captain) J. C. Pratt	Huron	23-09-54	11-02-55[**]

[*]Captain Charles relinquished the title to Commander Pratt while the two ships were together in Hong Kong. The absence of Captain Charles from the operational theatre explains the discrepancy.

[**] The title was abolished on this date.

Note: Dates given are those of arrival in operational theatre and the date of relinquishing the title. Rank given is the highest rank attained during the individual's period of service in Korea.

APPENDIX H

SERVICE OF RCN DESTROYERS IN KOREA 1950-1955

SHIP	DEPART CANADA	ARRIVE ASIA	DEPART ASIA	ARRIVE CANADA	COMMAND
ATHABASKAN	05-07-50	30-07-50	03-05-51	17-05-51	Pacific
	02-08-51	01-09-51	21-06-52	09-07-52	
	29-10-52	26-11-52	18-11-53	11-12-53	
CAYUGA	05-07-50	30-07-50	16-03-51	07-04-51	Pacific
	19-06-51	20-07-51	01-06-52	14-06-52	
	25-11-53	01-01-54	22-11-54	16-12-54	
CRUSADER	25-05-52	21-06-52	18-06-53	01-07-53	Pacific
	18-10-53	20-11-53	15-08-54	03-09-54	
SIOUX	05-07-50	30-07-50	15-01-51	04-02-51	Pacific
	08-04-51	30-04-51	14-02-52	08-03-52	
	07-11-54	14-12-54	07-09-55	24-09-55	
HAIDA	27-09-52	06-11-52	12-06-53	22-07-53[*]	Atlantic
	14-12-53	05-02-54	12-09-54	01-11-54[*]	
HURON	22-01-51	15-03-51	14-08-51	21-09-51	Atlantic
	29-04-53	18-06-53	05-02-54	17-03-54[*]	
	01-08-54	01-10-54	26-12-54	19-03-55[*]	
IROQUOIS	21-04-52	12-06-52	26-11-52	08-01-53	Atlantic
	29-04-53	18-06-53	01-01-54	10-02-54[*]	
	01-07-54	22-08-54	26-12-54	19-03-55[*]	
NOOTKA	25-11-50	14-01-51	20-07-51	21-08-51	Atlantic
	30-12-51	12-02-52	09-11-52	17-12-52[*]	

* Ship returned to Canada by way of the Suez Canal, thereby circumnavigating the globe.

223

APPENDIX I

BATTLE HONOURS

ATHABASKAN
Arctic 1943-1944
English Channel 1944
Korea 1950-1953

CAYUGA
Korea 1950-1953

NOOTKA
Korea 1951-1952

CRUSADER
Belgian Coast 1914-1916
Korea 1952-1953

HAIDA
Arctic 1943-1945
English Channel 1944
Normandy 1944
Biscay 1944
Korea 1952-1953

HURON
Arctic 1943-1945
English Channel 1944
Normandy 1944
Korea 1951-1953

IROQUOIS
Atlantic 1943
Artic 1943-1945
Bixcay 1943-1944
Norway 1945
Korea 1952-1953

SIOUX
Normandy 1944
Arctic 1944-1945
Atlantic 1945
Korea 1950-1952

APPENDIX J

EXCERPTS FROM THE ENQUIRY INTO THE GROUNDING OF HMCS *HURON*

The entire transcript of the enquiry includes all the testimony from all the witnesses and principals including that of the HDWS Radar and the ASDIC operators. It is extremely lengthy. The minutes of the hearing are available in the RCN Collection, *HMCS Huron*, 1953, National Archives in Ottawa.

The excerpts quoted below are directly taken from the original minutes with all testimony given as dictated. They contain the original grammar and spelling errors.

Questions and Answers to and from Lieutenant Commander T. J. Thomas, RCN:

Q. Will you tell the Board what your duties were on the night of 12 July?

A. I was to be Officer of the Watch for the Middle Watch.

Q. Were there any written orders or instructions for the conduct of the patrol?

A. Yes, two. The Commander Task Group 95.2's orders and the Captain's Night Order Book. [The Captain's Night Order Book is exhibited.]

Q. What was the condition of visibility when you took over the watch?

A. Approximately one cable. [One cable is equal to 608 linear feet. There are ten cables to one nautical mile. A nautical mile is 6080 feet as opposed to a land mile which is 5280 feet.]

Q. What reports had you made to the Captain regarding visibility?

A. I hadn't made any reports of any kind to the Captain during the watch.

Q. What compass checks were carried out during the watch?

A. The magnetic compass had been checked against the Gyro on course 230°.

Q. Was this compass check recorded?

A. No, it wasn't recorded.

Q. Did you keep a record of any subsequent checks?

A. No.

Q. Did you check the Gyro headind of the Radar sets with the Gyro compass?

A. I didn't.

Q. What Radars were being operated?

A. Sperry Radar on a continuous all-around sweep and 293 was available but not being used.

Q. Was there any reason Radar 293 was not being operated?

A. It was being operated in accordance with an EMC policy. [Electronic Emission Control Policy was 3 minutes every 15 minutes. 293 Radar was detectable by warning devices. It was assumed that the enemy had such devices so the 293 sets were used for short periods of time. HDWS Radar was not detectable and required no such precautions.]

Q. How were the ASDICS being used?

A. They were carrying out a mine detection sweep.

Questions and Answers put to Lt. G. H. Emerson:

Q. What was your duty the night of July 12?

A. I was second Officer of the Watch.

Q. Which watch did you have?

A. I had the Middle Watch.

Q. Where is the fix you took with Lt. Rowell? [Lieutenant Rowell had been 2nd Officer of the Watch during the First Watch, 2000-2359. His charts were up to the minute and correctly notated when taken over by Lieutenant Emerson.]

A. Its not there, sir.

Q. Did you make a record of that fix?

A. No, sir.

Q. When you took over the Watch did you keep *any* record of the fixings you took?

A. No, I didn't, sir.

Q. Were you operating the Radar yourself?

A. No, I wasn't.

Q. What report concerning the proximity to the island was made by the operator?

A. I'm not sure of the exact words but the report was that he thought we were getting close to the island.

Q. What range did you appear to be from the island when you took the ground?

A. 8 Cables, sir.

Q. When the ship was aground did you take a fix?

A. Yes, I did, sir.

Q. Where did the fix indicate the ship to be?

A. I can show you on the chart. [The fix is indicated as the most westerly point of Yong-Do. The chart is Exhibit "A".]

Q. Did you have anyone verify the fix at the time?

A. I can't remember, sir.

Q. Did you suspect a ranging error in the Sperry Radar?

A. I was aware that the Sperry was reading approximately 200 yards under true.

Questions and Answers put to Commander R. Chenoweth, RCN:

Q. Will you tell the Board, in general terms, what happened on the night of 12-13 July, 1953?

A. We were patrolling of Yong-Do doing a "Sweet Adeline" patrol which was running between the island and mainland. At approximately 2030 I went below and wrote up my night orders. I then discussed the patrol and star-shell firing position with my Operation Officer in the Operations Room then retired to my cabin at 2250. At approximately 2340 the Officer of the Watch spoke with me on the voice box and asked permission to fire two extra star-shells as per instructions. I enquired as to the visibility and was informed it was unchanged. Permission was then given to fire two star-shells. From the period until the ship grounded at 0038, 13 July I have no knowledge of the sequence of events leading up to the accident.

Q. How close did you expect the ship to pass the western end of Yong-Do on the patrol?

A. Between 1800 and 2000 yards.

Q. Who, by the arrangements you described, was responsible for the safe pilotage of the ship?

A. I hold the Officer in Charge of the Operations Room responsible for fixing the ship by radar.

Q. When you turned in did you leave any orders or instructions for the officers on the Bridge and in the Operations Room?

A. Yes, sir. [Witness produced Night Order Book. The Board accepted the Night Order Book as Exhibit "B".]

Q. At the time you turned in were the Radars and other navigational appliances working reliably.

A. Yes, sir.

Q. At what time were the compasses checked on the night of 12-13 July?

A. I will have to check the log. The last check was noted at 1700. [The ship's log was produced and accepted as Exhibit "D".]

Q. Were you satisfied that the chart in use was acceptable for blind pilotage?

A. It was not the best chart for that purpose. It was not the type of chart I would have chosen but was the only one available covering the whole area of patrol.

THE REPORT OF THE ENQUIRY BOARD

Chronological Summary of Events:

1. The three officers of the watch who took over the Middle Watch on 13 July were: 1st OOW Lt. Commander T. J. C. Thomas, RCN, 0-72695; 2nd OOW Lt. G. H. Emerson, RCN, 0-22372; 3rd OOW A/Sub-Lt. E. P. Webb, RCN (SSA), 0-76593. At this point the visibility was about two miles and patchy. The ship's position was reported to be on the HYDROPAC line in "Cadillac Two" patrol area and the ship on a course of 230°, speed 12 knots.

2. The 3rd OOW went down to the Operations Room and reported he saw the ship's position fixed by RADAR and plotted on the chart [Exhibit A]. He then returned to the Bridge.

3. At approximately 0020 the 2nd OOW in the Operations Room asked for a turn to part from the reciprocal, a course of 050° as they had reached the end of the patrol line. This alteration was carried out.

4. The 1st OOW visited the Operations Room but did not see the ship fixed. He then returned to the Bridge.

5. At 0030, with the 1st and 3rd O'sOW on the Bridge the 2nd OOW in the Operations Room asked for an alteration of 20° to 030° as they were slightly inside track.

6. The 1st OOW questioned this alteration because he knew his next alteration should be to starboard.

7. The 2nd OOW confirmed the alteration was necessary and the turn was executed to 030°.

8. The Sperry operator stated he reported the land was .4 miles away. The 2nd OOW told him to commence ranging on another part of Yang-Do which was .85 miles away and which the 2nd OOW probably mistook for the nearest land.

9. The Port and Starboard lookouts and the ASDIC operator detected land in the instant before impact but were unable to make reports before the ship grounded at 0038. (During the period between midnight and the grounding the visibility reduced from two miles to 1 cable.)

THE FINDINGS AND RECOMMENDATIONS OF THE BOARD OF ENQUIRY INTO THE GROUNDING OF HER MAJESTY'S CANADIAN SHIP "HURON". NIGHT OF 12/13 JULY, 1953.

a) We find HMCS *Huron* took the ground at 0038 13 July, 1953, in position 40°45'-3N, 129°31'-1 [the most westerly point of the island of Yong-Do] at a speed of 12 knots while probably on a course of 030°.

b) We find the ship went aground because of errors in blind pilotage.

c) We find it is not possible to re-establish the circumstances leading to the grounding because no written record are available VIZ:

   1) There is no notation of any alterations of course in the ship's log, officer of the watch's notebook or Navigator's Notebook although it is evident that two alterations of course were ordered and executed during the immediate grounding.
   2) There is no record on the chart in use of any fixes, nor is there written record of any fixing data in any of the notebooks or logs.
   3) Soundings were not being taken.

d) We find there is a history of neglect which indicates the ship's safety could have been jeopardized for a considerable period, VIZ:

   1) Two of the three officers on watch failed to sign the Captain's Night Orders although these with his Standing Orders were adequate for the patrol.
   2) There is no record of compass checks and "Compass Comparison Book" kept.
   3) A considerable change in the conditions of visibility occur[r]ed but neither the Captain or second Officer of the Watch in the Operations Room were notified of the change by the First Officer of the Watch.
   4) While lookouts had been placed on each side of the Bridge when visibility decreased there was no additional lookout kept.

5) One Radar was operating on an ECM [EMC] policy three minutes every fifteen minutes but when visibility decreased there appears to have been no reconsideration of the policy. Furthermore, the First Officer of the Watch was not aware of this policy.

6) The first principal in the use of Sperry Radar in blind pilotage, that the ship's head line must be painting, was neglected.

7) It was several *days* since the gyros had been checked for accuracy.

8) It was several days since the radars had been checked for ranging accuracy.

9) The radars were not checked for gyro accuracy with the Bridge.

10) A larger scale chart than the one in use was available but not used. The second Officer of the Watch was not aware it was available.

e) That the grounding was not caused by the failure or insufficient working condition of any navigational aid.

RECOMMENDATIONS

a) That disciplinary action be taken primarily in the case of the Second Officer of the Watch (Lieutenant G. H. Emerson) as being primarily responsible for the grounding.

b) That disciplinary action be taken in the case of the First Officer of the Watch (Lieutenant-Commander T. J. C. Thomas, RCN) because of failure to fulfil his duties in accordance with the regulations.

c) That disciplinary action be considered in the case of the Commanding Officer (Commander R. C. Chenowith, MBE, CD, RCN, 0-13420) mainly because of his ultimate responsibility for the safety of his ship but also because there appears to be flagrant disregard for normal Bridge and Operations Room customs and discipline in the ship.

(Signatures affixed)   W. M. Landymore
Captain, RCN

J. M. Cutts
Lieutenant, RCN

J. J. Brooks
Lieutenant, RCN

NOTES

CHAPTER ONE: Assault

1. *Facts About Korea* (Korean Overseas Information Service, 1983.) Koreans generally are identified with surname first.

2. The NK105 Brigade had 150 T-34 tanks when fighting commenced. Forty were employed in the initial assault, backing up seven infantry divisions.

3. LSVP is the designation for large craft designed to carry troops and/or vehicles. Full name is Landing Ship, Vehicles and Personnel.

CHAPTER TWO: Involvement

1. Blair Fraser, *The Search For Identity* (Toronto: Doubleday, 1967), p. 98. Ottawa finally bowed to public pressure over the issue of sending troops to Korea. On 7 August, Prime Minister Louis St. Laurent spoke to the nation on CBC Radio to announce Canada would send a contingent of special volunteers under the regimental colours of the Princess Patricia's Canadian Light Infantry (PPCLI).

2. *Fraser*, p. 98. In a speech to an Ottawa service club on 22 July, Lester B. Pearson stated in all seriousness that three destroyers were more than adequate as a contribution to the UN effort. "The destroyers are no mere token," he said. On hearing of Pearson's remark an unnamed official of the U.S. Embassy reacted, somewhat bitterly. "Okay, lets call it three tokens," he is reported to have said.

CHAPTER THREE: In All Respects, Ready

1. Commander Destroyers Pacific. Also known as Captain "D."

2. "Clean Sweepdown," *TIME CANADA*, 2 October 1950.

3. Admiral Rollo Mainguy, RCN, *The Mainguy Report. The Mainguy Report*, presented to NHQ by Admiral Mainguy in 1949, details the problems which beset the RCN prior to the mutinies of 1948. Copies are available in most public libraries.

4. On 26 June, I went to a barber shop in Victoria. The barber, knowing I was serving aboard *Cayuga* brought the topic of conversation around to Korea and asked what I thought of going over. I was hardly in on the navy's plans and replied I had heard only rumours. The barber then informed me not only when we would leave, but the very hour of departure.

5. So plentiful was the ale that a keg was removed by a group of stokers who manhandled it all the way to the ship and down to their mess. The

jostling, however, so agitated the contents that when the keg was opened the contents sprayed out to cover the compartment and its occupants with foaming beer. Brock, on his rounds the next morning, commented on the cloying odour of beer but declined to press the issue.

6. This seaman was killed in June 1951 in a motorcycle accident near his home in Mission, B.C. Although listed "in desertion" by the RCN he had not been apprehended. He was 21 years of age.

7. Thor Thorgrimsson and E. C. Russell, *Canadian Naval Operations in Korean Waters 1950-1955* (Ottawa: Queen's Printer, 1966), p. 4. Breach of naval etiquette was deliberate and made for appearances only. *Sioux*, though senior to *Athabaskan*, was smaller. It was felt the line would be more impressive kept to an order of size rather than the strict protocol of seniority.

8. CANAVHED to CTG 214.4. Signal 1220387/7/50. Original is in the National Archives, RCN Collection, *HMCS Cayuga File 1950*.

9. HMCS *Cayuga*, Ship's Log, 14 June 1950.

10. The ultimate fate of this unusual mascot was told to me during a telephone conversation with David Tyre in August 1989.

11. E. C. Russell, *Customs of the Canadian Armed Forces* (Ottawa: Deneau & Greenberg, 1980), p. 129. The parrot was mascot of *Gatineau* during the 1970s. Lestock, the coyote, was mascot of the 101st Regiment of Edmonton, which saw all its service in France from 1915 to 1918.

CHAPTER FOUR: Into The Fray

1. Thor Thorgrimsson and E. C. Russell, *Canadian Naval Operations in Korea*, p. 5. The ships steamed the 7413 nautical miles to Sasebo in nineteen days at an average speed of 16.2 knots.

2. W. Konig et al, *Battle Report: The War in Korea*, Recorded in various chapters throughout the book.

3. Charts were valid from July to 30 September 1950.

4. J. A. Field, *History of United Nations Naval Operations, Korea*, p. 365.

5. Thorgrimsson and Russell, *Canadian Naval Operations*, p. 11. Task Group 96.1 patrolled the east coast. TG95.2 patrolled the west. TG95.5 was the escort group. TG95.6 was the minesweeper flotilla. TG95.7 was the ROK naval force. TG95.10 was HMS *Ladybird* which was jetty-bound and served as the RN administrative unit in Sasebo. TG95.15 was a frigate flotilla.

6. Korean Information Service. *Facts About Korea*, 1983. *Do* and *To* are Korean words meaning island. They also mean the same thing if in lower case *do* and *to*. Capitalization signifies that the island is large. If large

the pronunciation rhymes with "slow"; if small the rhyme is with "blue." There seems no particular reason why some islands are designated *DO* or *TO* or why islands little bigger than rocks are *ni*, pronounced *neh* or *nee* depending on where they are. Only Koreans know for sure.

7. *Ibid.* Korea's best port is Pusan. The west coast has six ports, but only Inchon and Chinnampo are important. The east coast has twenty-six ports. Only Hungnam, Sonjin and Wonsan are of consequence.

8. *Sioux*, a "V" class ship, was not as heavily armed as the Tribals. She carried two 4.7-inch single-barrelled guns as main armament, one forward, one aft. It was also lighter in secondary armament, having only four 40mm Bofors and two single-barrelled 20mm Oerlikons on the bridge, one on each wing. Thus it took longer to dispatch multiple targets. *Sioux*, like *Crusader* who came to Korea some months later, was not really suited to the type of warfare experienced in Korea. The heavily-armed Tribals were ideal for surface action.

9. *HMCS Athabaskan, Report of Proceedings*, August 1950.

10. Tokchok-To is referred to as "Takuchaku" on naval maps. Its position is 37° 14'N; 126° 08'E. This publication uses *National Geographic* maps. If necessary, naval designations will be in brackets.

CHAPTER FIVE: Advance

1. The defending troops have been much maligned in most accounts of the war's earliest days. Very good accounts of the early stages can be found in Rene Cutforth's *Korean Reporter* (London, 1952), and in Marguerite Higgins' *War In Korea* (New York, 1951).

2. Attributed to Abraham Lincoln, reflecting on the news that the Union Army had been defeated at Antietam, though in a position to win, through a blunder by its commanding officer, General Ambrose E. Burnside. "Only Burnside could have managed such a coup, wringing one last spectacular defeat from the jaw of victory," retorted Lincoln.

3. Malcolm W. Cagle, Inchon—The Analysis of a Gamble (Annapolis: U. S. Naval Institute, 1957), p. 76.

4. Phillip Knightly, *The First Casualty* (London: Harcourt, Brace, 1975), p. 340. According to Knightly, the talk in the Tokyo Press club for days prior to the Inchon invasion was about the proposed operation. The members of the club referred to it as "Operation Common Knowledge."

5. TG 91.2 was under Brock's command during the invasion of Inchon.

6. "Gook" was first used as an identifier for North Korean soldiers in much the same manner as "bogey" was used in reference to unidentified aircraft. Before long the word became common and referred to any Korean.

7. Beijaa Bay is positioned at 37°12'N; 126°01'E.

8. Paryon-po is positioned at 36°22'N; 126°32'E.

9. Piun-to is positioned at 36°07'N; 126°35'E.

10. *HMCS Athabaskan, Report of Proceedings*, September 1950.

11. Malcolm W. Cagle, USNIP, March 1958 has some very interesting accounts under the title of *Errors in the Korean War*. Association of the U.S. Army. "MacArthur's Divided Command," December 1956 issue of *ARMY* is highly critical of General MacArthur and of his command at this time.

CHAPTER SIX: Long Days; Longer Nights

1. J. V. Brock, *The Dark Broad Seas, Volume I* (Toronto: McClelland & Stewart, 1981), pp. 227-8.

2. Phillip Knightly, *The First Casualty*, p. 335.

3. *Ibid*, p. 337.

4. *Ibid*, p. 337.

5. Canadian Archives, Ottawa, RCN Collection. Reports and Enquiries Division.

6. The blockade was strictly enforced but was kept low-key. On the west coast the enforced area was north of the 38th parallel to 39°35'N. On the east coast the area extended from the 38th parallel to 41°54'N.

7. Ross Monroe's reports from Korea were published on a regular basis in Southam papers from September 1950 to November 1950.

8. Department of National Defence, press release dated 15 November 1950. Published in most Canadian newspapers.

9. J. V. Brock, *The Dark Broad Seas*, p. 213.

CHAPTER SEVEN: The War Ends—Almost

1. *HMCS Athabaskan, Report of Proceedings*, November 1950.

2. Because of the extreme turn, the degree of roll was reported at 40 degrees. The height of the waves made this dangerous, but a slower turn would have caused the ship to run parallel to the waves for a longer period of time, which would have been riskier. The waves were running to a height even with the red maple leaf on the after funnel, eighteen feet above the upper deck.

3. *HMCS Athabaskan, Ship's Log*, 7 November 1950.

4. *HMCS Athabaskan, Report of Proceedings*, November 1950.

5. *HMCS Sioux, Report of Proceedings*, July 1951.

6. *Calgary Herald*, 9 December 1950.

7. Donald Stairs, *Diplomacy of Restraint* (Toronto: University of Toronto Press, 1966), p. 128. China actually entered the war during the second week of October. On 26 October Chinese troops engaged ROK infantry for the first time.

8. Messages between Ottawa and UN Headquarters from 1-15 November 1950 indicate two destroyers were to be recalled. The third was to remain in the Korean theatre of war for only a short time thereafter. (Letter from Chief of Naval Staff to Minister of National Defence, dated 21 November 1950. NS1950/40, Volume I. RCN Collection, National Archives, Ottawa.)

CHAPTER EIGHT: Chinnampo

1. J. V. Brock, *The Dark Broad Seas*, pp. 230-232.

2. Conversations with Leading Seaman Murray Blake, RAN, at Melbourne, Australia in March 1954. See also Norman Bartlett, *With The Australians In Korea*, pp. 160-161.

3. Brock, J. V. *The Dark Broad Seas*, p. 238.

4. Thorgrimsson and Russell, *Canadian Naval Operations*, p. 35. The ROKN minesweeper YMS.303, PC704 and YMS.308 all played important roles in the Chinnampo operation. Their crews took the little ships into the channel several times in search of the deadly mines. Their courage was never doubted, though at times their common sense was suspect as they deliberately searched for trouble. At one point the three captains informed Brock they intended to stay in Chinnampo to engage the Chinese in battle when the Reds came to the city. Brock, never known for his tolerance of those who might go against orders, kept them in line, but it was not an easy task.

5. All signals pertaining to the Chinnampo Operation are filed in the *Cayuga File 1950*, RCN Collection, National Archives, Ottawa.

6. *HMCS Sioux File 1950*, RCN Collection, National Archives.

7. Zone coded Area Shelter.

8. One fathom equals six feet.

9. *HMCS Sioux File 1950*, RCN Collection, National Archives, Ottawa.

10. The Daido-Ko.

11. J. V. Brock, *The Dark Broad Seas*, pp. 344-45.

12. *Ibid*, p. 247.

13. *HMCS Athabaskan, Report of Proceedings*, December 1950.

14. Thorgrimsson and Russell, *Canadian Naval Operations*, p. 35.

15. *HMCS Cayuga, Ship's Log*, 6 December. Entry of 0616.

16. "The Chinnampo Affair," *The Crowsnest* (RCN monthly magazine), February 1951. Author is identified only by initials A. J. P.

17. Fully detailed lists of ammunition expended by ships involved in the Chinnampo operation are available in the *HMCS Cayuga Battle Report* dated December 1950. See *Cayuga File 1950*, RCN Collection, National Archives, Ottawa.

18. *HMCS Cayuga, Report of Proceedings*, December 1950.

CHAPTER NINE: The Long Way Back

1. *United States Naval Institute Proceedings*, March 1958, p. 33 gives an excellent account of the pandemonium within the HQ of General MacArthur during the early days of the Chinese intervention.

2. General S. L. Marshall, U.S. Army, *The River and the Gauntlet*. An above-average account and in-depth study of the causes of the humiliation and defeat of the U.S. 8th Army. First published in 1953, General Marshall's book is highly recommended to the student of the Korean War annals. It was recently reprinted in paperback.

3. The vulgar expression "chew me," the most common rebuke in the RCN during the 1950s, was used mainly in good humour. Tone of voice was the indicator of the degree of anger. The suggestion that a shipmate might be homosexual was the ultimate insult.

CHAPTER TEN: Happy Holiday

1. E. C. Russell, *Customs of the Canadian Armed Forces*, pp. 115-116. During the days of wooden ships, storms and heavy seas often caused spars and masts to snap. Repairs took long, arduous hours and rum was sometimes issued as a reward for the hard work done by the crew. It was, however, necessary to account for the rum, so ships' captains often paid for it from their own funds rather than try to explain a gratuitous issue. The problem was solved in 1773 by Lieutenant James Burney, RN, commander of HMS *Adventure*. He recorded in his accounts book that a quantity of rum had been issued to his crew in order to "splice the main brace." No one in Admiralty thought to ask Burney what the entry meant. Others began to use the same ploy. Within a short time the term came into common use throughout the Royal Navy and, hence, the Commonwealth navies.

2. *Calgary Herald*, issue of 4 January 1951. A lengthy column was devoted to this gift. There seems, however, to be no official acknowledgment anywhere in the RCN Collections.

3. Since the end of the Korean War no Canadian warship has spent Christmas Day away from home port.

CHAPTER ELEVEN: Old Warriors; New Warriors

1. *HMCS Nootka, Ship's Log*, 11 January 1951. *Nootka File 1950*, RCN Collection, National Archives.

2. *HMCS Athabaskan, Report of Proceedings*, March 1951.

3. A Coston gun resembles a large-muzzle shotgun. It fires a wadded rope-knot to which is attached a long, light rope. The messengers are attached to the light rope.

4. *HMCS Athabaskan, Report of Proceedings*, March 1951.
   Ship's Log, 28 March 1951.
   HMCS Nootka, Report of Proceedings, March 1951.
   Ship's Log, 28 March 1951.

CHAPTER TWELVE: The Changing Of The Guard

1. *HMCS Huron, Report of Proceedings*, March 1951 and April 1951 (*Huron File 1950 RCN Collection, National Archives*).

2. TE 95.11 included ships of nearly all the contributing nations: RCN, RNZN, RN, RAN, USN plus ROKN and the Dutch destroyer *Van Galen*.

3. *HMCS Huron, Report of Proceedings*, June 1951.
   Report of Proceedings, July 1951.

4. Thorgrimsson and Russell, *Canadian Naval Operations*, p. 50. Only a few of the ships were attacked by enemy aircraft, none of them of the RCN contingent. An ROKN frigate reportedly came under attack by three Chinese YAKs. According to reports in Canadian records, the frigate shot down one of the planes and damaged a second while sustaining some minor structural damage.

5. A Horse's Neck was popular in the wardrooms. Made with gin or rye whisky, it is good on hot days. A tall glass is filled with crushed ice, two ounces of liquor is poured slowly over the ice and the glass is then filled with ginger ale. Stir gently and enjoy. Author.

6. *HMCS Sioux, Battle Report*, May-June 1951. The other members of TE95.12 were: HMNZS *Hawea*, HMS *Amethyst*, USS *Comstock*, USS *Glendale*, HMS *Ceylon* and a Columbian frigate the *Almirante Padilla*.

7. *HMCS Sioux, Report of Proceedings*, May 1951.

8. High Definition Warning System. (Developed by Sperry Limited.)

9. *HMCS Cayuga, Ship's Log,* 21/22 December 1951.

10. Identification Friend/Foe. A prearranged signal which quickly identified the various ships to each other.

11. Thorgrimsson and Russell, *Canadian Naval Operations,* p. 52.

12. Malcolm Cagle and Frank A. Manson, *The Sea War In Korea,* pp. 322-323. This work credits Commander Gay with formulating the plan for Operation Squeegee. *Nootka's Report of Proceedings,* May 1951, however, clearly indicates the plan had been that of the Canadian commander.

CHAPTER THIRTEEN: Happy Days

1. Rest and Recreation Leave (R&R) was misnamed, since in reality there was little rest. The Japanese resorts, to which the sailors flocked, catered to every whim. R&R became known to all as I&I—Intoxication and Intercourse.

2. Tiny crustaceans were sucked into the intake valves in such numbers that the lines became plugged. As it was not possible to clear the lines completely while at sea, freshwater production was seriously curtailed.

3. In 1952, when the present monarch ascended the throne, KRCN became QRCN—Queen's Regulations, Canadian Navy. QRCN became redundant in 1967 when Bill-C243 unified the forces.

4. Four cartons of American cigarettes, tied two on each leg, were easily hidden by the wide bell-bottoms of a sailor's trousers. Two or three trips ashore would earn a sailor enough yen to last two months under normal circumstances. Each carton was worth 3600 yen on the black market.

5. Basic Education Tests were equivalent to a Grade Ten level.

6. *HMCS Nootka, Reports of Proceedings,* April to June 1952.
   HMCS Athabaskan, Reports of Proceedings, May 1952.

CHAPTER FOURTEEN: Leopards, Salamanders and Donkeys

1. Thorgrimsson and Russell, *Canadian Naval Operations,* p.61.

2. James Plomer, RCN (retired), quoted in an interview with *Kingston Whig-Standard,* 10 June 1982.

3. Thorgrimsson and Russell, *Canadian Naval Operations,* p. 70. M/Sgt. H. Frost had been replaced by a Lieutenant Beaudette of the U.S. Army. He, in turn, was replaced by a Captain Patterson.

4. *HMCS Cayuga, Ship's Log*, 30 October 1951. Ship positioned at 38°04'N; 125°01.2'E.

5. The sinking of the two boats caused Sub-Lieutenant M. A. Martin, RCN, the officer in charge of boats, to lament loudly in feigned anguish: "My first command and it's sunk from under me. I shall be unlikely to get another." Martin did get other commands. He eventually rose to the rank of rear admiral, RCN.

6. *HMCS Cayuga, Battle Report*, 1-15 November 1951. The area was too confined for forward movement—a most fortunate circumstance. Had *Cayuga* moved forward, the shell which missed her forecastle would have struck amidships. Such a hit could have resulted in the ship's destruction.

7. *HMCS Cayuga, Battle Report*, 1-15 November, 1951.

8. Able Seaman R. J. Skavberg, RCN, enlisted in the navy at HMCS Tecumseh, the naval base at Calgary, Alberta, in April 1949. He joined the *Athabaskan* in June 1951.

9. Tefa-to appears on many naval charts as such, while on others it is named Taewha-Do, its proper name.

10. Plomer's report, classified top secret in 1951, shows the weak defensive positions of the various islands. Only the massive gathering of warships held the Chinese at bay. The Chinese quite probably took the naval strength as being indicative of the defences overall. The entire report would be of interest to students of the Korean conflict. It is found in the *HMCS Cayuga File, 1951*, RCN Collection.

11. *HMCS Sioux, Battle Report*, 1-15 December 1951.
    Ship's Log, Various entries from 11-16 December 1951.

12. *HMCS Sioux, Battle Report*, 16-31 December 1951.

13. *HMCS Cayuga, Report of Proceedings*, December 1951. *Cayuga* fired 247 rounds of HEDA 4-inch shells during the operation. The complete account of ammunition fired during Operation Cheerful is in *HMCS Cayuga Munitions Report*, December 1951, *Cayuga File 1951*.

14. *HMCS Cayuga, Report of Proceedings*, December 1951.

15. *HMCS Cayuga, Battle Report*, 16-31 December 1951.

16. *HMCS Cayuga, Report of Proceedings*, December 1951. *Cayuga* was trailing a thin line of oil all this time owing to her having popped two rivets at the waterline during her hasty retreat from The Slot on 30 October.

17. *HMCS Cayuga, Report of Proceedings*, December 1951. This report contains the original doggerel and the CTE's signal which was its inspiration.

CHAPTER FIFTEEN: All The World's A Stage

1. *HMCS Cayuga, Report of Proceedings,* October 1951.

2. James Plomer remained one of Demara's good friends through the years. In various interviews he readily praised the man he had known as Doctor Cyr. In 1979 Plomer was instrumental in obtaining for Demara a special pass from Immigration Canada which allowed Demara to attend *Cayuga's* reunion in Esquimalt.

3. The alleged bullet was never seen, and there is doubt it existed. Plomer and others always felt Demara had invented the bullet to add some spice to the story. He was never above boasting a bit. Petty Officer R. Hotchin expressed surprise at the mention of a bullet in the press release. Hotchin is unlikely to have missed such a removal as he had been on the scene for the entire period Demara was operating on the Koreans.

4. James Plomer, *Kingston Whig-Standard,* interview published 9 June 1982.

5. Thorgrimsson and Russell, *Canadian Naval Operations,* p. 69.

CHAPTER SIXTEEN: Shoot-Out at Package One

1. *HMCS Iroquois, Report of Proceedings,* July 1952.

2. The Dick Tracy Run, named after the comic strip hero, was the patrol assigned to various destroyers charged with recovering downed UN pilots.

3. Cock of the Walk was a title awarded the ship holding the highest standards in gunnery, seamanship and overall efficiency and was very highly prized.

4. CPO J. Stokke, RCN (retired). Personal files.

5. *HMCS Iroquois, Ship's Log,* 2 October 1952.

6. No pictures were taken by *Iroquois'* photographer as he was not on the bridge during the action.

7. *HMCS Crusader, Report of Proceedings,* October 1952.

CHAPTER SEVENTEEN: The Trainbusters Club

1. HMCShips *Huron, Cayuga* and *Sioux* bagged trains prior to June 1952. *Iroquois* destroyed one just a day before USS *Orleck* recorded her kill. Because of the timing, the earlier RCN kills did not qualify for membership in the TBC.

2. *HMCS Crusader, Report of Proceedings,* October 1952.

3. *HMCS Haida, Ship's Log,* 19 December 1952.

4. USS *The Sullivans* is now a permanent naval museum at Buffalo, N.Y.

5. *HMCS Haida, Ship's Log,* 19 December 1952.

6. The original signals produce interesting, and in some cases humorous, reading for anyone interested in RCN history. The signals are found in the RCN Collection, National Archives, Ottawa, under the *HMCS Crusader File, 1952.* Like most RCN records microfilming is not as yet complete, so a personal visit to the archives is necessary.

7. *HMCS Haida, Ship's Log,* 26-27 May 1953.

8. *HMCS Haida, Ship's Log,* 30 May 1953.

9. Thorgrimsson and Russell, *Canadian Naval Operations* p. 141 (Appendix C).

CHAPTER EIGHTEEN: Adeline Was Not So Sweet

1. *HMCS Huron, Report of Proceedings,* June 1953.

2. Conversations with Mr. William Mushing in 1984.

3. Ibid.

4. *HMCS Huron, Ship's Log,* 14 May 1953.

CHAPTER NINETEEN: Cease-Fire; Check All Guns

1. President Rhee tried to justify his rash move by claiming he had released only POWs who were anti-Communist. Most were rounded up within a few days, but the fragile truce talks were nearly destroyed by Rhee's action.

2. *HMCS Iroquois, Patrol Report,* July and August 1953.

3. *HMCS Athabaskan, Report of Proceedings,* August 1953.

SELECT BIBLIOGRAPHY

BOOKS

Allen, Ralph. *Ordeal By Fire*. New York: Doubleday, 1961.

Barlett, Norman. *With The Australians in Korea*. Sydney, 1955.

Brock, Jeffry V. *The Dark Broad Seas, Vol. 1*. Toronto: McClelland and Stewart, 1981.

Cagle, Malcolm. *Inchon—The Analysis of a Gamble*. Annapolis: U.S. Naval Institute, 1954.

Cagle, Malcolm and Frank A. Manson. *The Sea War in Korea*. Annapolis: U.S. Naval Institute, 1957.

Crichton, Robert. *The Great Imposter*. New York: Random House, 1959.

Cummins, Geraldine. *Unseen Adventures*. London: Ryder Press, 1959.

Fraser, Blair. *The Search For Identity*. Toronto: Doubleday, 1967.

_____. *MacKenzie King: The Incredible Canadian*. London: Longmans and Green, 1953.

Knightly, Phillip. *The First Casualty*. London: Harcourt Brace, 1975.

Marshall, S. L. *The River and The Gauntlet*. New York: Doubleday, 1953.

Melady, John. *Korea: Canada's Forgotten War*. Toronto: MacMillan of Canada, 1983.

Paige, Glenn. *The Korean Decision*. New York: Free Press, 1966.

Russell, E. C. *Customs of the Canadian Armed Forces*. Ottawa: Deneau and Greenberg, 1980.

Stairs, Donald. *The Diplomacy of Restraint*. Toronto: University of Toronto Press, 1966.

Thorgrimsson, Thor and E. C. Russell. *Canadian Naval Operations in Korean Waters 1950-1955*. Ottawa: Queen's Printer, 1966.

Wood, Herbert F. *Strange Battleground: The Operations in Korea*. Ottawa: Queen's Printer, 1966.

MAGAZINE ARTICLES, INFORMATION BULLETINS, NAVAL REPORTS AND DOCUMENTS

Battle Reports. All ships. Individual Files, 1950-1955. National Archives of Canada, Ottawa, Ontario.

Boards of Enquiries. HMCS *Sioux*, January 1951. National Archives of Canada, Ottawa, Ontario.

HMCS *Huron*, July 1953. National Archives of Canada, Ottawa, Ontario.

"Clean Sweepdown." *TIME* (CANADA), 2 October 1950. Article covering proposed changes to the Royal Canadian Navy as recommended by the *Mainguy Report.*

Fraser, Blair. "The Secret Life of MacKenzie King, Spiritualist." *Maclean's Magazine*, 15 December 1951.

Korean Overseas Information Services. *Facts About Korea.* Seoul, 1983.

Mainguy, RCN, Rear Admiral Rollo. *The Mainguy Report.* Ottawa: Queen's Printer, 1949.

Patrol Reports. All ships. Individual Files, 1950-1955. National Archives of Canada, Ottawa, Ontario.

Reports of Proceedings. All ships. Individual Files, 1950-1955. National Archives of Canada, Ottawa, Ontario.

Ship's Logs. All ships. Individual Files, 1950-1955. National Archives of Canada, Ottawa, Ontario.

Author's Note: Letters, memoranda and minutes of proceedings are all available in the files of individual ships.

The National Archives has not as yet completed the work of microfilming the RCN collection. All files are available, but they are still in the files of individual ships. Usually a one-day notice is required to gain access to these files and boxes. Some of the files are numbered in volumes.

RECOMMENDED READING

Cutforth, Rene. *Korean Reporter.* London: Wingate, 1952.

Ferhenbach, T. R. *This Kind of War.* New York: MacMillan, 1963.

Goulden, Joseph, C. *Korea: The Untold Story.* New York: Times Books, The New York Times Book Company, 1982.

Guttman, Allen. *Korea and The Theory of Limited War.* Lexington, Mass.: D. C. Heath, 1967.

Higgins, Marguerite. *War in Korea.* New York: Doubleday, 1951.

Leckie, Robert. *Conflict: The History of The Korean War 1950-53.* New York: G. P. Putnam's Sons, 1962.

Macpherson, Ken and John Burgess. *The Ships of Canada's Naval Forces, 1910-1985.* Toronto: Collins, 1985.

Miller, Merle. *Plain Speaking: An Oral Biography of Harry S. Truman.* New York: Berkley. 1973.

Ress, David. *Korea: The Limited War.* London: MacMillan, 1964.

Smith, Robert. *MacArthur In Korea: The Naked Emperor.* New York: Simon and Shuster, 1982.

Stevens, G. R. *The Royal Canadian Regiment, Vol. 2, 1933-1966.* London, Ontario: London Printing and Lithographing, 1967.

Princess Patricia's Canadian Light Infantry: 1917-1957, Vol. 3. Griesbach, Alberta: Historical Committee of The Regiment, undated.

Ridgeway, Matthew. *The Korean War.* New York: Doubleday, 1967.

INDEX

245